UNDERSTANDING VEDANTA
A CONTEMPORARY APPROACH

A Collection of Essays to Introduce Vedanta

This collection of essays is based upon Shankara's teaching which, despite age-old controversies surrounding their radical vision of a singular reality, remain the most rigorously developed and commonly taught form of Vedanta

Understanding Vedanta
A Contemporary Approach

A Collection of Essays to Introduce Vedanta

DHRUV S. KAJI

New Age Books

New Delhi (India)

UNDERSTANDING VEDANTA

Published by
NEW AGE BOOKS
A-44, Naraina Industrial Area, Phase-I
New Delhi–110 028 (INDIA)
E-mail: nab@newagebooksindia.com
Website: www.newagebooksindia.com

ISBN: 978-81-7822-396-4

First Edition: Delhi, 2012

Printed and published by
RP Jain for New Age Books
A-44, Naraina Industrial Area
Phase-1, New Delhi 110 028. India

UNDERSTANDING VEDANTA

A Contemporary Approach

A collection of essays to introduce Vedanta

Dhruv S. Kaji

CONTENTS

With Gratitude

To a fascinating life which has been a wonderful teacher. Among its many blessings, I specially want to mention my mother who demonstrated love and courage through all circumstances and my father who brought home the virtues of clear thinking and discipline. No words can express my gratitude to:

Prof. S.A. Upadhyaya

Mr. Ramesh S. Balsekar

Swami Dayananda Saraswati

Swami Tadatmananda Saraswati

Swami Tattvavidananda Saraswati

teachers of Vedanta who have made life meaningful.

Preface

The aircraft was on its final descent when the striped threshold of runway 27 at Elstree started moving towards the bottom of the wind-screen; its gradual disappearance from view meant that I was too high. If I continued, the plane would either over-shoot the runway or touchdown dangerously fast. *"Golf sierra lima going around"* I informed the tower with frustration as I opened throttle to circle back for another attempt at landing. And my long-suffering instructor once again said to me, *"Remember, a good landing can only come from a good approach."* Today, as I work towards a better understanding of myself, it strikes me that the need to set up a correct approach is equally applicable to the teachings of Vedanta. And hence this book which is meant to provide a contemporary approach to wisdom from an age-old tradition.

For an aircraft preparing to land, a good approach means being in line with the runway at the correct height, speed and distance. Whatever further that is necessary for touching down becomes much easier if this initial set-up is proper. For many of us, our journey on the path of Vedanta becomes unduly demanding because of a defective approach. We come to this subject without properly understanding its true purpose and the rationale behind the methods it uses; this lack of understanding is frequently compounded by prejudices and false expectations. It is not surprising that when the challenges of Vedanta are thus aggravated, disappointment or rejection are the likely outcome – we, in other words, fail to make a good landing.

The collection of essays in this book contains what I have found to be a valuable approach to Vedanta's wisdom.

Happy landings.

You should know your self ......

Brihadaranyaka Upanishad

The unexamined life is not worth living

Socrates

There is no darkness but ignorance

Shakespeare

AN INTRODUCTION

Vedanta is the name given to the end portion of the Hindu scriptures called the Vedas; unlike the bulk of these scriptures, the focus of their last section is not religion but extraordinary insights into the real nature of things. Vedanta addresses people who need a meaning to their lives beyond pleasure, wealth, power, fame or religion. Its subject-matter is our own reality which it says is misunderstood by most of us.

Vedanta's purpose is to give us freedom from our constant sense of inadequacy. It does this by helping us discover natural fullness which it says is intrinsic to all. To benefit from Vedanta's teachings, its students need some level of intellectual competence and mental equipoise. Wisdom similar to Vedanta's is also available in other cultures through aspects such as Taoism, mystical streams of Christianity and Sufism; however, Vedanta has better-developed traditions and unique methods for preserving and imparting the knowledge it contains.

A few caveats are appropriate at the outset. First, the objective of this book is to only provide an introduction to the subject; so, even though you will find references to important teachings of Vedanta, this is not an attempt to set them out fully.

Second, it should be kept in mind that no book, however exhaustive, can truly teach Vedanta. This is because Vedanta is not information but a path to be personally walked, a life to be actually lived in keeping with its vision. As we all know, not even the best of travel guides can replace a real journey. In Vedanta's case, its wisdom remains of limited use unless it is distilled in the crucible of our own effort and experience.

Third, I write as a student; while I certainly hope that you will take away some useful insights from this book, it must be noted that the content here is neither based on scholarship nor on a life at an exalted plane. I write mainly because this is an effective way of improving my own understanding; but, as I write, I frequently remember the truth of what Francois de la Rochefoucauld once said: *"It is easier to be wise for others than for ourselves"*.

Last, my understanding of Vedanta is inevitably coloured by my own objectives and limitations. The exceptional person who completes the entire journey of Vedanta does this on the basis of great wisdom and the life-style of a saint. As Ralph Waldo Emerson put it, *"Life is a festival only to the wise"*. My abilities are more modest and my life is not a perpetual festival; yet, I am immensely grateful for the sense of ease and contentment which the pursuit of Vedanta has brought in. I have no doubt that the benefits of Vedanta are valuable even for those of us with feet of clay, who may never walk its full path.

Why yet another book on Vedanta when a large number is already available? There are, of course, several scholarly works which go about their task brilliantly, with a detailed exposition of the subject. But many introductory books here are written in a manner which makes them difficult to relate to. For instance, such books are peppered with words (usually beginning in the upper case) like *Bliss Divine, Eternal Life* and *Sacred Self*. As most of us are not quite finished with our struggle for earthly bliss, the goal of Bliss Divine seems a bit far-fetched; as none of us knows anything which is truly eternal, the promise of Eternal Life is none too clear; and the Self we know is, of course, far from Sacred!

These books often also contain grand exhortations, of which the more common ones are *"Free yourself of all desires"* and *"Act without any expectation"*; many of us who are just embarking on an exploration of Vedanta are doubtful about our ability to lead lives based on such noble dictums.

Expressions and ideas like these have to be very carefully employed by authors, and only after setting out their full context and rationale; unfortunately, this is not always done.

The need for greater clarity on the part of authors applies to other important areas in Vedanta as well. For instance, when Vedanta talks about the process by which our universe is supposed to have been created or about the much-bandied *karma* theory, it has to be pointed out that such material does not share the sanctity of its key teachings; it is included only to provisionally answer initial questions of students. Even more important, it is necessary to clearly tell modern readers that Vedanta's basic insight (of a single reality being all that actually exists) is not capable of being conclusively proved. There are good and logical reasons why this is so but the fact remains that Vedanta cannot make us share its core vision by arguments alone, just as genuine appreciation of music cannot be brought to us purely by scholarly explanations. When such matters are not fully explained, the result is unnecessary confusion. Often, therefore, we begin to feel that Vedanta is too abstruse or esoteric and we may be better off with only an ethical or, perhaps, a religious life.

But an ethical or a religious life, by itself, does not solve the basic human problem of constantly seeking happiness without ever reaching that goal – only a grasp of the essential unity of things, which is revealed by Vedanta, can do this. And the fundamental message of Vedanta, despite its great implications, is actually quite simple and capable of being shared. Therefore, all of us can and should benefit from Vedanta if we approach it properly.

In response to these impressions of mine, I have set out some aspects of Vedanta in the form of essays which I hope will be easy to understand. ('Easy' is, of course, a subjective term and some of you will find the material in this book to be disappointingly elementary while some others may find the same material taxing their patience with too many details.) Keeping in mind a reader who is a product of present-day westernised education, I have tried to keep the general tone contemporary and practical. Relatively few Sanskrit words have been used in the body of these essays with many others having been relegated to the footnotes. Diacritical marks (such as the two dots over the 'i' in *naïve* which alter the usual sound value of that letter), conventionally used when Sanskrit words are written in the Roman alphabet, have been omitted here to reduce a sense of alienation.

As you read, you will find repetition of several aspects of Vedanta over a number of essays; this is deliberate because restatement is useful for better understanding and, in the case of this book, it is also necessary to make each essay self-contained. Similarly, some stock illustrations and analogies (such as the appearance of an imaginary snake instead of the rope and of water being the common truth behind both the ocean and its waves) have been repeatedly used as they are traditional and appropriate. One term which has been used in several places is *God* and it may create immediate doubts or disdain for those who consider themselves to be atheists or agnostics; if you are one of them, you may find it worthwhile to first read the section "Does God Exist?" from the essay titled "Some Big Questions".

It should also be noted that the original texts of Vedanta have been differently interpreted by a number of great teachers of the past, of whom the most notable have been Shankara, Ramanuja and Madhva. This collection of essays is based upon Shankara's teachings which, despite age-old controversies surrounding their radical vision of a singular reality, remain the most rigorously developed and commonly taught form of Vedanta.

A few of the essays here are based upon work done much earlier. The entire collection has greatly benefitted from valuable suggestions made by Swami Tattvavidananda Saraswati, a renowned teacher, by Raghu, a fellow-student for many years and by Kersi Khambatta, a man of many facets who has just begun to explore Vedanta; all have been very generous with their time and patience as they reviewed this material.

For a newcomer to Vedanta, care is needed as one is being introduced to this subject in order not to miss or dismiss new ways of looking at things just because they are alien to our conditioning. We are used to dealing with things within a certain frame of size, time and experience. For this reason, we find it difficult to comprehend the size of galaxies or of sub-atomic particles; we cannot relate to time in picoseconds or in billions of years; we cannot grasp the idea of time and space being one continuum. Vedanta's key insight goes out even further and postulates a single reality as the common truth behind all existence. While its vision never denies the fact that a world of diversity is vividly experienced by us, it denies any absolute reality to this experience; it goes on to erase the apparently fundamental distinction between an observer and what he observes. It should therefore not be surprising that we face difficulty in coming to grips with Vedanta's core teachings.

Also, the process of assimilating this singular reality involves our trying to understand the consciousness because of which we perceive and understand things. Because we have to necessarily use consciousness to understand anything, including consciousness itself, this attempt faces inherent obstacles – we would encounter similar problems if we attempted to lift ourselves up by our own boot-straps or if our eyes tried to observe themselves. It is for this reason that all of Vedanta's wisdom cannot be reduced to a set of bullet points; a certain amount of receptivity, patience and contemplation is required for the vision of Vedanta to progress from dubious, second-hand information to a live experience of a profound truth.

From this, it follows that books such as this one are not meant to be efficiently skimmed through to merely extract data. Vedanta needs to be read in small portions over a period of time and with greater focus on obtaining a feel for its overall vision, as against getting trapped into dissecting every single detail or coming up with quick counter-arguments against each one of its ideas.

On the other hand, there is no need to approach Vedanta with labels like 'Eastern' or 'Hindu' and then automatically consider it to be impenetrably mysterious. As said earlier, Vedanta involves unusual and subtle ideas; however, nothing in Vedanta offends logic or contradicts our valid experiences. Also, our greatest difficulties in reaping full benefit from Vedanta do not arise from problems of logic and understanding; they arise from our unwillingness to reduce the turbulence in our minds which renders them opaque. Vedanta requires an adequately prepared mind which is neither in internal turmoil nor in conflict with its surroundings; it also needs a healthy ego which is receptive to the possibility that our personalities may not be as important as we take them to be. These requirements are often glossed over. However, one of the most encouraging features of Vedanta is that even its introductory teachings bring in great benefits in terms of attitudinal changes as well as the realisation that the truth may be different from our usual ideas.

Finally, it should be borne in mind that it is not unusual for many of us to fail in relating to Vedanta's offering at a given point in our lives. This has been so over the ages and if a person does not zealously embrace Vedanta immediately upon being introduced to it, nothing judgemental needs to be read into this. Vedanta's goal is our own happiness and since all our activities are directed towards experiencing happiness, all of us are already on Vedanta's path to some extent, even if we do not recognise this.

During the several years over which I have had the good fortune of pursuing Vedanta under the guidance of exceptional teachers, I have found my own life becoming more rewarding; I have also developed better understanding and immense respect for the scheme of wisdom contained in my culture, to which I had not paid any attention earlier. I hope that as you read this book, you begin to feel the true spirit of Vedanta which I have come to admire and love and find some things in it which add value to your own lives.

WHO NEEDS PHILOSOPHY?

Vedanta is not philosophy in the usual meaning of that word but, yet, it is considered to be so. Therefore, it is important to consider to relevance of philosophy in general; this is especially so when philosophy seems to be rapidly falling out of favour and is often written-off as being useless.

Dictionaries term Vedanta as a school of Hindu philosophy. The word 'philosophy' carries a connotation which was well-captured by the American historian Henry Adams when he said, *"Philosophy is unintelligible answers to insoluble problems!"* Philosophers are usually thought to be reclusive academics who endlessly debate abstract issues.

The matters which philosophy is supposed to deal with are represented by Big Questions like:

What is the purpose of life?
Is there God?
Do we have free-will or are we ruled by destiny?

Our general impression is that these questions have been discussed since time immemorial, without getting anywhere near convincing answers. Based upon such impressions, we keep philosophy at a safe distance and get on with our practical lives; we feel that we are better off by doing, experiencing and achieving things, instead of wasting time in sterile speculation. The relevance of philosophy in general therefore needs to be addressed first, even before we come to Vedanta.

To begin with, philosophy is about thinking and human beings think for the same reason that birds fly and fish swim: they are uniquely designed to do so. And, for any human being, questions about the meaning of his life and the nature of the world are bound to arise, even if infrequently. Many believe that such fundamental questions (or metaphysical questions as they are called) are less important than practical questions like how to amass a personal fortune or how to alleviate suffering of the down-trodden. There are entire cultures, such as the Chinese, whose major systems of thought focus almost entirely on proper action as against questioning the real nature of things. However, ethics ultimately need some kind of underpinning from metaphysics. If, for instance, we are told to be fair and compassionate, it would be perfectly reasonable for us to ask why we should have to behave in this manner, especially if we happen to be rich and powerful. Our question can find a final answer only by understanding the true nature of things which gives value to specific behaviour and relates it to our own well-being. It is philosophy which helps us to find meaningful ways in which to explore such questions.

'Philosophy' is a combination of two Greek words: *philo* which means love and *sophia* which means wisdom. It thus means love of wisdom. But this is only a direct and limited meaning; let us dissect it a little further. Love represents commitment because, without commitment, there is no real love. Wisdom involves gaining insight into the real nature of something. Putting the two together, commitment to gaining insight into ... what? As we know, the focus of philosophy is human life. Thus, philosophy means a commitment to gaining insights into our lives. This is not as abstract as love for wisdom in general; in fact, most of us would concede that it could be useful to gain some insights into our own lives.

And these insights do not always have to be about the so-called big questions. After all, we do not get up each morning to earnestly look into the mirror and ask, "Why am I here?"! However, from time to time, we all need answers to questions like:

> *Is it selfish to seek my own happiness?*
> *How do I deal with my frequent anger?*
> *Why are my relationships so unfulfilling?*
> *Can I be happy without serious wealth?*

The approach and discipline of philosophy help us to find answers for several such questions and doubts. In fact, philosophy's most important task is to help us answer the question: "How should I live?"

A vital thing about philosophy is that it is not an optional matter for any of us; it is an integral part of human existence. Philosophy involves using individual experiences to develop generalised conclusions. What does this mean? Let us look at an instance where a child first touches a flame. The pain it suffers is a single experience which it may forget in time. But after a few more experiences of being singed by fire, it forms a broad-based conclusion: fire burns. After this, it does not have to stick its finger into every flame to re-learn the same lesson; it can now use its common knowledge about fire to protect itself from harm.

While philosophy operates on a more profound plane, it too is based on the fact that we cannot practically deal with every thought, issue or event in our lives as an individual occurrence. Unless we have a conceptual frame-work of across-the-board conclusions, we would be like a new-born baby who stares at everything in ignorant wonder or a person who keeps on re-inventing wheels. A general set of conclusions is therefore indispensable in our lives. Even though many of our conclusions are not fully thought through and may lack validity, we often rely and operate on the basis of generalised convictions like:

> *I don't believe in destiny but only in my effort and skill.*
> *This is wrong because it is selfish.*
> *Don't be so sure – nobody can be certain of anything.*
> *You always reap the consequences of your deeds.*

Does any of this sound familiar? Each one of these statements is an example of a philosophical statement because it is a general conclusion about our lives, which we repeatedly use to deal with individual issues. In fact, even the statement that "Philosophy is useless" is itself a philosophical statement. So, to paraphrase Aristotle, our actual choice is never between philosophy and no philosophy but only between bad philosophy and good philosophy.

What is bad philosophy? The noted Russian-American novelist and philosopher, Ayn Rand, provides an answer when she says that if we never pause to work out our philosophy by a rational process of thought and logic, we may unreflectively absorb some baseless conclusions, unknown contradictions, nebulous hopes and empty platitudes from our surroundings; we may then use these without concern about their source, validity, context or consequences. Such a rag-tag and random collection of ideas becomes our 'philosophy' and forms the basis for many of our vital decisions.

If proper philosophy is necessary for a meaningful life, do lives based upon the infirm ground of bad philosophy always end up in disaster? Our actual experience is quite the opposite and our lives seem to proceed in a reasonably satisfactory manner even without a well-structured philosophy. How does this happen?

There are good reasons why many of us are able to go through life without being ruined by the lack of a cogent philosophy of our own. Perhaps the most significant reason here is the source of many of our usual attitudes and habits. Our lives are still largely based on values and behaviour patterns which have been handed down to us. The importance of ethics, some relevance of worship and the dangers of improper life-styles are all part of our collective psyche.[1] These are the synthesis of the experience and intelligence of a large number of people over the years. This collective philosophy becomes available to us through our background and environment. Much as the average pilot is protected in flight by adhering to check-lists and by staying within limits developed by expert test-pilots, we avoid many troubles in our lives by following (even unconsciously) the philosophy built into the tenets of our cultures and religions.

Another factor which protects us is good luck or grace, or whatever else we may want to call that unknown factor in all our lives. An instance of this is a true story of an air-crash in the Pyrenees, in Europe. A small aircraft crashed in a desolate part of these mountains. The survivors used a torn map from the plane's wreckage to head to the nearest village which, to their great relief, they soon reached. It was discovered only later that the map they had relied upon was not of the Pyrenees at all, but of a region of the Alps. It was sheer luck that the features on the map coincided with their surroundings and that a village happened to be in the direction in which the survivors had

---

1 I can see despairing parents of rebellious teenagers shaking their heads in total disagreement with this statement! But the most difficult of teenagers become remarkably orthodox once they develop a personal agenda of their own.

walked. And with luck we may be naturally even-tempered, wealthy (perhaps through inheritance or marriage) and enjoy good health; as we comfortably sail through life we may wonder what this fuss over philosophy is all about. Some of our lives are like this: we go through moderate ups and downs, but are lucky enough to avoid running into major problems, where our lack of a sensible philosophy would extract a heavy price.

But this reliance upon traditional ways of life and upon chance to protect us is not without its own dangers. We live in times where the role of institutions like families and religion is diminishing. Our sense of individuality is becoming more unbridled and the tempering effect of traditional values is waning. We are no longer content to remain the ordinary pilots who follow check-lists; each one of us wants to be the test-pilot who is allowed to push beyond the envelope of conventional safety. Further, as Bertrand Russell (the famous British Nobel Prize-winning author and thinker) points out, most of us do not feel contentedly rich; many of us are not born good-natured; many of us have uneasy passions; health is a blessing which no one can be sure of preserving; marriage and children are not invariable sources of bliss. In this situation, we have genuine need to develop a sound, personal philosophy, if we want to live happily.

Quite apart from these dangers, there is an insidious way in which the lack of proper philosophy detracts from our lives. To understand this, let us look at two simple analogies. The first is of a person who leads a comfortable life, filled with conveniences and luxuries, but who does nothing to ensure physical fitness. The second is of another person who enjoys eating out at restaurants but sticks to the same cuisine, often to the extent of ordering the same things on the menu of the same restaurant.

The person who never gets any physical exercise may manage to remain functional; however, with passing time, there is no doubt that his strength and fitness will be compromised. Staying away from philosophy is, for our mental muscles, the same thing as staying away from exercise for our physical muscles. Just as a well-toned body stands erect and proud, philosophy makes our mental posture reliably firm and upright. Philosophy develops and maintains our capabilities of being able to analyse complex issues, assess alternatives and use logic properly. These are vital skills, both in daily living as well as when confronted with large issues. Ultimately, philosophy brings in that nebulous quality called wisdom; wisdom is difficult to define but it brings both depth and practicality into our lives.

Coming to the second analogy, philosophy expands our entire sphere of thinking and opens up new avenues. A person ordering the same things in the same restaurant may continue to enjoy his habit-driven choices, but he misses out on a new world of eclectic and exciting cuisines. A life without an element of philosophy, which Socrates called 'the unexamined life', is like that: a life based on a narrow selection of options presented to us by our environment, family, friends and simple habit. It was because of unexamined ideas that European mariners in the Middle Ages did not sail too far to the west because of the fear of falling off the edge of the earth. To live life in a small cocoon is the waste of opportunities to explore, experience and enjoy the countless other possibilities that our lives offer. The price we pay for the unexamined life is, in some ways, life itself.

Finally, it is important to understand that while Vedanta uses analysis and logic in ways similar to western philosophy, its entire orientation and objectives are different. Unlike conventional philosophy, which is a quest for truths outside of the observer,[2] Vedanta's aim is to show an underlying unity between the observed and observer. Also, philosophy's primary focus is on the establishment of absolute truths for truth's sake; while Vedanta is also undoubtedly concerned with the truth, its commitment is not to the truth as an end in itself but as a means for us to find personal happiness. In this way, Vedanta is different and much more individually relevant to us than conventional philosophy.

---

2 Some major areas covered by conventional philosophy include epistemology (How do I get knowledge of the word?), ethics (How do I conduct myself in the world?) and theology (What is the nature of God?).

WHAT IS VEDANTA?

There seem to be as many views about Vedanta as those of the proverbial group of blind men about an elephant! This essay provides an over-view of Vedanta's nature and relevance.

We often have some prior notions about Vedanta even before we make an effort to understand it. For instance, for some of us Vedanta is Hindu religion, for some others it is mystical philosophy and for yet others, it is an ascetic way of life. But these are fragmentary views which do not capture the whole. In its essence, Vedanta is a solution to our problem of perpetually seeking happiness. Why should the pursuit of happiness be considered a problem at all? After all, don't we all seek happiness on a regular basis, day in and day out? But it is this constant seeking which is the crux of our problem. We continuously seek happiness because not one of us feels fulfilled for too long: there is always something which can be added to (or subtracted from) our lives to make us feel more completely happy. Because we are never fully satisfied with our current situation, our entire life is an endless effort to become different in one way or another: from poor to rich, from rich to famous, from fat to thin, from ignorant to knowledgeable, from diseased to healthy, from having a bad boss to having a good boss, and so on and so forth, without any end. It is this life of coercive and perpetual becoming (called *samsara* in Sanskrit) which Vedanta addresses.

What is wrong with a life of trying to be different from whatever we presently are? The first problem here is one of freedom – we all like to choose the ways in which we act but if the need to change becomes compelling then we lose that freedom. The second problem is that a life of continuous change requires constant effort which is tiring; it also leads to fear and anger because no amount of effort ever ensures that life remains in line with our wishes. And finally, for some of us, a life of perpetually trying to become happy seems as pointless as a journey on a treadmill: despite a lot of expended effort and time, one continues to remain in the same place, i.e. a person who is yet always wanting. Vedanta comes in only when we develop some doubts about our usual approach to being happy, when we want to go beyond a constant and compulsive state of trying to be happy.

Vedanta's objective is also to make us happy. But its solution is different from our usual recipes such as making more money, going on a more exciting vacation or entering into a more satisfying relationship. Vedanta does not focus upon our individual wants but challenges the assumption that we really are the wanting persons we experience ourselves to be. The purpose of the core teachings of Vedanta is to help us discover a constant substratum of contentment and peace which is integral to us and which remains unaffected by all our pending agendas and unfulfilled desires. The discovery of something which is already with us may not sound like a big deal but the fact is that our most vexing problems are resolved simply by this change in the understanding of the nature of our own selves.

Here, one may ask why something integral to our own selves should remain unknown; after all, if there is one thing we know really well, it is our own self. To understand why self-knowledge is not readily available, we have to start from the time we are born. We all begin our lives with a completely clean slate in terms of knowledge; apart from some in-built instincts such as suckling for food and recoiling from pain, we are born ignorant. This ignorance can be divided into two basic categories: ignorance of the world and ignorance of our own self. As we grow up, our faculties develop and we use them to shed our initial ignorance. Thus, we learn about objects, places, processes and concepts; we also get to know more and more about our own bodies and the various facets of our minds. However, in this process we do not learn anything about our own real self which Vedanta says is different from our bodies and minds.

Why do we not learn anything about our real self? Vedanta's answer (which it establishes by using reason) is that the true nature of our self is pure consciousness or awareness. Our faculties work very well for knowing things that can be an object in our awareness. They cannot work for obtaining knowledge of awareness itself. This is because knowing anything necessarily implies a knowing awareness separate from the object or thought which is known. Whatever is known can never be the knower. Thus, we can never know awareness because it is the same awareness which makes things known to us. This is similar to the fact that our eyes cannot see themselves. We can, therefore, go from birth to death with our initial self-ignorance completely intact, even though we may have made great progress in demolishing our ignorance in other areas. At this point one may well ask, "So why bother? Why is the demolition of this self-ignorance so important, when I have conquered ignorance in all other areas?"

Vedanta's response is that 'knowledge in all other areas' is only lower knowledge.[3] Such knowledge never fully resolves our struggle for happiness. It also distracts us from real knowledge worth having: knowledge of our own self which can provide the answer to our endless search for happiness.

The lack of self-knowledge actually becomes a problem of false conclusions. Despite being ignorant of our true nature, we do not simply conclude that "I do not know who I am"; we make the natural mistake of taking the things we know most intimately – our own bodies and minds – to be our real selves. In our daily language, when we say "I am tall" or "I am sad", we show the complete identification we have with our physical and mental attributes. Our bodies and minds are relatively limited and insignificant. When we take them to be our real selves, their limitations seem to become our own limitations. Our instinctive efforts to overcome these limitations then become a desperate and unending struggle. It is to overcome the limitations of our bodies and minds that we so assiduously try to become stronger, healthier, richer, more famous, more loved, better informed and so on, unto our dying day. Our entire life, instead of remaining a gift, becomes a serious battle and we lose our natural sense of freedom and spontaneity.

This is where Vedanta comes in to remind us that whatever is known cannot be the one who knows. Thus, our deepest truth has to be more than our bodies or our minds, both of which are known to us. Once this is clear to us, we may still

---

3 Termed *apara vidya* in Sanskrit.

superficially continue with our usual efforts; however, now the actual results we achieve in augmenting and pleasing our physical form and personality, no longer remain the sole determinants of our happiness.

It is obviously not enough for us to just understand what we are not. Nor is it the sole purpose of Vedanta to convince us that our bodies and minds are alien or inconsequential. Its initial rejection of our bodies and minds is a transitory point; it is only meant to help us overcome some of our false conclusions. After doing this, Vedanta comes to its next task of helping us to understand what we really are. For this purpose, Vedanta has to work in a special way because we cannot know ourselves in the way in which we get to know anything else. Even though we cannot directly use our eyes to see themselves, we can use a mirror to observe them. Similarly, the teachings of Vedanta operate like a word-mirror which, when used appropriately, result in the removal of ignorance surrounding our own selves.

Because we live as an integral part of creation, Vedanta then goes on to explore the nature of the reality underlying the entire universe. It finally unfolds a vision of our true nature which is stunning in its scope and consequences. In its most breathtaking revelation, Vedanta postulates that all things which exist (including us, the individuals) are not really independent entities which they seem to be; they all appear in and consist of a single, unchanging and conscious reality. Because this reality is single (or 'one without a second' as stated in Vedantic texts) it is described as *advaita* or non-dual; it is the truth of everything and Vedanta promises that its abiding knowledge liberates us from all our notions of limitation.

Of course, Vedanta does not stop with a convenient statement like "Everything is one reality" which may sound profound but actually does nothing for us in our daily lives; Vedanta goes on to provide us with processes which help us to experience the consequences of this startling insight and obtain personal benefit. And, moreover, it does this without recourse to thoughts and ideas which offend logic or contradict our valid experiences.

This insight into fundamental oneness is also shared by other cultures and geographies, as is evident in Taoism of China, in Sufism aspects of Islam and in mystical streams of Christianity; however, Vedanta has developed unique methods of preserving and propagating its wisdom and making it more practically accessible.

The knowledge that Vedanta offers does not work instantly or for all of us; it requires an eligible student with the right attitude, properly guided over a period of time. However, where it works even partially, it has the effect of removing a large layer of illusions and unnecessary suffering from our lives. Lives touched by the spirit of Vedanta become fuller and Vedanta becomes their biggest blessing.

Etymology and History

Etymologically, Vedanta stands for the end-portion of humankind's oldest scriptures, the Vedas.[4] (Antah means 'end' in Sanskrit and veda + antah becomes vedanta.) The word 'end' also means 'goal' and, in this alternative sense, Vedanta has connotations of being the goal or culmination of the voluminous contents of all the Vedas. The end-portion of the Vedas is also called the Upanishads[5] and so the term Vedanta is synonymous with the term Upanishads. The Upanishads are not set out as well-structured philosophical treatises but contain a record of scattered insights and experiences which occurred to *rishis* (seers or sages) of ancient India. Even though this material appears vague, contradictory and confusing in parts, the overall perspective of reality it provides is sublime and startling.

No one quite knows how many Upanishads existed once upon a time, but one hundred and eight of them, of vastly varying size, survive till today. According to historians, the earliest ones are reckoned to go back to 2,500 BCE but Hindu traditionalists do not recognise any such time-frame because, in their vision, the

---

4 The Vedas are in four large compilations known as *Rig, Yajur, Sama* and *Atharva.*

5 'Upanishad' is a combination of three words: *upa* meaning something very near, i.e. our own self, *ni* meaning unambiguous or well-established and *shad* meaning destruction of something unwanted, i.e. unhappiness.

entire Vedas are *anadi* or timeless and *apaureshya* or of divine origin. This vision is not as culturally chauvinistic or esoteric as it may sound. It is based on the insight that all knowledge is part of creation since its very inception – we only discover from time-to-time that which is already there. After all, the law of gravitation existed even before the apple fell in front of Newton. Therefore, in ancient India, the identity of discoverers of knowledge and the time and place of their discoveries had been traditionally regarded as being irrelevant. Because the Vedas are nothing but a collection of knowledge (*veda* is derived from the root word *vid* meaning to know), there is no record of who complied them and when.

Out of the available Upanishads, ten[6] are considered to be the principal ones because Adi Shankara, a renowned sage and teacher from the 8th century CE, wrote elaborate commentaries on them. Individual Upanishads appear to be dissimilar at a superficial level because of differing approaches, emphasis on particular ideas and writing styles but there is, in fact, a basic unity in their underlying thrust.

Apart from being another name for the Upanishads, the term Vedanta also has a broader meaning when it is used to refer to an entire classical school of Indian philosophy.[7] In this sense, it includes not only the contents of the Upanishads but many other subsequent texts and the interpretations of a number of great scholar-teachers. Thus, the Bhagavad Gita[8] and the writings of Adi Shankara are vital parts of Vedanta, even though they are not part of the Vedas.

One fact which needs to be mentioned here is that while we focus on advaita Vedanta as explained by Shankara, there are other interpretations of the contents of the Upanishads. Out

---

6 *Isha, Katha, Kena, Prasna, Mundaka, Mandukya, Taittiriya, Aitareya, Chandogya* and *Brihadaranyaka.*

7 Just to make matters more confusing, Vedanta (as a school of philosophy) also goes by another name: *uttara mimasa!*

8 A well known composition found in the epic Mahabharata; even though the Bhagavad Gita is not part of the Vedas, it is a key text for teaching Vedanta.

of these, the two most significant ones are *visisht advaita* (qualified non-dualism) of Ramanuja and *dvaita* (dualism) of Madhva. Both these are dualistic and theistic to a smaller and larger extent, respectively; they are more palatable because they offer greater scope for devotion and because they avoid some of thedifficulties which advaita Vedanta faces in explaining the cause of the perceived world. However, advaita Vedanta is the oldest, the most rigorously developed and the dominant form of Vedanta.

A very important fact about Vedanta which we should not lose sight of is that, at its heart, it is a remedy for our compulsive and endless effort to be other than what we are. If we forget this, we may start looking for definitive answers to abstract questions such as "Why is there any existence at all?" or "When, how and why did this universe come into being?"; but such questions are not Vedanta's focus. Vedanta does not claim to be a grand explanation for all our questions; what it does is to take us to a point where awareness of the enormity of our own reality makes all questions trivial and permits us to be comfortable even in the face of unanswered questions.

One last thing we should deal with here is the issue of the relevance of Vedanta because, to some extent, this is implicit in the question "What is Vedanta?". Vedanta has always been relevant for human beings because it deals with our universal search for happiness. But it is more relevant to us today because of the accelerating pace of our lives which makes the quest for true happiness even more challenging.

To some of us, any comment about the hectic pace of our current lives sounds like the lament of an ageing generation which is unable to cope with change. There is some truth in this because, as people get older, there is a natural tendency to indulge in warm and comforting nostalgia; many older people in each generation always see the seeds of disaster in the headlong pace and licentiousness of the succeeding generation.[9] As

---

9 An inscription on an Assyrian clay tablet, dating back to 2,800 BCE says:"Our earth is degenerate in these latter days; bribery and corruption are common; children no longer obey their parents; and the end of the world is evidently approaching."

someone has wittily said in the context of older people being too judgemental, "*Good advice is something you give once you are too old to set a bad example*"! But even after making allowance for the foibles and predilections of age, we cannot ignore the increasingly scorching pace of our lives and its consequences.

Growing aspirations, more intense competition and amazing technological capabilities all spur us into faster and more frantic action in many areas of our lives. There are, of course, very real benefits of accelerating change and development which have made us the healthiest, the best informed and the most liberated individuals ever, with an incredible range of choices and powers. However, the age-old rule that there is no free lunch continues to operate. Payment has to be made for the benefits we have, even if this payment is in an indirect or intangible form. So, there is continuous and rapid proliferation in the number of things we must keep learning to feel useful and productive; the variety of activities we get involved in at work and at home grows exponentially; the increasing number of options available to us makes even trivial decisions agonising; the amount of information available on all subjects swamps both our minds and our time; the level of competition – whether to get into college or to get a job or even to get theatre tickets – puts relentless pressures.

This pace and pressure have led to several changes in our ways of thinking and in our choices. We are almost forced to look for quick fixes rather than long-term solutions, even in fundamentally important areas of life. Increasing specialisation is a natural reaction to the increasing complexity of our lives; the resulting tunnel-vision, even though euphemistically labelled as 'focused', makes it difficult to take an integrated view of life as a whole. Even as we are more informed about global issues and their consequences, our concerns seem to get progressively more self-centred on the plane of day-to-day living. The power of increasingly trivial irritations to upset our equilibrium is remarkable. Our attention spans are getting shorter and our relationships more brittle. Even our vacations are packed with activities and agendas to 'optimise' them. The unpressured time required for our minds to objectively evaluate our goals and actions is now getting almost impossible to obtain. And, unfortunately, many of us seem unable to make the connection between our neglect and failure on this front and the fact that a sense of tranquility and wholesomeness eludes us in spite of our great progress on so many other fronts.[10]

It is in this scenario that Vedanta becomes particularly vital. It helps us to see that a large part of our constant running is not towards a clear objective but a reflection of our inner restlessness. Vedanta suggests that we are in a tearing hurry because of our fears: fear that we will lose out on something even though we do not quite know what we will lose; fear of being silent and with our own selves because that may force us to reflect on what we are doing and why.

The teachings of Vedanta encourage us to look at a bigger picture where we do not have to take every little thing so seriously. How does looking at a bigger picture help us? This can be perhaps better understood by considering a common experience of taking a picture with a camera. Let us take an instance where we are standing on a hill-top and looking at a vista of a tree-filled slope, going down to meet the sea. As we gaze upon this view, it appears fine and nothing is out of order. However, as soon as we shoot the same sight through a camera's lens, problems suddenly arise. The previously unnoticeable twig of a nearby bush looms disturbingly large in the photograph because it was too close to the lens; the forested slope appears to be only sparsely wooded in the image because a small barren patch has unintentionally gained prominence; the expanse of sea in the picture seems disproportionately large in relation to the narrow strip of the sky because of the way in the camera was angled.

What alters the original perfection of the vista? It is the artificial boundaries, caused by the camera's limitations, which distort natural wholeness and create problems when there were none

---

10 According to global drug sales data for 2010 (from Pharma Exec), drugs to deal with diseases caused by wrong life-styles (such as cardio and cerebro-vascular disease and gastric ulcers) and with diseases of the mind (such as mood disorders and schizophrenia) constituted the largest segment of total sales.

previously. These distortions and disturbances immediately cease when the large picture – the view as a whole – is seen. Vedanta, by helping us to counter the restrictive boundaries created by the conditioning in our minds, also helps us to regain a natural wholeness where there is nothing fundamentally wrong.

With Vedanta we learn that while there is good reason to plan for tomorrow, it should not always be at the cost of living fully today. While we may not see this, things go on silently and peacefully in the universe without any contradictions; things happen in nature in spite of us and not because of us. By making us realise this, Vedanta provides some space within us in which we can relax and experience a deep sense of peace. Even though this may sound quixotic and dreamy, the consequences of being able to shed our compulsive drives are real and remarkable. And Vedanta, properly pursued, guides us towards this state.

WRONG NOTIONS GALORE

The number of misconceptions about Vedanta is legion. This essay talks about some of the more common ones which are important to get over, if Vedanta is to be meaningfully explored. Vedanta is an ancient body of knowledge, based upon texts in an archaic language couched in unfamiliar terms and sometimes talked about by those whose own understanding is none too clear. It is, therefore, not surprising that many false notions have grown around it. It is useful to consider at least some major misconceptions about Vedanta because, without this, we may either reject Vedanta prematurely or have some unrealistic expectations as we pursue it.

Vedanta is Religion or Philosophy

Vedanta is frequently understood to be no different from the Hindu religion. Religions are based on unverifiable beliefs (such as that there is an almighty being called God sitting in heaven, that there is a hell for sinners and so on); they appeal to faith and are not dependent on knowledge; they contain dogmas and use prescriptions. Vedanta, on the other hand, is knowledge-based and gives us a direct experience of its teachings. It contains no set creed; the prescriptions it seems to contain are really only descriptions of what many people have found relevant in their own journeys towards a personal truth. It has an over-lay of Hindu religion only because the way of life prescribed under the vedic religion is useful for the pursuit of Vedanta. In a strict sense, one need not be a follower of Hinduism or of any other religion and nor is there absolute necessity to relate to any particular God to learn the lessons of Vedanta.[11]

---

11 It must be borne in mind that this dispensability of God is only at the conceptual level. None of us is an intellectual purist at all times and we have to deal with other aspects of our mental make-up including our emotions. Vedanta recognises that without developing a proper understanding of God and establishing an emotional connection with him, our preparation for the journey of Vedanta is likely to be incomplete. But the God of Vedanta is very different from the anthropomorphic notion of God which most theologies hold out; the understanding of God here is unique and beneficial, without requiring blind adherence to any set form or ritual.

To the extent that Vedanta examines our world-view and fundamental aspects of our lives, it can be called philosophy. However, philosophy focuses on abstract truths for the sake of the truth itself, while Vedanta's commitment is towards us, the individuals; its objective is to help us solve our problem of perpetually trying to be other than whatever we currently are, in the hope of finding lasting happiness. This orientation of Vedanta makes it very different from what we conventionally understand by the term philosophy.[12]

Vedanta is Fatalistic

It is frequently held that Vedanta breeds a fatalistic attitude. Fatalism is an attitude caused by accepting the premise that all events are pre-determined and that human beings are powerless to change them. Vedanta is supposed to preach such a doctrine via the theory of *karma*. However, the karma theory is not even part of the core teachings of Vedanta. And, even for those who accept the karma theory, nowhere does it suggest that sitting back and letting events overcome us, is the correct course to follow.

Vedanta actually emphasises that free will is the only pragmatic basis for leading our lives. At the same time, it highlights the fact that the actual result following any action is not determined by that action alone but also by a complex set of other known and unknown factors. And we all have experience of this. We may use our best efforts to run our business successfully but an unexpected technological break-through in a distant corner of the world renders our product obsolete. Or we may go to a bus-stop to get to work but a ride in the car of a passing friend makes our journey quicker and enjoyable. Not recognizing the effect of factors beyond our own inputs can lead to misplaced pride, guilt or anger. By exhorting us to action and by reminding us that our own action is only one of the factors which shapes the final outcome, Vedanta acts as a valuable guide to make our lives purposeful as well as emotionally balanced.

---

12 In Sanskrit there is no equivalent of the word 'philosophy' and the word *darshana*, which is used instead, means 'vision' and implies a 'point of view' – the emphasis is not on the total grasp of grand truths but on enough understanding, from the limited perspective of helping us solve our problem of finding happiness.

Asceticism and Renunciation

Does Vedanta preach asceticism and renunciation? A 'Yes' here seems justified by upanishadic statements[13] as well as by writings of great teachers (such as Shankara's famous Bhaja Govindam[14]) and poets (such as Bhartruhari's Vairagya Shatakam[15]) which all extol the virtues of renunciation.

The actual objective of texts like these is not to encourage everyone to don a loincloth, pick up a begging bowl and wander off alone into the sunset. Some of this writing is poetry with its license; some of it is designed to shock people out of a complacent way of thinking. We need to see the whole context of such compositions; only then do we understand that the issue is not renunciation as a physical act, but as an attitude. What is vital is an objective valuation of our concerns, possessions and goals. And our valuations do change with maturity and learning. A father who used to be upset about lost toys in his own childhood, may now look gently amused when his child throws a tantrum about some misplaced trifles; or a driving sense of envy and competition with which one may have started one's career, can sublimate over time leaving just deep peace and contentment. We all develop an attitude of indifference to some previously dear objects or attitudes as a result of our growth; this is mature discrimination, not renunciation.

But what about people who don orange robes and become wandering mendicants? One has to recognise that a small number

---

13 For instance the often recited verse from the Mahanarayana Upanishad which begins by saying:" Not by actions, not by having children, not by wealth but only by renunciation is the immortal end achieved..."

14 As an example,Verse 18 reads: "Who can disturb a man's happiness if he can be happy living in the open halls of temples or under the trees, lying on the bare ground wrapped in skins, having given up every possession and enjoyment?"

15 Look at Verse 31, again as an example: "In enjoyment, there is fear of disease; in social position, the fear of being displaced; in wealth, the fear of hostile kings; in honour, the fear of humiliation; in power, the fear of foes; in beauty, the fear of old age; in scriptural learning, the fear of opposing views; in virtue, the fear of seducers; in body, the fear of death.All things of this world connected with man are subject to fear; renunciation alone is fearlessness."

of people in all cultures have a mental make-up which encourages them to seek opportunities for intensive contemplation in solitude, without distractions from any other agenda. Such people may become monks, *bhikshus* or *sanyasis*. This does not mean that all people who wish to benefit from Vedanta have to opt out of the normal mode of living. In fact the Bhagavad Gita goes to considerable length in pointing out that, for a majority of people, the path of carrying on normal activities with the right understanding is far better than becoming a renunciate.

Act without Expectation

A common misunderstanding, based upon a well-known *shloka* from the Bhagavad Gita[16] is that Vedanta wants us to act appropriately but without any expectation of results. This, in turn, is taken to mean that we should have no purpose in mind to be achieved as we do anything. Such a notion is obviously not realistic because, after all, as we board a flight scheduled to go to London we do expect the aircraft to get there and, as we teach a class, we do expect students to obtain some understanding. All action is geared towards a practical outcome and this cannot be a problem.

What this verse of the Gita highlights is the important message that when we focus on the pleasure or ego-gratification which we hope to derive from our actions, we are doing ourselves a disservice. The reasons for this are many. When a part of our mind is already savouring the enjoyment of our anticipated success, this is necessarily at the cost of some diversion from the work on hand. Further, it is not very wise to live in a future which may remain illusory, at the cost of not fully living the present. And, most important, focus on the fruits of one's efforts is based on the assumption that joy comes to us only from a favourable outcome. However, Vedanta's central message is that our true nature is always fulfilled. Therefore, hankering for temporary and superficial pleasures (which may come if our efforts are successful) actually keeps us away from discovering our already-existing state of wholeness.

---

16 Verse 2(47): *karmanyeva adhikaraste ma phaleshu kadachana*...you only have the right to act but no entitlement to results.

It is for these reasons that the Gita asks us to find fulfilment in doing whatever is appropriate, without obsession with the enjoyment of future results. This is called *karma-yoga* and its objective is to lead us to a level of equanimity required for the deeper insights of Vedanta to become meaningful. However, this does not imply that our actions should not have any goals; the problem is not in planning for the future and working towards a specific practical outcome but in pinning our personal joy and satisfaction only upon such outcome.

Is the World Illusory?

One of the more popular one-liners quoted from the writings of Adi Shankara is *brahma satyam jagan mithya*, which is often translated as *the ultimate reality is the only truth and the world is illusory*. Leaving aside the bit about the ultimate reality, it is the second part of this statement (about the world being illusory) which causes misconceptions and provokes humour. The misconception is that Vedanta tries to solve all our problems by the simple trick of dismissing the world as being unreal. The humour is reflected in clever questions such as "How come my toe hurts when I stub it against this illusory table?"

Mithya is a special and technical term of Vedanta, used for referring to anything that is dependent on something else for its existence. To use a stock illustration, a clay cup appears to exist independently with its own form, function and name. However, the cup's existence is entirely grounded in the clay from which it was formed; while the cup cannot exist without the clay, the clay will continue to exist even when the cup-form is destroyed. In the parlance of Vedanta, the cup would be termed mithya while, in relation to this cup, clay would be called *satyam* or real; this does not mean that the cup is non-existent or illusory at the level of our experience.

Vedanta says that the world which we experience is as real as our bodies & minds and has to be dealt with accordingly — Vedanta is not a method which will help us to cleverly side-step the practical world. However, Vedanta awakens us to a higher level of reality where our personalities and the world which we experience, both subside into the common reality which is their basis. This is similar to bangles, chains and earrings being seen as only gold by the bullion-trader and, in that bigger vision, the forms and names of individual ornaments losing their meaning. It is only when Vedanta's highest vision becomes our own that the world loses its capability of seriously affecting us and thus becomes superficial.

Perfection and Goodness

Let us move on to another type of misconception about Vedanta. This misconception revolves around notions of perfection and goodness.

It is not the intention of Vedanta to mass-produce enlightened clones. All persons who have received and fully understood the knowledge of Vedanta need not look and behave like the Buddha — in the vedantic scheme of things there is scope for feeling physical and emotional pain, for the mind to have preferences and for occasional flashes of temper, even at the end of its journey. There is of course a tremendous difference between a person who has completed this journey and a person who has not, but enlightenment does not mean erasure of individuality at the superficial level.

Coming to the notion of an ideal world which is only good, Vedanta makes it clear that the world exists entirely in polarity. All our states and even all our thoughts occur because of their opposites. There is death only because of birth, a notion of beauty only because of a simultaneous notion of ugliness. We cannot have a world which is purely good because we cannot even conceive of good unless evil is present. To attempt to have a world with its polarities removed is like trying to have a single-sided coin.

There can of course be periods in history or some individual lives where the quality of goodness dominates. However, on a larger scale of time and space, there has to be a balance between not only good and evil but also between all other opposites. Any hope of retaining only the good will never be realised by the very nature of the world. That is why despite numerous saints (and, in some traditions, God himself) having done their work on this earth, evil continues quite unabated. Vedanta recognises that creation has to be based on polar opposites and helps us to understand and deal with them. While it encourages goodness, its primary aim is not to fulfil the impractical notion of a perfect world.

Bliss

Many are attracted to Vedanta by the prospect of an experience of bliss which is supposed to far outstrip any other joyful experience which we have had so far. That Vedanta will provide such an experience is a notion which arises from the frequent use of the word *ananda* (which literally does mean joy) in Vedantic texts. However, the implication of ananda here is to be understood in conjunction with another inter-related term, *ananta*, which means 'limitless'. Anything without limits implies fullness (because nothing more can be added to something which is already limitless) and, so, ananda actually refers to a natural and constant sense of fulfilment, independent of any specific experience. Vedanta's promise is not a taste of some extra-ordinary brand of happiness but the personal discovery of our very own nature as always being without any lack and, therefore, at complete peace by itself. This is very different from a joyous experience arising from an event or situation, which comes and goes in time.

Therapy

It is often believed that Vedanta is specialised therapy, meant only for those who have either met with grave misfortune or are not able to successfully handle the floods and ebbs of the tides of ordinary life. People who suffer from dysfunctionality in important areas (such as severe physical or mental disease, financial failure or inability to sustain normal relationships) need professional help outside of Vedanta. While it is true that many turn to Vedanta only when disillusioned as a result of problems and reverses[17] a significantly dysfunctional person is unlikely to have enough mental elbow-room for the subtle teachings of

---

17 In this context, someone has said that religion is for those who fear hell while Vedanta is for those who have actually been there!

Vedanta to gain a foot-hold. This is why a modern teacher of Vedanta says, *"Vedanta is for normally abnormal people"*! We all suffer from completely wrong notions about the real nature of the world as well as of our own selves and Vedanta is a solution to the problems created by such notions; however, it is not a replacement for conventional solutions for other serious ailments which have to be sorted out irrespective of the pursuit of Vedanta.

Many More Wrong Notions

Questions about the meaning of our lives and our search for happiness are perennial and universal. Yet, there is often hesitation in approaching the issues that Vedanta raises here. Many of us just do not want to think seriously about these matters. As Bertrand Russell once said, somewhat superciliously, *"Most people would rather die than think; in fact, they do."* Then, there is also the risk of de-stabilising comfortable notions or the possibility of discovering that years of effort in a particular direction may have been misguided. Coupled with such fears, there is often intimidation by the language and terminology employed by Vedanta. These factors inhibit the understanding of its true spirit and provide ground for many wrong notions.

Often, teachers of Vedanta who are supposed to remove ignorance, actually add to false notions; some do it out of ignorance of the subject or its teaching methods and some out of ulterior motives.

In fact, there is no end to the sources and variety of misconceptions about Vedanta. It is important to obtain proper guidance and put in sufficient effort to gain a better feel for the actual nature of this subject at the outset; only then can one continue this pursuit meaningfully.

THE END OF ALL ROADS
All We Want is Happiness

All our aspirations and efforts are centred on happiness and this essay deals with what is at the core of Vedanta: our search for happiness.

The ancient Romans had the grand but fallacious notion that their city was the goal of all roads. But, when we look at the paths of human endeavour, we find that there is indeed a single, constant and universal end: happiness.

The ways in which we seek happiness are many. Hindu scriptures classify our usual efforts to experience happiness under three broad categories: *artha, kama* and *dharma*.[18] Artha is everything we do to ensure our own survival and obtain security. The most obvious instances of artha are our economic activities. Kama is all that we do to seek pleasure on the physical, emotional and intellectual planes. A vacation, a gourmet meal or going to a concert are all based on kama. Dharma includes ethical conduct, religious activities and charitable work.

Security and pleasures are obviously centred on our own immediate happiness. Most of us also include elements of dharma in our lives because that too is expected to bring us personal happiness of a long-term nature. Even our wrong activities are based on the same goal of happiness; the difference is that here we are unable to initially see that such activities will, directly or indirectly, lead us to unhappiness.

The Brihadaranyaka Upanishad categorically proclaims that the personal experience of happiness is the goal of all our efforts, by boldly stating: *atmanastu kamaya sarvam priyam bhavati* - everything is dear only for the sake of oneself. But we do not need scriptural authority to tell us this - a little honest reflection on our own motivations will lead us to the same conclusion. Whether we run a business for private gain or we see our life's mission as the alleviation of the pain and poverty of others, the expected pay-off in all our activities is the same: we hope to feel good, contented and satisfied.

---

18 *Moksha* or liberation is also usually listed as our fourth goals but it is a completely different type of pursuit.

What kind of happiness is our goal? Here again, our experience provides the answer. We are not content with limited happiness. We want a healthy body and an intelligent mind; we want growing and varied skills, knowledge and experiences; we want money along with job satisfaction; we want love and respect from our families as well as from friends and colleagues; we want pleasant memories and a pleasant future; we want an on-going life of security, pleasures and integrity not only for ourselves but also for our children and, in time, for our children's children. As a renowned Vedanta teacher says, tongue-in-cheek, that at the very least we all want to be thinner, richer and more famous than what we are today!

What we really want is an unbroken experience of a pleased and contented self in all situations, at all times, in all places and in all aspects. And this, of course, is an impossibly tall order. After all, who amongst us is permanently and fully happy? Who amongst us has no feelings of guilt, regrets, hostility and fear? Who amongst us has no wish-list which stops us from feeling completely fulfilled?

Propelled by our natural urges, we cannot but strive for happiness. But even our greatest efforts do not completely meet our never-ending desires and overcome the varied obstacles that life throws up on our path. Our lives, therefore, remain moments of pride, satisfaction and joy, replaced by periods of disappointment, regret, guilt, fear and anger, in an on-going cycle. This see-saw continues because, despite all our doings, life stubbornly refuses to settle down in a manner which permits us to be totally and continuously happy. Yet, our hopes keep on conquering our own experiences and we battle on, without a meaningful pause to look at a different approach.

Suppression of Desires

Some traditions, other than Vedanta, suggest that because all our desires cannot be fully and permanently met, true happiness can only come from the simple suppression of desires. But desires are like emotions: they arise without our volition and cannot be eliminated by an act of will, not at least in the short run. For instance, we know that we cannot generate genuine sadness on demand; by the same token, we cannot just will away our sadness once it has arisen, despite our strong desire to be rid of it. And this is similarly true of our desires to own, to consume, to experience, to be loved and so on.

Mere suppression of our desires, without any deeper understanding, can actually be counter-productive because suppressed desires may be driven inwards where they may accumulate and fester, to later surface with redoubled vigour. The many instances of ascetics indulging in perversions and misusing their hold over their followers often have their root in desires which have been masked only to project a certain image.

Rise of Discrimination

Some of us, however, are not comfortable with the idea of life being an endless trek towards the apparently unreachable goal of total fulfilment. Just as our natural hunger pre-supposes the existence of food, some of us instinctively sense that our natural urge to find unchanging happiness indicates that there must be a way of reaching this goal. This is a very critical juncture in our journey towards happiness, a point where we are no longer content to live with a compromise and are ready to question the game-plan of life which we have been using so far. Very often, we reach this point when we are greatly troubled by misfortunes or when we are able to take on board some good advice. Whatever may be our reasons, we now begin to use more discrimination and understanding, as against doing more of the same things which we have so far been doing. We begin to realise, as Einstein pointed out, that insanity lies in doing the same thing over and over again but expecting different results. This is the beginning of Vedanta and, whether we realise it immediately or not, we are now on a completely different path to our goal of happiness.

Sources of Happiness

Vedanta, once it enters our lives, helps us to analyse our attempts to obtain happiness. It first points out that all our usual attempts ✱ are based on the assumption that happiness is contained in things outside of us and is experienced when our desires for possessions, relationships and experiences are fulfilled. Vedanta then shows us that this basic assumption is wrong.

That happiness is not integral to any outside object can be seen by considering a few simple experiences. If our shiny new car contains a certain amount of happiness in itself, why does some of it evaporate as soon as our undeserving neighbour gets a shinier, bigger car? If loud music contains joy, why is it a source of pleasure on one occasion and a positive annoyance on another? The notion that happiness arises upon fulfilment of our desires is the classic fallacy of after this and, therefore, because of this.[19] While fulfilment of desires certainly provides an experience of happiness this does not establish any invariable concomitance. What desire is fulfilled when we feel good while looking at the starry vault of the sky on a magical night? Which one of our needs is met when we dissolve into carefree laughter upon hearing a great joke?

In view of such experiences, Vedanta points out the need to re-examine our usual conclusions about the sources of our happiness.

Graduated Solutions

Whatever may be the actual source of our happiness, our pending desires are undoubtedly issues which continue to bother us. If all our desires can never be fully met or eliminated, how can we ever hope to be totally happy? Vedanta's offers us graduated solutions here with the objective of first lessening the consequences of desires in our minds before finally addressing them with its knowledge.

Many of our desires are natural and they provide us with the motivation to do things. For someone who is just beginning on the path of self-growth, the problem is not in the simple existence of such desires; problems arise when these desires acquire enough force to deny a person the freedom to act rationally and ethically. It is over-powering and compulsive desires which cause anger, fear and hostility which, in turn, may tempt us to employ illegitimate means. Here, Vedanta relies upon the codes

---

19 This fallacy is often better known in its Latin form: *post hoc ergo propter hoc.*

of dharma to modify and balance such problematic desires. Vedanta further depends upon dharma to encourage a way of life which reduces our sense of individual agency or doership, in which the strength of our desires is rooted.

For a more prepared and committed seeker, real Vedanta starts by showing the complete disconnect between what we want – total and abiding happiness – and the very limited results we achieve in trying to fulfil our small and changing desires. And, in its most fundamental approach, Vedanta does not dwell on our desires at all, but helps us to see that our true nature is already fulfilled, and thus makes desires irrelevant. Let us briefly look at each of these four approaches.

Refining Our Desires

We all remember that when we were children, we placed great value on the acquisition of trifles like marbles. Then, as we grew older, we became quite indifferent to marbles because something more valuable, like electronic games, became desirable. We did not have to give up our desire for marbles but we outgrew that desire. This is dharma's first approach, where it helps us to grow away from cruder desires by turning us towards more refined ones.

Some of our pursuits, by the very nature of things, are more harmonious and growth-oriented than others. For instance, when our desire is to acquire more money, the fulfilment of this desire is at the cost of someone else losing an equivalent amount of money; also, accumulated wealth may give us a sense of arrogance as well as a continuous fear of loss. On the other hand, a desire to acquire knowledge of, say, Sanskrit can be a win-win situation where we gain without anyone else incurring a reciprocal loss; further, once we have learnt Sanskrit, there is no fear of loss and our knowledge actually grows if we share it by teaching someone else.

This is not to imply that wealth acquisition is evil and that learning Sanskrit is noble. A Sanskrit scholar can, as a result of his learning, become more arrogant than someone who has accumulated a fortune with hard work. But the fact remains that some activities tend to be better for our own long-term welfare than others. Many traditional values and ways of life were meant to nudge us in their direction and help us to balance our not-so-helpful pursuits. Instances of such prescriptions included injunctions to conduct ritual worship thrice a day (reinforcing humility & gratitude as well as occupying time which could have been spent in doing something superficial or selfish), follow the family occupation (reducing aggressive competition), treat all natural resources as sacred (inhibiting pollution of rivers & lakes or wanton destruction of forests) and, above all, venerate knowledge and people with learning.[20] With changing times some of these prescriptions have become irrelevant or impractical but the problems they addressed still remain.

Toning Down of the Ego

The second approach of dharma is to reduce the sense of personal doership or ego. A sharply-etched sense of *me* and *mine* means more pride, regret, guilt, fear and hostility and, consequently, greater pressure behind our desires. One way to modulate our ego is by reflection over our successes and failures; this shows how small a role we actually play in events in our lives. We may, for instance, feel rather proud that we were able to stop smoking and look down upon our friend who was not able to give up this habit, despite his trying. The pride in our achievement may seem justified because we used our will-power to successfully achieve our goal. But from where did we obtain our wonderful will-power? What did we ourselves do to create it? Is it not an aspect of our mind brought about by our genes, by our upbringing and by our environment? If we say that we personally cultivated our will-power by rational thinking and determined practice, the same questions can be asked about the source of our rationality and determination. If we look deeply and objectively at any result or situation in our lives, it becomes clear that we, as individuals, had a remarkably small role in bringing it about.[21]

---

20 Those of you brought up in India may recall days when doctors and lawyers were inordinately respected, even by the very wealthy and the powerful, because their professions signified a lot of learning.

21 It should be clarified, however, that there are good reasons why this fact does not provide an excuse for us to do anything or to do nothing.

The more traditional way of checking the ego is by bringing religion into our lives, by cultivating and nurturing a relationship with God or Ishwara. Once Ishwara meaningfully enters a person's life after proper understanding,[22] the consequences are many. Understanding Ishwara to be the natural order which determines actual results, goes a long way in reducing stress and fear while doing things, and in moderating pride and arrogance upon achievements. When things do not go our way, there is reduced hostility towards obstructive people and circumstances, because they are not seen as being purposefully evil but as elements of the overall natural order.

The approaches of refining our desires and moderating our egos work for many of us. This is especially so for those of us who are already blessed with desires which do not readily gain a de-stabilising momentum. On the other hand, some of us do have particularly powerful desires and over-grown egos; some of us are unable to form a helpful relationship with Ishwara. We, too, need help and Vedanta fortunately extends more fundamental help to us.

Discrimination

A student on the path of Vedanta would have already tried very hard to gain lasting happiness by the obvious method of trying to fulfil all his desires; he would have realised that despite occasional or even frequent success here, one yet continues to remain lacking, wanting and basically unfulfilled. New and different desires arise continuously; desires which are thwarted generate anger & hostility; desires which are fulfilled bring greed for more, apart from tiredness in the efforts expended. Thus, Vedanta actually begins when it is clear that trying to cater to desires cannot be the primary plan for being totally happy. Vedanta's teachings help us to ponder over our past experiences and strengthen this discrimination, bringing about reduction in the hold of our usual desires.

---

22 The section titled "Does God Exist?" in the essay "Some Big Questions" deals with the rational understanding of God, which goes beyond faith or belief.

Understanding Ourselves

The core teachings of Vedanta point to a solution which is based not only on moderating our desires and egos but on a dramatic shift in the understanding of our own selves. From this changed perspective, we are made to see ourselves to be already full and complete, and this knocks out the very foundation of our desires. The unfolding of these teachings is a complex and time-consuming process which requires a certain level of preparedness and the guidance of a good teacher. All we can do here is to take a quick look at their general nature.

Our desires acquire over-whelming force because we see ourselves as fundamentally limited and lacking. This, in turn, happens because we consider ourselves to be defined by our own bodies and minds which are, indeed, limited and lacking. It is because of such identification that we conclude, for instance, that we are short and forgetful when our body is of less than average height and our memory is weak. Our struggle to get over such limitations can never come to an end because no matter how clever and hard-working we may be, our bodies and minds remain limited, lacking and vulnerable. Even as we buy high-heels and go to a memory-improvement course to feel taller and be less forgetful, a sense of being fat or angry or bored steps in. The only possible way in which this struggle can end is by the discovery that what we really are is not confined to our body-mind structure and that our reality does not, in fact, suffer from the limitations which we have been struggling against. This is a radically different approach because it is not rooted in doing something and not in becoming different but is based on getting rid of a wrong identification, by correct understanding.

Why should we ever believe that we are other than our bodies and minds? Here, we have to bring in a clear and consistent rule which we all know: in any knower-known relationship, the known is always different from the knower.[23] To take a deliberately trivial example, I know the pencil I am writing with; I am the knower and the pencil is the known. Because I am different from the

---

23 The Sanskrit term for this discrimination is *drik drishya viveka*.

pencil, I do not take myself to be red and blunt even though I know this pencil to be red and blunt. I may prefer my pencil to be yellow and sharp and work towards that goal but, whether I succeed or not, what I am is not at all affected. This preference is therefore not a matter for a desperate, life-long struggle; I have ease and freedom despite my preference, because I am not the pencil but the knower of the pencil.

On the other hand, when we know our body to be aged and our mind to be slow, we take ourselves to be old and dull and then feel immensely pressured in our attempts to remain young and energetic. But then we are the knowers of our bodies and the knowers of our minds. How else would we know anything about the state of our bodies and minds? So even here, there is a clear distinction between knower and known and the known can never be the knower. Just as the qualities and limitations of my pencil are not my qualities and limitations, I have no valid reason for seeing myself as being defined by the attributes of my body and mind. And this is often reiterated when we say "my body" and "my mind" – what is mine can never be myself.

This understanding may sound very startling (because it means that our bodies and minds are as different from us as the pencil is) but once it is clear and constant, it brings about a dramatic change in the force behind our desires. After we realise that our truth is not restricted to our bodies and minds, we can yet work on preserving and augmenting our physical and mental aspects. But, now there is no undue tension as we go about these activities, no dramatic pride if we succeed and no great fear or anger if we fail. The actual process of getting over our instinctive and age-old body-mind identification is, of course, far more involved and time-consuming than this simple over-view. And great discipline, together with constant reminders of Vedanta's teachings, is needed before the new understanding of our own selves is firm and constant.

Vedanta does not stop at just helping us to disentangle ourselves from our invalid identification. If we are other than our bodies and minds, it is obviously important to know what we actually are or, in other words, what is really meant when we say "I".

✷ Vedanta goes on to unfold the nature of the real "I", the knower, and shows us that our true nature is pure awareness which is intrinsically free of any limitation. This realisation is a long journey which goes through several phases of learning and stabilization. It is then that it becomes clear that while we appear to obtain happiness from outside by fulfilment of desires, we are already and completely fulfilled at all times by our very nature. We lose sight of this and feel unhappy because of the continuous 'clamour of our desiring mind, which veils our own reality.

Because our real nature is unchanging and boundless awareness, we can never be really unhappy – the unhappiness we experience is in and of our limited minds. In fact, because happiness is intrinsic to us, it cannot be captured, travelled to, earned, worn or consumed. When a particular desire is fulfilled, no external happiness is brought in; all that happens is that the strident movements of our wanting mind are briefly stilled and, in that lull, we are at one with our own fulfilled and peaceful nature. This is why a star-spangled night, capable of temporarily stilling our demanding mind by its beauty and mystery, brings us an experience of our inherent fullness and joy; and this is despite the fact that nothing in our circumstances has changed and not one of our desires has been met. But this magic ends when our mind picks up another desire and, in its renewed frenzy, again obscures our own core. Our fundamental problem is, thus, in the mind and the solution is also in the mind; Vedanta works on our mind by both helping us to process our emotions and desires (to reduce mental clamour) as well as by changing our understanding of our own reality.

Vedanta finally goes beyond the knowledge of the true nature of our own selves; it moves on to an understanding of the nature of the world which we experience and deal with. It unfolds a startling unity between the reality of our own selves and the reality underlying the world. The end result for those who complete this journey is true freedom or moksha - freedom from a life of compulsive striving to be other than what we are, freedom to have and pursue agendas at the level of our bodies and minds without pride, regrets, fear and anger.

These great teachings of Vedanta do not work for everyone because all of us do not have the inclination or the required aptitude. Even for those who are relatively prepared for Vedanta, there is considerable difficulty in putting these teachings into practice during every moment of their lives. On the other hand, even a limited understanding of Vedanta has remarkably beneficial consequences in all aspects of our lives.

THE ROLE OF DHARMA
CONCEPTUAL FRAME-WORK
Dharma is Objectivity

Dharma is the threshold between our temporal needs for security & pleasures and our spiritual need to find natural freedom. The intention of this essay is to convey a sense of dharma's underlying rationale and spirit.

In the vision of Hindu scriptures, all human activities can be categorised under just four basic goals: security or *artha*, pleasures or *kama*, appropriate conduct & attitude or *dharma* and liberation from a mistaken self-identity or *moksha*. The goal of dharma holds the pivotal position in this list of four because if our natural search for security and pleasure has to be truly successful, it must be kept within the ambit of appropriateness; similarly, we will not be ready to tackle wrong notions about our own selves, without first integrating the rectitude and balance of dharma into our lives.

Our desires for security and pleasure are varied and endless; under their pressure we frequently choose inappropriate attitudes and conduct which ultimately bring us grief. If we pause to think about the underlying causes of our unhappiness or suffering, we will find that many of them are centred on distorted conclusions and values; these distortions arise because we tend to look at things through the lens of subjectivity, through a veil of our conditioning and compulsive desires.

Money is an example of one of our most common distortions caused by unbridled desire. Money has a certain intrinsic value and can provide us with many opportunities and freedom. But when we look upon a person as being refined just because he is rich or when we believe that happiness will arise only when we make a fortune, we are imputing values to money which it really does not have. As a result of our contorted view we may be motivated to relentlessly pursue wealth, often at the cost of our own physical and mental well-being. And this distortion can branch out into several more shoots. For instance, once we get fixated on money because of its assumed values, a person may appear inimical merely because his path happens to bring him in natural competition with us or we may judge him as a failure just because he is less wealthy compared to us.

Similarly, there is distortion when a man looks upon a woman's appearance as the most significant attribute which she brings to a marriage. There is distortion when we believe that our brand of religion is the only acceptable one. There is distortion when we look upon nature as being made solely for our plunder and when we look upon other people as mere instruments to serve our needs. There is also distortion when we try to go through life believing that we can get away scot-free, despite ignoring the legitimate needs and limits of our own bodies and minds.

Such distortions are damaging because they are based on a mistaken view or a wrong understanding of the reality of a specific situation. If we were to believe that we could counter the force of gravity by flapping our hands as we jumped off a cliff or that we could continuously spend money beyond our means, we would come to obvious grief. In the same way, our mistaken views about the world, wrong habits of life and deficient ethics also bring in difficulties and pain in our individual lives (though less emphatic than flying off a cliff); further, they detract from the society in which we live. The purpose of dharma is to reduce our subjectivity and distortions in order to enhance our own, long-term happiness.

Dharma is Natural Order

When we talk about a false view of anything, this can only be with reference to its true nature. And, in its broadest sense, dharma is the name given to the proper and innate nature of things. This meaning is reflected in the etymology of the word which is derived from the Sanskrit root-word *dhr*. The meaning of this root is *to hold* or *to support* and, so, the most general meaning of dharma is that which holds the world together, that which supports existence.

How does dharma hold or support existence? This may become clearer by expressing it differently: dharma is the name for the order found throughout the universe, which makes things what they are. Let us look at some examples. There is an orderly force of gravitation which stops the earth from flying off its orbit and ensures that apples always fall downwards from a tree; there are precise laws of evaporation, convection and condensation which sustain the life-giving connection between oceans and rain-fall; only chickens come from a hen's eggs and our eyes are always to be found on our faces and, that too, in the same location; in all atoms, electrons remain in orbit round their nuclei. All these are instances of the order which we find in nature; it is this order which we refer to when we say that the dharma of fire is to burn.

Such order is not restricted to phenomena which are the province of physics, chemistry and biology but extends to all other facets of our lives. A different kind of order, which is no less natural and includes things like mutual respect and accommodation, is necessary to sustain our social structures such as nations, communities and families. We, as individual human beings, are subject to yet another kind of universal order which operates within our minds; the fact that no one likes being hurt, that we feel guilty when we cheat a friend and that we feel good when someone helps us are all reflections of the natural order which resides in our inner recesses.

While the broad meaning of dharma is natural order, we obviously have greater concern with that part of the order which is specific to us. We, therefore, most commonly use the word dharma to denote conduct and attitudes of individuals which are in keeping with the universal order pertaining to human beings, to a way of living which is naturally right for us.

It is important that we understand dharma as something which is self-generated rather than imposed. To do this, we must get away from the limited view of dharma as a form of social control through which entrenched traditions exercise tyranny over individual lives. The basic intention of dharma is not to limit individuality for the sake of blind conformity. On the other hand, dharma is not a field of boundless individual creativity. This is because while we are obviously capable of thinking for ourselves, we may not always personally come up with answers which are compatible with our own, long-term wellness; this can happen due to the pressure of the need for quick gratification or the inability to think through to ultimate outcomes. Such distortions in our thinking become evident in instances when a student opts for a night out rather than preparing for an important test the next day or in the case of a person with an extra fondness for alcohol who fails to see any merit in moderation. Therefore, we need to keep in mind the fact that thinking for ourselves is not incompatible with the existence of specific and appropriate answers, which we will discover only with proper thinking.

Human Choice

You will have noticed that nothing that we have said about dharma so far explains why only some of our actions and attitudes constitute dharma while others do not. If dharma refers to natural order, can we really say that the compassion of a saint is natural order while the cruelty of a terrorist is not? The fact is that, in the broadest sense, there can never be any *adharma* or anything contrary to dharma. At the loftiest plane, everything is always as it should be; there is never any deviation from the natural order because the deviation itself is part of nature.

However, as soon as we come to individual human-beings, we have to talk about the possibility of deviating from dharma. Why does this happen? Why do we need a narrower meaning of dharma here, where only some conduct and attitudes are considered right? The answer lies in the vital difference between human-beings compared with other objects in creation. This difference is in the self-consciousness of a human-being.

We are not only conscious of our surroundings but also conscious of our own selves in a special way which gives us our unique sense of individual identity. Such self-consciousness and identity do not seem to occur in other living beings and this is why the winner of a beauty pageant feels proud and triumphant but the Derby-winning horse does not display any such feelings. This individual identity of ours is accompanied by a sense of free-will; we see ourselves as the wilful authors of actions which occur through our bodies and minds. It is our self-awareness and the attendant experience of free-will which makes dharma relevant for human-beings.

When someone unnecessarily hurts us, he knows that it is part of natural order that no one likes to be hurt. This knowledge is unambiguous because he, himself, never likes to be hurt. Further, with his free-will, he could have chosen not to hurt us. If the tables had been reversed, he would have wanted and expected us not to hurt him; it is, therefore, only reciprocally appropriate that he should not hurt us. This logic does not apply to the rest of nature because animals and things are always guided by impersonal instincts, without any sense of individuality empowered by volition. Therefore, a fire does not deviate from its dharma even as it wreaks havoc and causes misery. Animals also never fall from dharma; a tiger does not go against dharma even as it kills its victim. To follow dharma or not is a uniquely human option because of our unique experience of self-identity accompanied with free-will.

Dharma's Direct Pay-Off

We experience a warm glow of satisfaction when we do something which is naturally right, such as helping an injured stranger on the road or owning up to a lie. Conversely, when we do something to others which is intrinsically wrong, we experience guilt and regret. This is a result of our very make-up.[24] Similarly, when we go against natural balance by, for instance, over-loading our own bodies with junk-food or by getting carried away by a single, obsessive pursuit, there are obvious negative outcomes. Further, because we do not exist in isolation, it is difficult for us to be happy in a ravaged environment, where people have been dehumanised and where nature has been rapaciously exploited.

A large part of codified dharma lays down this common-

---

24 Charles Darwin, in his book The Descent of Man, extended his theory of evolution by natural selection to human behaviour. According to this view, people who are helpful and show consideration towards others gain from reciprocal behaviour and this gives them a better chance of survival and longevity. Over a period of time, people exhibiting such behaviour proliferate and their genetic disposition becomes the societal norm.

sense understanding in specific terms, to encourage us to live appropriately. This is not to stop us from having a good time and not because the natural order will collapse without our co-operation; the only objective of dharma's tenets is to support our happiness and keep us from damaging ourselves out of ignorance and carelessness. This aspect of dharma is very important in our day-to-day lives but because it is constantly emphasised in books and by several teachers, we do not need to examine it in detail here.

Dharma Creates an Integrated Personality

The direct consequences of dharma are fairly obvious. However, the greatest value of dharma's prescriptions lies in the fact that it tries to create within us an integrated person capable of experiencing fulfilment. Dharma's deepest concern is not with what we actually do but with the kind of persons we are; its focus is the state of our minds. It is the failure to understand this aspect of dharma which leads us to the heedless pursuit of short-term pleasures and temporary security. In doing this we pay a fundamental price which we may not understand, unless we first understand the central role our ego plays here.

Our ego is that facet of our mind which gives us our individuality.[25] Our ego is the "I" which takes delivery of happenings associated with our body and mind. When we enjoy a meal, we do not feel that "My tongue and my stomach had a good meal" but that "I had a good meal". Similarly we say "I am tall" or "I am pleased" and not "My body is tall" or "My mind knows pleasure". The ego is actually nothing but a product of our own mind, a thought of self-referral which stands apart from all other thoughts. The ego is not our inner-most reality; our actual essence is awareness because of which we know our ego and its changing states – at times swollen and demanding and, at other times, mellow and small. However, because awareness

---

25 We often take the word 'ego' to mean an exaggerated sense of self-importance but this is only a secondary meaning. It is interesting to note that the Sanskrit word for ego – *ahamkara* – is very accurate because it literally means the 'I, the doer'; 'ego' is used here in this sense to denote only a sense of being a separate individual and not to denote anything undesirable or harmful.

cannot be known by itself, the ego wrongly gets to play the role of being our core reality. Instead of awareness, it is our ego which we refer to as "I" and this gives the ego a crucial role to play in our experience of happiness.

For us to be happy it is not enough to be just the recipients of pleasant sensations or possessors of good fortune; it is also necessary for our ego to be healthy and intact. For instance, we know of occasions when a beautifully cooked meal gave us no joy because our ego had been pained by a disparaging remark made by somebody about us; we are acquainted with people who are unable to feel blessed despite having a remarkable fortune; we meet people who are always annoyed or fearful even without adequate cause. The most basic and common reason for a general lack of feeling good, even when we are free of any specific reason for our unease, is a dysfunctional ego. The ego also includes our sub-conscious: a hidden pigeon-hole in our mind where we automatically tuck away unpleasant emotions like hurt, anger and guilt, which we do not want to confront. When the sub-conscious is loaded with a large amount of negative emotions, such emotions emerge involuntarily from time-to-time to keep us away from feeling positive and contented.

A troubled ego often puts hidden pressure on us to do inappropriate things, against the call of our own intelligence. This is what Duryodhana, a misguided prince in the large Hindu epic called the Mahabharata, was referring to when he lamented to Lord Krishna that he knew what was right but was unable to do it and he knew what was wrong but was unable to stay away from it – it was as if there was a powerful being seated within him and directing his behaviour.[26] The thrust of a large part of dharma is to help us here, by encouraging the development of integrated and wholesome egos without which we cannot experience abiding fulfilment.

---

26 *janami dharmam na ca me pravrittih, janamyadharmam na ca me nivrittih; kenapi devena hrudi sthitena yatha niyuktosmi tatha karomi.*

The Ego's Health

The creation and nurture of a healthy personality is not a simple matter because egos are fragile by their very nature. The most direct way in which we can damage our egos is by doing something which is contrary to what we naturally know to be right. Any deviation in our actual conduct from the call of our own instinctive knowledge, because of indifference or obsessive needs, creates a dichotomy. This happens because the ego, playing the role of the real "I", assumes responsibility for our actions and faces the inherent contradiction which arises when what we do is different from what we should have done. Such contradictions divide us at the very root of our individuality and this has consequences, even though the damage may not appear to be significant in the short-run.

A damaged ego can generate an exaggerated sense of personal success or failure, even in areas where there is no valid reason for us to take matters so personally. It is an unhealthy ego which makes some of us feel exceptionally clever if a stock-market punt works in our favour, without acknowledging the role of good luck. On the other hand, such an ego can also make some others conclude 'No one loves me' just because people around them do not always pander to their whims; it can give yet others an irrational sense of failure and guilt when the future proves even one of their originally sensible decisions to have been wrong in hind-sight.

The ego is also affected by the continuous stream of thoughts, memories and emotions which arise in our minds. Because these mental movements are spontaneous, they are impossible to immediately control by using our will. For instance, as we read these words, if we were suddenly asked 'Be angry' or 'Be sad' there is no way in which we could comply because emotions such as anger or sadness do not arise when we wish them to arise. And, by the same coin, emotions, memories and thoughts do not disappear when we wish them to disappear. Our ego is powerless here and all it can do is to ascribe the mind's state of the moment to itself; we, therefore, feel that 'I am angry' or 'I am sad' even though the "I" had nothing to do with the arising of the anger or the sadness.

The problem of maintaining the ego's health gets further compounded by the fact that the ego has no objective needs in itself. What it does is to make continuous comparisons with past levels (dredged from memory), future scenarios (predicted by using mental faculties) and with others around us. So, "Today's concert was good but not as good as last week's" or "There is enough saving now but what if markets collapse?" and the new car is good only till the neighbour gets a better one. Living in the past or the future denies us the only reality which is the present; living by comparisons with others is like trying to navigate while using a reference point which is itself moving.

Because of wrong conduct, because of spontaneous movements in our minds and because of the insecurity generated by constant comparison, it is possible for the ego to be hurt and lose its resilience; we then have problems which psychologists call neuroses – a lack of self-worth or a sense of false sin and guilt. On the other hand, just as a malignant disease can provoke parts of our bodies to hideous growth, the ego can also go to the other extreme of aggrandization; we then have problems which psychologists call character disorders – the notion that the world is out to serve us and that the fulfilment of any and all of our desires is the only thing which matters.

Dharma seeks to provide a balance between deprivation and the unfettered growth of the ego by looking at all aspects which affect it. The thrust of important portions of dharma is to bring about behaviour which is not only in keeping with our knowledge of right and wrong but which also provides mechanisms to deal with excessive emotions. Many aspects of traditional dharma, such as demonstrating unconditional respect to elders, performing elaborate ceremonies at significant events like marriages and deaths, working and marrying in keeping with one's family background and showing esteem for knowledge were all based on the understanding that egos have to be nourished as well as kept in check and that emotions have to be modulated, if one wants to live a life of balance and contentment.

Role of Religion

In addition to physical and emotional aspects, human beings also have other needs which dharma has to cater to. These include need for a larger meaning to our lives as well as a safety-net of support and comfort. This now brings us to the important question of why God and religion are part and parcel of dharma. (The aspects of dharma which deal with God may cause problems for readers who consider themselves to be atheists or agnostics. For such people it would be helpful to first read the section 'Does God Exist?' in the essay titled 'Some Big Questions'; they may be pleasantly surprised to discover that Vedanta would agree with their rejection of the supernatural and mysterious Gods of most theologies.)

Religion involves our dealings with God. Without some acceptance of the concept of God, we would have no sense of commonality with the rest of the world and would remain just its exploiters; we would also have to take all of creation as a random happening, in spite of its amazing complexity and functionality. But a religious person readily finds connectivity and meaning in life from his relationship with God. He can see dharma not only as a natural part of his life but he can also see his life itself as a natural part of something larger.

All religions deal with understanding and relating to God, using different approaches. The Hindu view of God, at its highest level, is unique because it is not restricted to the conventional notion of a magical being sitting in heaven. But the proper understanding of God is not our subject here. For the time being, let us just say that even as we push the frontiers of science to unravel the mysteries of creation, we have to accept the not fully known but yet obvious order underlying our complex universe. In a sense, we can say that God is the way in which we acknowledge this order and integrate it with our individual lives.

Apart from providing meaning and integration, religion plays a vital role in the processing of our emotions, especially when they become turbulent. As infants, we start by looking upon our parents as infallible anchors in our lives; later we look to other people and institutions for our need to find safety and security. However, nothing human can meet this need fully because all other human beings themselves have their own insecurity and changing personal agendas. The only place we can turn to with total openness, trust and love is to the altar of God; it is only here that we can discharge our emotions without shame or fear of reciprocal payment.

Leaving aside the need for God in times of disturbance and insecurity, we have to recognise that even in our daily lives there is continuous accumulation of negative and annoying emotions. As we inter-act with people and situations, our minds gather small amounts of anger, hurt, jealousy and disappointment just as our bodies gather sweat and grime every day. If we did not shower regularly, the dirt and odour of our bodies would begin to get intolerable; similarly, if we do not regularly cleanse our minds of petty and undesirable emotions; they can accumulate and have serious consequences by affecting our basic attitude. Here again, relating to God in regular prayer has a cleansing and calming effect and promotes gentler emotions like humility and gratitude.

Proper understanding of God also plays a vital role in modulating the sway of emotions which continuously arise in response to the results of our own actions. When the actual results of our actions are equal to or more than our expectations, feelings of elation and pride tend to arise; when the actual results are less than or contrary to our expectations, we may feel dejected and be afflicted by guilt, regrets and hostility. A religious person has advantage here because, in his vision, God is not separate from the natural order which prevails in producing a specific result and thus becomes the giver of all results. This attitude and understanding go a long way in tempering emotional gyrations.

Relating to God for our emotional needs becomes more effective if we have taken the time and effort to develop a genuine understanding of God. Apart from understanding, most of us also need a symbolic representation of God which gets more powerful as we imbue it with regular reverence and worship. Statues, portraits and abstract symbols are used to provide a focus for our actions and emotions in relating to God; this is similar to a flag being used as a symbol for a country and as a focal point for feelings like national pride and patriotism. A large part of dharma therefore deals with ritual conduct towards the symbolic representations of God, to give them meaning and vitality.

To Sum Up So Far

We have, until now, seen that dharma not only contributes to our direct happiness but, more important, it makes us into integrated persons who are capable of experiencing happiness. Dharma does this by promoting conduct which is in consonance with our natural knowledge of right and wrong as well as by providing healthy ways of dealing with our emotions and egos; religion is a crucial part of dharma because, without religion, full integration of our personalities and proper processing of our emotions is difficult. The consequences of a life of dharma are ✗ the balanced growth of an individual in his material, emotional and spiritual aspects as well as the well-being of the society in which the individual exists.

Deviation from Dharma

Lack of concern about dharma may not appear personally relevant in the short-run. We may relentlessly pursue our pleasures and security without too much thought towards their long-term consequences on our bodies and minds; the resulting achievements may provide satisfaction despite their wrongness or imbalance. But, deep down, our instincts and our knowledge of right and wrong persist. When we do something wrong there is no escape from the resulting contradiction at the core of our individuality, even though we may use bluster, copious consumption and ceaseless activity to hide our guilt and to numb our divided ego. This is why dharma is a goal which over-rides the goals of pleasure and security. While our quest for happiness makes us seek pleasures and security, such seeking has to be within the ambit of dharma, if true happiness is to be achieved.

Once we ignore important elements of dharma, especially those which deal with our internal make-up, there are important consequences even though they may not be obvious. As we carry on with an apparently normal life, the health of our carelessly handled ego may become like the health of a chronic asthmatic's airways. As a result of recurrent allergic reactions and infections, an asthmatic's air-passages remain inflamed and constricted. Over a period of time he gets used to this problem and his ordinary life seems unaffected despite his compromised breathing capacity. But the disease is actually always present, just short of being manifest and painful. When there is even a slight change in the conditions which this person faces – a little increase in pollution, a bit of extra physical exertion – then the remaining narrow margin of tolerance is rapidly used up and the result is a full-blown attack of asthma.

We can transgress dharma by blindly catering to every desire, pandering to every emotion and satisfying every whim, without considering their appropriateness or of the means used to achieve them. We can omit to do anything which will moderate our desires, process our emotions and soften our egos. Such transgressions of dharma can inflame and constrict our mind to the level of a major, potential disease. The whole world may then be seen by us to exist only to cater to our needs. We may be able to see only our rights and no duties. In this state, our experiences of happiness rest on a very narrow and unstable base. Just a slight push is now needed for us to lose our equilibrium; a small provocation can trigger disproportionate consequences of anger and anguish.

To successfully handle life, we need internal space and resilience within us. These are lost when we fan our desires and egos to over-powering levels; we now have no choice but to meet their compulsive needs. It is then that our natural sense of spontaneity and freedom begins to evaporate. Every person, every event, every desire has to be guarded against or dealt with very seriously because he or it can easily tip the balance from happiness to unhappiness. In this process, privileges and gifts become necessities; gratitude and awe are replaced by fear and anger. Under pressure to fulfil our assumed needs, we end up defining our joys and liberty in almost entirely material terms, because they are obvious and provide immediate gratification.

As Alan Watts (an acclaimed British interpreter of Eastern

philosophies) points out, once we have barricaded ourselves in a very narrow zone of comfort, everything within this zone becomes a necessity which must be had; we then need increasing means to ensure the availability of these assumed necessities. Our working hours and the levels of stress increase. We make sure we are always on call so that we can remain competitive and are seen to be working harder than our colleagues who are trying to work harder than us. We sacrifice aspects of our family life as well as our less materialistic growth impulses. We yet need joy, but having blocked up the natural spaces within us where joy may surface if we gave it a chance, we now need to buy joy through packaged entertainment, flaunt-worthy possessions and adrenalin-pumping, artificial thrills. When this recipe falters, we can always turn to therapy but preferably of the quick fix variety so that we do not fall too far back in the race, even as we seek help. And, of course, the buying of such 'joys' and therapy needs more resources and so the cycle continues and escalates.

Naturally, our children imbibe this life-style and attitudes. Schools become places for remorseless testing and permanent examinations to prepare for a life of visceral competition and self-protection. We then complain that education has not remained the same and that teachers do not seem to be joyous in the once noble profession of teaching.

In this way, a life in which dharma has not been intelligently and fully woven can seem normal and progressive at one level and yet leave the core person involved in it without true happiness. It requires discrimination and effort to understand and derive dharma's benefit in terms of our personal fulfilment. As an ancient saying goes, *dharmo rakshati rakshitaha* – dharma protects those who protect it. Dharma is meant to safeguard and enrich us but it is not a one-way street: to reap dharma's benefit we also need to protect and propagate it, by understanding it, by integrating it with our own lives, by reflecting it in our personal conduct and attitudes.

Mercifully, our lack of understanding of the true value of dharma does not drive us to completely inappropriate ways of living. Natural moderation of our emotions, the resilience of our ego, the effect of social conditioning and our own good sense combine to provide some balance. While total disaster is avoided what is yet lost is very special and precious: an in-built tempering of mental swings, a sense of empathy and good will, a zest for life in its many facets, an abiding feeling that life is a privilege to be enjoyed and grateful for, a sense of awe, wonder and humility. These are some of the simple and natural joys which get lost and forgotten when we snap our ties with dharma. And while dharma as a source of such happiness may sound impractical and Utopian, it is surprising how small a tilt in our perspective and just slightly better appreciation of the true worth of dharma can bring about a sea-change in our internal equilibrium; the result is a capacity to experience a different type of wholesomeness and a more abiding happiness.

Our natural pursuits of pleasure and security are common with all other animals. But, in addition to our bodies and minds, we also have a unique self-awareness which makes the goal of dharma relevant to our happiness. As this is a special human feature shared by no other creature, dharma is a uniquely human goal. In fact, a human being completely unconcerned with dharma is not only endangering his own happiness but is also missing out from participating in an essential element of humanity. Just as an aeroplane which never leaves the ground is a waste, a human being who does not aspire and reach for dharma is also a sad waste.

CODIFICATION OF DHARMA

For the benefit of people who do not have the time or inclination to explore the conceptual framework of dharma, practical guidelines are available for use in day-to-day living. Where do we find these tenets of dharma set out for our compliance? Is there a ready-made list? As far as Hindu scriptures go, different types of codes to serve specific needs are available from different sources.

Varna Ashrama Dharma

There are many lists of Do's and Don'ts in Hindu scriptures which are specific to an individual's place and stage in life (*varna ashrama dharma*). The scriptures which focus on such codes of conduct are known as *dharma shastras* and the Manu Smriti is a good example. However, these detailed lists contain what we may term as the evolved super-structure of dharma and not its foundation. Such codes were developed for the convenience and guidance of the average person at a given time and place. They are not the final expressions of absolute righteousness; they were never meant to be inflexibly applied to all situations. Untold harm has been done, especially among the weak and poor in India, by treating these codes as rigid and then conveniently interpreting and enforcing them for the benefit of a few.[27]

Apart from exploitation of people, some out-dated aspects of codes like the Manu Smriti have brought a lack of credibility for Hinduism as a whole. After all, who in today's age can look up with conviction to a set of regulations which says, amongst other things, that you cannot marry somebody outside your own caste or that the rightful place of a woman is under the thumb of a man? The Manu Smriti does not consist only of such archaic

---

27 One aspect which has gained notoriety here is *varna dharma* which is understood as the caste system freezing an individual's status and occupation purely based on birth. *Varna* really is the categorization of individuals based upon their personal qualities, professions and family backgrounds. In its original concept, the emphasis in this scheme was first on personal qualities, then on actual occupation and only then on birth; the dominance of the factor of birth came much later and distorted the original spirit.

dictums but these do tend to over-shadow its good and valid prescriptions, at least in popular perception.

Samanya Dharma

More general tenets of Hindu dharma, which are not affected by caste and gender, are termed *samanya* (common) *dharma*. The attributes which are usually included here are *ahimsa*, *satyam*, *asteyam*, *shaucham* and *indriyanighram*. These terms, respectively, mean non-injury, truthfulness, non-covetousness (for things belonging to others), purity and control over one's senses. These are easy to understand, difficult to put into practice in their true spirit and form the bed-rock of ethical behaviour.

Pancha Mahayagna

One of the ways in which the codes of dharma have reiterated the inter-connection of our lives with the rest of creation and the gratitude we constantly owe to others is by an injunction to regularly perform the *pancha mahayagna* or the five great sacrifices. This daily ritual consists of:

- *deva yagna* – We are all dependent on the forces and bounty of nature for our existence; this is to be recognised by ritually sanctifying aspects of nature (such as the sun, fire, wind, rivers and trees) and by offering daily worship to divine beings (*devas*) which are the symbolic sources of such largesse.

- *rishi yagna* – This is also called *brahma yagna* and is based on the fact that knowledge comes to us in an unbroken stream going back to the sages (*rishis*) who compiled the vedas; the way to express gratitude here and repay this debt is by studying some aspects of the scriptures every day and also by teaching whatever one has learnt.

- *pitru yagna* – A man owes his very birth to his parents and to an endless line of ancestors; he acknowledges this lineage by being of service to his parents, by giving ritual offerings (*tarpana*) to his forefathers on their death anniversaries and, finally, by parenting his own children.[28]

- *nara yagna* – We are social creatures dependent upon inter-action and help from other human-beings; dharma requires us to be aware of this fact and demonstrate such awareness by offering food, shelter and hospitality to guests[29] and to those people who are in need of our help.

- *bhuta yagna* – Our inter-connection and dependence is not only restricted to humans but to all other living creatures, ranging from the cow which provides food, fuel and motive-power to the lowly earthworm without which the soil will not regenerate and be fit for cultivation; the requirement to feed some creatures everyday is symbolic of this connection.[30]

By performing these five great sacrifices daily, a man realises that he is part of a greater whole; dharma tries to encourage this understanding by holding out that the fruits of heaven cannot be attained without repaying these debts we owe to creation. What is important in the mandate to perform the pancha mahayagna is not some ancient ritual in itself but the underlying spirit which,

---

28 It is interesting to note that the Sanskrit words for a son and a daughter are *putra* and *putri* respectively. These words are derived from two other words: *put* which is the name of one of the several levels of hell in Hindu mythology where people who commit the 'sin' of not parenting a child are sent after their deaths and *trayate* which means to protect. Thus, *putra* or *putri* refers to someone who protects you from being consigned to hell, within a tradition which considered becoming a parent to be an important duty.

29 It is the Taittiriya Upanishad which contains the rather well-known statement *atithi devo bhava* meaning 'treat guests like gods'.

30 Even in big cities in India today, there are several households where the first *roti* (bread) cooked everyday is fed to crows.

for our own good, must not be lost upon us even today. Now, more than ever, we need to be acutely aware of our dependence on all aspects of our fragile planet, conserve and renew finite resources and treat all living and non-living things with the care, concern and humility which the pancha mahayagnas had once brought into lives.

The setting out of even more evolved values occurs in philosophical scriptures such as the Bhagavad Gita (where a list of twenty values is given in Chapter 13) or Patanjali's Yoga Sutras (where a list of ten Do's and Don'ts is found under the headings of Yama and Niyama) or Shankaracharya's Vivekchudamani (where a list of six items of conduct and attitude appears). The emphasis here is not on some inflexible absolutes or frenzied attempts to reach super-human perfection; the tone is one of encouragement of certain behaviour and attitudes which others had found useful during their own journey towards growth in maturity and knowledge. In fact, what is really important in such scriptures is not the list of specifics they contain but the overall attitude they encourage and the raised perspective they lead us to.

Pravritti and Nivritti Dharma

Traditional codes of conduct and values can also be divided into two categories depending upon their target: one which is more relevant for those for whom the principal focus is accumulating wealth and enjoying pleasures (*pravritti dharma*) and the other which is appropriate for those who are in a singular search of growth and evolution on a more spiritual plane (*nivritti dharma*). Pravritti dharma emphasises the appropriateness of actions which are deliberate and will-based, while nivritti dharma is more concerned with promoting attitudes which will refine even our spontaneous thoughts and desires.

Bhagavad Gita

Perhaps the finest scripture, which contains a combination of practical ethics and sublime truths in a work of great beauty and efficacy, is the Bhagavad Gita. The Gita continues to provide guidance, solace and encouragement for people of different mind-sets and helps them to intelligently respond in a variety of situations. If one had to refer to or rely upon a single Hindu scripture, that scripture would have to be the Bhagavad Gita.

Vedas

When we come to the even more ancient scriptures, the Vedas, we actually find no detailed and comprehensive codes of conduct. There is no equivalent of the biblical Ten Commandments in the Vedas though several individual statements about desirable conduct (such as 'speak the truth', 'treat parents like gods' and 'give in charity') are sprinkled at various places. The Vedas are the oldest religious scriptures known to mankind and they are the voluminous source scriptures of Hinduism. The fact that despite their antiquity, importance and size, the Vedas do not lay out an unambiguous list of what to do and what not to do is very significant. This omission in the Vedas recognises the fact that human lives are very complex and dynamic. The Vedas, therefore, do not attempt the impossible task of setting out a comprehensive and infallible list of moral absolutes.

Let us look at very simple examples to illustrate the impracticality of moral injunctions. The Yajur Veda contains the statement *satyam vada* which means 'Speak the truth'. However, if dharma was restricted to compliance with absolutes such as this, what should one do if a murderer asked for the whereabouts of his intended victim? Or should one disclose to a very young person that a potentially fatal disease has been detected in him? We, of course, should have a value for being truthful but human life and emotions are also valuable. Thus, the practice of dharma has a lot to do with the whole context of a given situation.[31] This issue is highlighted in epics like the Mahabharata, in which many of its central characters have to decide between several valid but opposing alternatives. (Incidentally, the fact that dharma is dynamic and not absolute is also incorporated in the Buddhist tradition which depicts dharma as a turning wheel – the Ashoka chakra on the Indian flag).

---

31 *sandharbha*, as it is termed in Sanskrit.

Ahimsa, the Basic Tenet

It would obviously be of great help to us if we could have some over-riding principle to come to the right decision when faced with conflicts between two or more individually desirable values. Instead of concentrating on specifics, Hindu dharma wisely enunciates a guiding principle for the application of dharma in daily life: *ahimsa paramo dharma*. This one statement captures the essence of a large part of dharma in actual practice.

Ahimsa literally means 'non-violence' but implies 'non-injury'; *parama* means 'the highest'. Thus, this statement says 'Non-injury is the highest dharma'. We must remember that this is not a simple injunction against any violence because, at times, one may have to engage in violence to prevent greater injury (such as a war waged against a tyrant). Conversely, one can gravely injure someone without using any physical violence, such as by using hurtful words or by betraying faith. The spirit of ahimsa lies in trying to live with causing minimum possible injury (not 'no injury' because the very process of living inevitably causes injury to someone, even if inadvertently). The concept of ahimsa is to be applied not only to other human-beings but to all things – we should not be squashing insects and breaking off leaves (and, perhaps, not even mindlessly kicking stones).

Once ahimsa becomes the touchstone for determining our conduct and attitudes, following the spirit of dharma becomes simpler. In any given situation, we need to try and assess what would cause the least injury to all concerned and then act accordingly. It is now easy to see why it would be dharma to tell a lie in order to save a victim from his prospective murderer or postpone discussing the possibility of death with a person too young to deal with it meaningfully. Similarly, it is not difficult to understand why a person who has total value for ahimsa is a vegetarian – he wants to live causing least possible injury and he sees that the killing of animals causes more pain compared to the plucking of fruits or the harvesting of grains.

To look at ahimsa from a different perspective, we can also approach it with the age-old question: "What is the purpose of life?" One obvious answer to this question is that the basic and natural purpose of life is to live. But what does living mean? We all know that living implies growth because stasis or atrophy is the hallmark of death. We can, therefore, say that any action of ours which impedes the growth of a living being is against the natural order of things or against dharma.

In respect of human beings, growth is not limited to their bodies but extends to their minds. We impede this special growth in respect of human beings when we hurt their emotions, stifle their intellects or attack their egos; such acts would be against ahimsa and dharma.

Ahimsa Also Applies to Our Own Selves

One aspect of ahimsa which we sometimes ignore is in respect of our own selves. Some of us get so fixated on a few of the many roles that we all have to play that the balanced nurturing of other aspects of our personality is omitted. Thus, a girl may do all the right things expected out of a daughter while she is with her parents; once she gets married, she may make immense sacrifices in areas of her personal interest in order to do full justice to her roles as wife and daughter-in-law; she may then devote several years of her life in single-mindedly catering to the needs of her children. In this whole process, she may completely ignore her other intellectual or spiritual needs and justify this omission by the belief that she is selflessly carrying out her dharma towards her family.

There is no denying the fact that many of our roles do require effort and sacrifice on our part. However, the fact that we have duties towards others does not permit us to always forget that we also have duties to our own selves. Our personal growth requires some skills and extra effort in balancing other people's expectations and multiple demands on our limited resources; if we simply abdicate our responsibility to ourselves, we have certainly gone against dharma to some extent.

One other factor which is important here, but not often recognised, is the insidious role of the ego even in a person who is always sacrificing his wants and aspirations for the sake of others. To understand this, let us first look at how we display a work of art such as a painting. If a painting is bold and bright, we may hang it up on a wall without too much concern about its frame or back-drop – the painting itself stands out and is noticed. However, when we have a more subdued painting we are likely to place it in a bolder frame and with a contrasting back-drop, so that even this less obvious painting effectively stands out. Our egos also want to be displayed and noticed. The flamboyant ones announce themselves by holding out their colourful personalities and achievements while the duller ones draw attention to themselves by contrast with their surroundings.

A perpetual martyr may seem self-effacing but is, in fact, trying to draw attention to himself by pointing out the strong and powerful environment around him which over-shadows his own dreams and wishes – it is "Look at the POOR me" versus "Look at the GREAT me". In both cases, though the emphasis is different, the object is 'me'. And too much involvement with 'me' and 'mine' is not conducive to our evolution. Any act or attitude that ultimately promotes egoity, however subtly, is adharma in its highest sense.

Dharma Requires Skill

In a situation where we must make a choice between our own growth and our duty to others, there is always a risk of our choosing a pleasure-enhancing or ego-aggrandizing path, under the guise of self-growth. True growth should propel us towards more intelligent living where our ego is not over-grown and where our personal likes and dislikes do not always force us into action against the call of our reason. To grow in dharma by balancing our personal needs against the needs of others is a difficult and delicate task. The Bhagavad Gita recognises this when it says that skill in action is yoga[32] – the skill referred to here is not a vocational skill but the skill needed for determining the path of dharma at every juncture. To help us in this process, we need to be honest to ourselves, reflect upon our motivations and, above all, seek help from good friends and proper teachers.

---

32 *yogah karmasu kaushalam.*

Substance Over Form

Keeping in mind that this journey along the path of dharma is life-long, one need not become harshly judgemental towards every flicker of movement from our emotions and egos. Emotions and egos are perfectly natural, they too need sustenance (perhaps even an occasional binge!) and, with all our intelligence and good-will, we will certainly make mistakes and wrong choices. Rather than get too stuck on some specific action or event, we should focus more on our underlying attitude. Once we are committed to dharma because we see its value for our growth and happiness, it does not matter so much if progress consists of one step backwards for two steps forwards.

Not Dry as Dust

While on the topic of incorporating dharma in our lives, it is not helpful if dharma remains an abstract matter which is either laboured or mechanical. For dharma to be a vibrant and spontaneous part of our lives, it is necessary that some emotions supplement our understanding. While dispassion has a role to play in our other pursuits, only scholars in ivory towers should try to be dispassionate about dharma. The natural order we are talking about is not separate from us but we are part of it; our compliance with dharma is not only a function of a cost-benefit analysis but because we feel its natural goodness. One important way to involve our emotions with dharma is by its association with personalities; it is in this context that development of a relationship with a guru and the worship of personified representations of God occupy important places in Hindu dharma.

PROBLEM BEYOND DHARMA

Dharma is Limited

Dharma encourages us to live a life of balance and objectivity, in keeping with the natural order which is applicable to all of us. If we follow the spirit of dharma, there is no doubt that we will find more happiness and fulfilment in our lives. There are, of course, difficulties in staying on the path of dharma even for a well-meaning person. Often we are tempted by short-term gratifications; also, a de-stabilising event (such as a large financial loss) puts pressure on us to adopt unworthy means. At times our emotional connection with Ishwara fails us; there are many people whose life-long devotion evaporates in the face of a calamity such as the premature death of a loved person.

But, despite such pressures, if we do manage to stay on dharma's path, our elemental urges (which make us struggle to survive forever, to continuously know more and to always be happy) yet remain unaddressed. Obviously no one is immortal and no one knows everything he wants to know; further, when we look into the lives of even those who are venerated as pinnacles of rectitude and religiosity, we do not find an eternal ocean of perpetual bliss. (Leave aside people, even the Gods in our mythology were not able to always get what they wanted and suffered from anger and disappointment!) In order to deal with the problem of perpetually wanting to become different from the mortal, ignorant and unfulfilled creatures that we find ourselves to be, we need to go beyond dharma and look at a completely different approach which Vedanta offers.

Three Traits

In the context of man's highest destiny not ending with dharma, it is relevant to look at the concept of *trigunas* or the three basic qualities of our mental make-up. The scriptures state that we all have these three attributes but in widely varying proportions:

- *tamas* -   characterised by somnolence, dullness, ignorance, delusion and lack of any worthwhile goal.

- *rajas* -   manifested as driving ambitions, hyper-activity, lack of balance & moderation, greed, envy and anger.

- *sattva* -   denoted by balance, moderation, compassion, gratitude, objectivity and harmony.

The goal of dharma, in relation to these three fundamental orientations, is to first motivate a pre-dominantly tamasic person to rise above rudimentary urges. This is done by holding out artha (security) and kama (pleasures) as valid objectives worth striving for and also by drawing such persons into social and religious duties with the consequent need to earn resources and enter into meaningful interactions with others. The objective here is to increase their level of rajas, in order to overcome indifference and lassitude.

However, too much rajas is not good because it leads to endless desires and frenzied activity, without any discrimination. So, dharma then deals with a predominantly rajasic person. The emphasis for such a person is on keeping his pursuit of securities and pleasures within the ambit of dharma. He is encouraged to give importance to education as well as to the role of patriarchs and priests in his life; his tendency to acquire and hoard is sought to be balanced by holding out the virtues of contributing and giving; his competitive urges are moderated by encouraging him to work and live within the norms of his own community; his ego is sublimated by giving religion a large role in his life as well as by instilling the understanding that fruits of his actions are not something conquered entirely on his own but a gift (*prasada*) from a benevolent God.

Finally, persons in whom tamas and rajas have been brought to their optimum, what naturally comes to the forefront is the quality of sattva; such people have graduated from being ordinary people with ordinary motivations to become extra-ordinary people who have attained harmony and balance, who have empathy and compassion for others and who are not in frantic competition to garner money, power or name. People like these often become monks or priests or teachers; their objectivity and love for knowledge is likely to propel them in the direction of Vedanta.[33]

While developing a sattvic person is dharma's goal, Vedanta's goal is to take a person beyond concern with these three qualities.[34] What does this mean? It does not mean that Vedanta considers tamas, rajas and sattva as being irrelevant. Each of these qualities is necessary in its right place for living in this world: for instance, a person completely lacking tamas may not be able to rest at all, a person without any rajas would find no motivation to get out of bed every morning and a person without an iota of sattva would be like a wild beast, not equipped with the minimum qualities required to live in society. But, for a refined person in whom a life of dharma has brought the quality of sattva to the forefront, Vedanta tries to further elevate him to a perspective from where these three qualities are stripped off any fundamental significance.

Vedanta does this by showing that our reality is greater than the mind in which tamas, rajas and sattva arise. The state of our mind is important to the extent that only an adequately prepared mind will be receptive to Vedanta's wisdom; however, because our true nature is not the mind, it is never affected by our mental state. If one does not understand this, it is possible for a person's journey of growth to stop at the mental level of sattva: he may consider his task done when he lives an ethical life devoted to religion and charity and, instead of transcending his ego, he may actually develop a very powerful ego filled with self-importance based upon the rectitude of his life.[35] Coming to a halt here keeps us well away from our ultimate objective which is the discovery of our deepest truth beyond the mind and the ego.

Shiva's Story

That Vedanta's goal is to take us beyond the play of our mind and the ego is portrayed in a story from the *puranas* about Shiva

---

33 I must hasten to clarify that all people who study Vedanta, especially today, are by no means pre-dominantly sattvic.

34 *triguna atita*.

35 This type of self-righteous ego is termed *sattvic ahamkara*.

as *Tripurantaka* or the destroyer of the three cities.[36] The story is about three great cities, made with walls of iron, silver and gold respectively, which were populated with ungodly people (*asuras*). All these cities were in constant orbit at three different levels in the universe. They were protected by a boon so that they could not be destroyed except by a single arrow; for this to happen, all three had to be in alignment and this would be an almost impossible occurrence because they were always moving in relation to each other. It was Shiva who ultimately brought about their destruction by shooting an arrow at them at the precise and rare moment when they happened to be in line with each other.

On a more interpretive plane, the iron, silver and gold of the three cities represent, respectively, the tamas, rajas and sattva within each one of us. (Iron, as a base metal, stands for our baser qualities; silver stands for wealth which motivates us into perpetual and greedy action; gold, being untarnishable and considered to be the noblest of all metals, denotes our finest qualities.) Our ultimate objective is not to progress from tamas to sattva but to go beyond all qualities because even the quality of sattva carries a seed of ego and duality; this is depicted by portraying even the golden city as containing evil and needing destruction.

This goal can only be achieved when these three qualities are in alignment (by being in appropriate proportions) and when good fortune or grace is available in the form of penetrative insight (represented by Shiva's arrow). Dharma brings about the required alignment of mental qualities by promoting a life of balance and objectivity and Vedanta provides the necessary insight through the wisdom of its teachings; this then takes us beyond the realm of qualities to our pure and natural state where there is no duality at all.

Vedanta Needs Dharma

Vedanta's answer to our need for evolution beyond sattva is knowledge-based and, in a strict sense, it is a complete solution in

---

36 This form of Shiva, also known as *Tripuravijayi* (or conqueror of the three cities), is the subject matter of many beautiful Chola bronze images where Shiva is depicted as an imperiously upright figure with a large bow in his hand.

itself. However, Vedanta's potential does not become available to us unless we have first prepared ourselves by leading a life of dharma. The situation here can be compared with the cooking of rice where it is fire which actually cooks; but without a pot and water, the use of fire alone will not produce any edible result. So, for the fire of Vedanta's knowledge to work we need the pot and water of dharma.

To express this in different words, the seeds of Vedanta do not readily sprout in minds which do not possess objectivity, maturity, stability and clarity; we can cultivate such a mind only by actions and attitudes based on dharma. If dharma is not given due place in our lives it not only leads to our failure in finding conventional happiness but also leads to our failure in benefitting from the great truths of Vedanta. In this way, dharma and Vedanta are inextricably tied up.

Are All Religions the Same?

It is sometimes believed that all religions say the same thing and lead us to the same goal. Such a conclusion needs to be examined more carefully to make sure that we do not readily accept something just because it sounds liberal.

Religions consist of three major and distinct elements:

- Theism and beliefs
- Modes of worship
- Life-style and conduct

Religions also have associated with them something else which is called spirituality. Spirituality, in its broadest sense, refers to the recognition of the ultimate or innermost reality[37]. All these elements vary greatly over different religions.

Each major religion has its own vision of God. Beliefs about the nature of heaven, hell, life after death and the fate of non-

---

37 The primary dictionary meaning of 'spirituality' refers to the spirit as being something different from the body which survives even after the body dies; but, in the context of Vedanta which holds that all divisions are superficial, spirituality means personal awareness of the underlying unity behind every single thing.

believers are also different in each religion. Modes of worship and life-style are specific to different cultures.

The one area of commonality in most religions covers basic ethics and conduct in human relationships. All religions support the dictum 'Do unto others what you want others to do unto you' because this is in keeping with universal human needs to be loved, helped and protected from harm. However, even in this area there are significant differences. Religions have their own ideas of accommodating contrary beliefs and they can uphold contrasting standards of conduct towards believers and non-believers; further, some religions extend their concept of consideration and non-injury to all living beings while others restrict it to only human-beings, with animals being regarded as undeserving of such kindness; many major religions take the aggressive conversion of people of other faiths to their fold as holy duty while others do not.

Where, perhaps, some deeper commonality can be found is in the area of spirituality. But while all cultures have spiritual aspects, such aspects are often not part of their mainstream religions; in fact, in the history of religions like Christianity and Islam there have been many cases of people with spiritual leanings (the so-called 'mystics') who have been condemned as being dangerous heretics. Vedanta has been fortunate in being preserved in a religious culture which actually recognises spiritual evolution as being the ultimate goal.

But it should be noted that even amongst the main religions of India (Hinduism, Buddhism and Jainism), the vision of the spiritual goal is not identical. For instance, a school of Buddhism conceives ultimate reality as nothingness or emptiness (*shunyavada*); such nihilism is in complete contrast to Vedanta's vision of reality being fullness without any limits (*purnata*). Further, both Buddhism and Jainism concentrate on appropriate attitudes and conduct to escape suffering in this world while Vedanta focuses more on everyone's intrinsic fullness which it says can be accessed primarily with proper understanding.

And even within Vedanta itself there are differences in the

vision of *advaita* as set out by Adi Shankara, *visisht advaita* as propounded by Ramanuja and *dvaita* championed by Madhva; these differences are not quibbling matters but affect the basic understanding of reality, the goal of life and the way of reaching that goal.

Therefore, while religions and religious philosophies encourage worship of divinity and uphold a set of universally accepted human conduct and attitudes, they are quite different in their ideas about the nature of that divinity and the underlying spiritual vision. We should guard against blindly accepting the claim that all religions are the same, just because we want to be open-minded. As the acclaimed modern thinker Richard Dawkins once observed (rather caustically), *"By all means let's be open-minded but not so open-minded that our brains fall out."*

Finally

We can understand the true role of dharma only once we are well on the way of Vedanta. It is when the vision of Vedanta starts getting clearer to us that we realise, first, how critical it is to lead a life based on dharma and, second, that the actual goal for any human being is *moksha* – liberation from a mistake in understanding our own true nature.

Once we are able to see this perspective, our definition of 'good' becomes anything which helps us to gain self-knowledge while 'bad' becomes whatever that inhibits such knowledge; artha, kama and even dharma, no longer remain goals for us but become a means to our only real end. But it is not that dharma disappears with the dawn of Vedanta's knowledge. When Vedanta's teachings succeed in removing the ignorance surrounding our own self, the pressure within us to do anything wrong dissipates and actions which occur through our bodies and minds are then always naturally right and in keeping with dharma; the quality of sattva which we need to initially cultivate by using our efforts, now spontaneously flows from us. In a way, the means also become the end.

DESIRES, EXPECTATIONS AND VALUES
Often Misunderstood

Some aspects of desires have been covered in other essays. However, fuller understanding of the role of desires in our lives is critical if the pursuit of Vedanta is to bear fruit.

Desires, expectations and values are inter-related matters which have a great bearing on our journey of growth. Many of us, especially those with a Hindu background, often carry ideas such as:

• The path to happiness promised by Vedanta requires us to become completely desire-free.

• All our activities should be in keeping with *karma yoga*, which is taken to mean that we should work without any expectation of results.

• There is no chance of benefitting from Vedanta without bringing back a whole host of ancestral values into our lives.

Such conclusions can easily become a damper on anyone's enthusiasm as he or she attempts to learn something from Vedanta. While becoming desire-free is certainly a tidy solution to problems caused by endless wants, many doubt their abilities to reach such an utopian state; many are also not quite ready to turn their backs upon the world which, despite its problems, has a lot of worthwhile and rewarding things to offer. Similarly, not everyone is convinced that he or she can perform any activity without some expectations about its outcome. Last, while there may be several problems with our current values, achieving ethical perfection in the traditional sense seems an unrealistically tall order. If these issues are not sensibly resolved, we can easily be discouraged from looking beyond our usual recipe of eat, drink and be merry.

To put these issues in perspective, we can begin with the criticism we read about our modern life-styles, values and attitudes. Many of these views are subjective, coming from a purely personal view-point. Criticism in these areas tends to get sharper with the increasing age of the commentator. This happens because gradual change around us accumulates almost unnoticed during the first 50 or 60 years of our lives, till it reaches a critical mass; then, the considerable variation in the way of life between when we were younger and now, suddenly hits us. This is when we exclaim "Oh my God! What is this world coming to?" From then onwards we can only see impending disaster and find solace in dreamily talking about the 'good old days' when things were so different, so good.

This is nothing new: the well-known Yoga Vashishtha (an ancient book which contains the teachings of the rishi Vashishtha to the young prince Rama) begins by be-moaning the state of the world – even then, morals were seen to be slipping, values changing for the worse and conduct becoming inappropriate to the point where the collapse of civilised society was apparently just round the corner!

On the other hand, provided one does not get too maudlin or despondent, there is a lot to be gained by understanding changes in societal trends, which will highlight areas where one may have to make extra effort to foster one's inner growth.

Ancient Setting

The ancient setting in which the Vedic way of life evolved was an agricultural society. Agriculture created need for large joint families so that work could be divided and peak-loads (such as sowing, transplanting and harvesting) could be handled. This, together with the fact that migration was uncommon, created a sense of community within families as well within local areas. Agriculture being so weather-dependent also brought home the effect of natural forces on everyone's well-being. The constant presence of several family elders and occupations which were hereditary did not leave much scope for individual choice and validation. And, even though most people were never formally exposed to Vedanta's teachings, a common religion and culture imprinted two major aspects of its vision on society as a whole:

- Everything is sacred; nothing is to be misused because nothing is separate from Ishwara.

- Every person, being only a manifestation of Ishwara, is essentially whole and divine.

These ideas had large impact on traditional life-styles, aspirations and attitudes.

Current Scenario

Things have naturally changed since then. Geographic and occupational mobility are now normal, families break up easily and connections with a shared past get readily snapped. Further, industrial and post-industrial societies are able to sustain and improve output by use of technology. In this set-up, we are less affected by natural forces and feel a sense of greater control over our lives. Given the importance of technology and scale in our economies, success becomes increasingly measured only in terms of economic output. Any time spent in sitting back or in contemplating (i.e. in not directly increasing tangible output) is considered a move away from success.

Also, large and complex economic systems require continuously increasing levels of consumption to remain viable. This is achieved by systematically validating and encouraging all our desires, continuously feeding our egos and weaning us away from any notions of thrift and moderation; we see manifestations of this in wasteful portions in restaurants, in packaging which has become more important than the contents, in advertising blitzes which convince us that our happiness depends upon a certain shape of a car or on a particular brand of shoes and that each and everyone of our desires is legitimate, whose immediate fulfilment is owed to us by the world.

This attitude spills over to music, dance, vacations and relationships. The recipe now is: hurry, obtain, optimise, consume and defend. In this set-up, it is difficult to find a place for philosophical and cultural learning; ironically, such education was less important when society did not give too many choices to individuals in terms of conduct, occupation and religion. But, in today's individualistic society, it is easy to lose connection with a cultural background and what is lost is not only some specific behaviour or ritual but an entire vision carried by that culture.

If that vision is valid and helpful, a great loss can occur unless special effort is made to preserve and propagate it. The traditional vision of Hindu culture, apart from the idea of the sacredness of everything, also emphasises the importance of managing our emotions and modulating our egos, by advocating moderation and balance; the loss of such vision has marked effect on our attitudes and conduct.

When we define success only as possession and consumption, we aggrandise the culture of societies which have such 'success'. But culture has to provide for all human needs, including emotional and spiritual ones. After all, our needs to find lasting peace and to be connected with something constant and infallible are as real and important as our other needs, perhaps more so. However, we now tend to gravitate towards beacons which symbolise over-development in only the physical, the intellectual and the ego-based aspects of our lives, without any emphasis on all-round balance.

In our current state of minds, we are less fascinated by the every-day marvels and miracles of nature: a magnificent peacock produced from the unremarkable contents of an egg does not draw our attention as much as a car which does 0 to 100 kph in less than 5 seconds. We are also losing our ability to enjoy things for what they intrinsically are; for some of us now, great art or fine wines or the latest marvels of technology are only part of a veneer of sophistication and more a statement of the size, brand and cost of our inventory. There is nothing wrong by itself in having high-performance cars or vintage wines or an art collection (provided, of course, that one does this without transgressing ethics or neglecting other responsibilities). Problems arise when we buy that car only to show that we have 'arrived', when we have no real interest in its performance and the underlying engineering, when our mind is already working on the next acquisition which will wow people around us, even as we take the delivery of this car.

Problem of Desires

When we seek to feel good only by our acquisitions and experiences, we get trapped into a tense and frustrated life because:

- Wants are never-ending and they proliferate in variety and intensity, often depending upon the choices of others whom we try to emulate.

- Wants are never fulfilled only by the availability of the desired object but also require our bodies to be healthy and our minds to be receptive. Some of these factors are outside our control: even a great meal is not enjoyable if we have a tooth-ache or if we are hurt by our hostess paying more attention to some other guest.

- Wants are a zero-sum game because the achievement of any want is always at the cost of something else expended or foregone; at a given point in time the price we pay for a particular thing may seem well worth it but, in the long run, this spending and getting cancel out each other. This is why, despite great success in meeting so many wants, the pressure of our pending desires remains substantially unchanged.

Based on these factors, Benedictine monks in medieval Europe had held that even the rich were never ever rich enough; it is for the same reasons that Ramana Maharishi said that while this world can meet everyone's needs, even the entire universe cannot fulfil a single person's wants.

An example of people committed to the fulfilment of ever-increasing material wants was seen in the late Roman world. Many there were devoted to endless consumption and possessions including exotic food, fine clothes and grand houses. They were also obsessed with their physical health, spending more time in baths and health clubs than in temples and libraries. A man could earn fame and acceptance just by spending more than his neighbours; if one was famous enough, the fact that one may have a dubious character was ignored or forgiven. Like the *carvakas* of ancient India, Romans of the 4th century cared most about success which was interpreted as being ahead for today and let tomorrow take care of itself. They were remarkably proud, greedy and vain – in short, very much like some of us today who have a misplaced sense of entitlement and complacence.

However, all that has been said so far should not be taken as a generalised stand against today's economic and social systems. First of all, Vedanta's focus is not on economic and social changes at the systemic level but on the development of personal capabilities within us, to maintain our sense of fullness and peace even within a problematic environment. In a way, Vedanta has characteristics of capitalism where individuals are encouraged to work assiduously on their personal deliverance: a Vedanta story extols the good sense of an individual putting on leather foot-wear on his own feet instead of trying to carpet an entire kingdom with leather.

Second, today's global markets are associated with free societies which have spurred material and social progress and increased overall communication and co-operation. There are, of course, grave dangers if free markets are released from all rules and are left to be governed only by the greed of the most powerful. But we should also be aware that the additional wealth and capabilities we have today only amplify some of our own latent tendencies towards being self-centred and acquisitive. Therefore, as we try to bring in overall improvements in our society, we should never forget to simultaneously work on our personal attitudes and understanding; this is where Vedanta's focus is.

Desires Need Intelligent Handling

All this also does not mean that our desires are reprehensible in general and that our initial task in life has to be the stamping out of all our wants. In fact, the Bhagavad Gita has Lord Krishna saying *bhuteshu kamosmi*, which literally means 'I am in the form of desires in beings'.[38] A later Hindu scripture speaks of *iccha-shakti* – the power to desire – as a special privilege for mankind.

---

38 It needs to be noted that the context in which this statement is made in the Gita makes it clear that its intention is not to promote or validate all desires.

Thus, desires seem to be elevated to a divine gift, a form of Ishwara, even by ancient texts.

But then how does this reconcile with the fact that desires are also compared with fire which can never say no to more fuel and which leaves destruction in its wake? Scriptural passages pointing out the danger of desires and the need to control them far outnumber the portions which take a more tolerant view.

To resolve this apparent contradiction we have to understand that desires can be both a privilege and a curse, just as a fire can both cook our dinner and burn down our house. Desires are perfectly natural; they arise spontaneously and, without them, we would not be motivated to do anything or enjoy our magnificent world of objects and experiences. However, without some understanding, desires can go out of hand and instead of remaining privileges they can become our masters which over-rule our own intelligence – like the proverbial tail wagging the dog. As Spinoza put it, "*The true slave is he who is led away by his pleasures and can neither see what is good for him nor act accordingly.*"

We also have to understand that the place of desires in our lives changes, depending upon the stage of life and maturity that we happen to be at. When we are children (or child-like, as many adults remain), any and all of our desires seem justified and have to be necessarily fulfilled – even by throwing a tantrum or by robbing a bank. As we grow in maturity, we realise the importance of keeping our desires in check so that they remain within our legitimate means as well as within reasonable moral and legal constraints of civilised society.

Regulation of Desires

Traditionally, the initial regulation of desires in society was achieved by the presence of priests and patriarchs and also by the influence of detailed codes of accepted conduct. What we need now is not merely a list of do's and don'ts but a better understanding of the spirit behind such prescriptions. In this context, a modern teacher of Vedanta talks about the so-called ABC of desires; while this is not directly based on a scriptural passage, it is very helpful for someone at a preparatory stage of Vedanta.

The 'A' in this ABC stands for appropriateness. Appropriateness of a desire is not determined by some arbitrary standard but by understanding the natural laws which govern our world, including our own bodies and minds. For desires not to damage us, they need to be in keeping with the natural order called dharma and we are legitimately entitled to pursue only *dharma aviruddha kama* or those desires not opposed to dharma. This is not for the sake of some abstract or moral goal but in our own, long-term interest because rubbing against the natural order will only lacerate us.

The 'B' stands for balance, even within our legitimate desires. Just as our different muscles have all to be exercised to remain fit, the entire body of our desires has to be kept in balance by not over-emphasising or neglecting any one aspect. One important balance here is between our need to possess and consume versus the need to give and share. While we are entitled to earn, save and enjoy the fruits of our labours, we need to balance this by contributing and helping. Balance also has to be achieved between our material and non-material desires – growth in our emotional and spiritual aspects should be given our time and energy, despite the endless call of our more material wants; this is because, in the long run, material achievements alone do not satisfy many of our deeper needs.

Finally, the 'C' here stands for cleanliness. Fulfilling desires involves effort, where energy is expended on both physical and mental levels. When an engine generates power, polluting and noxious by-products arise; as we work towards fulfilment of our desires, we too generate undesirable by-products like anger, jealousy, hostility and guilt. Just as we put filters and catalytic convertors on our car engines, we also have to deliberately incorporate appropriate conduct and attitudes into our lives, which will process our negative emotions.

This approach of modulating our desires is useful at the initial stages of our journey of life. As we grow in maturity and understanding, our concern with desires (including appropriate, balanced and clean ones) must, of course, lessen upon the arising of the discernment that there is no real and valid connection between our efforts to fulfil desires and our goal of lasting happiness. As Nagarjuna (the ancient Buddhist philosopher) put it, *"There is pleasure when a sore is scratched but to be without sores is more pleasurable still; just so, there are pleasures in worldly desires but to be without desires is more pleasurable still"*. And progress on Vedanta's path, leading to the discovery of our intrinsic peace and fullness, requires that desires lose their powerful hold on our minds for this discovery to dawn and abide.

Vedanta and Desires

As we continue to grow, it becomes apparent to some of us that no amount of propriety in our desires removes the sense of being small, limited and insignificant individuals; some of us then turn to Vedanta which offers a solution to this fundamental problem. It is interesting to note that the starting point of the chain leading to Vedanta is, in fact, desires. Desires lead to actions which produce results and generate experiences. These provide us with the raw material for discerning that all experiences are temporary and limited. We then come to the point where the only desire we consider worthwhile is the desire to find permanent freedom from being wanting in general and this makes us eligible for the wisdom of Vedanta.[39]

Can the variety and strength of a person's usual desires continue unchanged while pursuing Vedanta? Underlying our usual desires (such as to be richer, healthier, more famous, more knowledgeable and more loved) are a mortal body, an insecure ego and unfulfilled emotions. Vedanta, on the other hand, says that our reality is unchanging and boundless awareness; it is the wrong identification with our limited physical and mental aspects which leads to our desires gaining so much force. Vedanta also shows us that our compulsive struggle to overcome such

---

39 Students of Vedanta are classified as *manda adhikari*, *madhyama adhikari* and *uttama adhikari*, in ascending order of discrimination (*viveka*) and dispassion (*vairagya*). Unfortunately, some people who listen to Vedanta today are not *adhikaris* at all because of unchanging focus on usual wants and pursuits.

limitations is misplaced because it will never fully succeed – instead, what we should focus on is a better understanding of our true nature which is always free of any sort of limitation. Too much concern with the fulfilment of desires just reinforces the notion that we are nothing but our bodies and minds; therefore, holding on to both Vedanta and the usual force of all our desires will be as useful as alternatively digging a hole and filling it up, or reading a book on healthy eating as we eat a large plateful of greasy food.

Expectations and Preferences

Apart from desires, the question of preferences and expectations is also subject to a lot of misunderstanding. It is almost impossible for us to have no preferences or an expected goal in mind. Thus, we may prefer tea over coffee and, when we take a medicine, we do expect to feel better. In this context, Vedanta tells us to remember that while action is within our purview, the result of our action is outside our control; this is because the actual result of any of our actions is a product of a host of other factors, above and beyond our own efforts. This means that when the result of our action presents itself, there is no justification for great personal pride (if things have gone well) or for dejection and guilt (if things have not gone so well). We can develop this healthy attitude by analysing our own successes and failures objectively and seeing for ourselves that our effort is only one of the inputs which go into bringing about a particular result. If one has a religious inclination, we can also look upon Ishwara as the set of natural laws which cover the creation of a particular result in response to our action; we can, then, gracefully accept all results as *prasada* – a hallowed gift – from the Lord.

Because of his discriminative understanding, a more evolved pursuer of Vedanta would no longer be driven to seek the small rewards of his own actions. Here, we have to be careful in understanding the difference between the harmless expectation of a practical outcome from an action (*prayojanam*) and the problematic anticipation of individual gratification (*phalam*). So, as one teaches a class, the expectation that students will understand and benefit is natural (and creates no harm as long as one understands that the expectation may or may not be met); on the other hand, if the focus of the teaching is on the personal accolades that the teacher will get for his brilliance and, perhaps, some bonus remuneration, then this creates problems because it reinforces the mistaken identification with his body and mind. In other words, when advice given to a person seeking evolution it is not against an expected outcome but against the hankering for ego or sense gratification.

Values

Coming to our value system, there is no need for a desperate attempt to comply with every letter of ancient codes, portions of which may have become dated and irrelevant. If we understand both the privileges and the dangers inherent in our desires and if we have the maturity to accept the results of our actions in the proper spirit, then we will have no difficulty in following a value system which will be appropriate, even if it deviates from some traditional prescriptions. An example of intelligently modifying traditional values in keeping with changing times is provided by some contemporary teachers of Vedanta. These gurus venerate traditions and understand their spirit so well that they have no problem in giving *diksha* to qualified women (i.e. ritually ordain them as *sanyasis*) even though this is prohibited by medieval norms; their concern now, and rightly so, is with the maturity of the seeker and not with gender.

On the other hand, flexibility in values and codes of conduct can degenerate into carelessness, laziness and exploitation. While it may now not be practical or necessary to perform a religious ritual and seek forgiveness prior to the felling of every tree, this should not lead us to mindless plunder of nature. To take another instance, in portions of modern Indian society many fortunate women are now freed from the drudgery and the subservient role that they would have had to suffer in the past; this should not lead them to waste their comfortable lives, without doing anything worthwhile.

Similarly, we now have grown-up children who want freedom from family norms and obligations but also want to stay with their parents and be supported even after getting married – they are 'western' when it comes to defending their rights and limiting their duties but they become traditional Indians when it comes to accepting the safety and comfort of their extended family's infrastructure.

While some of this is inevitable in the process of transition, when such 'division of labour' (you put in the effort and I will take the fruits!) is taken too far and when appropriate new values, roles and responsibilities are not brought in to replace the discarded ones, society and the environment suffer, relationships sour and unnecessary pain is caused.

On a Personal Note

The traditional teachings of Vedanta begin on the assumption that the seeker's desires, preferences and values have been already processed to be in line with Vedanta's requirements. There are occasionally some people who get into Vedanta without such preparation and yet manage to quickly and almost effortlessly absorb its true spirit. These are envious examples but their record does not offer anything practical, beyond inspiration, to the rest of us; after all, the fact that Mozart completed his first symphony at the age of nine is not of much use to an ordinary mortal struggling to learn music.

For a prepared and committed seeker, traditional Vedanta envisages only two basic life-styles:

- A life of formal renunciation (called *sanyasa*) for the few who are cut out to be monks and want to pursue self-growth without any other distractions or agendas.

- A more usual life but without focus on personal gratification (called *karma yoga*) for someone who needs to live conventionally but only as a means of preparing his mind for the wisdom of Vedanta.[40]

Both these options are very demanding because they require a seeker to turn his back on what the rest of the world considers to be the only worthwhile goals (money, pleasures & fame)

---

40 For *antahkarana shuddhi*, as it is termed in Sanskrit.

and to become indifferent to what were, hitherto, the very reasons for living. But classical Vedanta expected its students to be already endowed with tremendous wisdom and discipline as well as being totally committed to solving the fundamental human problem of perpetually feeling inadequate; further, many Vedanta texts were written by teachers who were themselves renunciates, like Shankara, and were addressed to persons with similar inclinations.

Lacking even the primary qualifications for entry into Vedanta as I did, the enormity of Vedanta's real requirements never struck me as I put in my toes to test its waters. But this was actually helpful because had I any inkling of the rigorous expectations of this task, I would have perhaps retreated instead of plunging in. This is why some contemporary teachers do not emphasise the full requirements of Vedanta at the outset; they understand that not only do many modern entrants lack the required preparation but some may never become suitably qualified even after years of studying Vedanta.

But this does not mean that Vedanta is of no benefit to such students. While the full fruits of Vedanta are available only to the fully qualified seeker, this ancient wisdom blesses its seekers not only by its core teachings but also by its initial exposure which provides remarkably important and useful insights; further, it leads us to wise and kind people, re-connects us with a valuable culture and gives us a great sense of hope.

However, studying Vedanta without having earned the required qualities raises several issues. In my own case, I conveniently glossed over any ethical, attitudinal and life-style changes and tried to rely only on intellectual prowess (upon which I had placed excessive emphasis) to crack the nut of Vedanta. Our intellectual efforts here can equip us with fascinating concepts, an impressive vocabulary and involved logic; they may even qualify us to write erudite-sounding books. But Vedanta is meant to help us experience a natural sense of fullness and compassion in actual living and not for delivering lectures or for participating in debates. And its real purpose is not achieved till our egos, emotions, desires and attitudes are suitably modulated, to bring to fruition the knowledge contained in Vedanta.

The study of Vedanta without too much concern for what is compatible with this pursuit in other aspects of life can lead to a peculiar stalemate where, despite a lot of effort and apparent progress, one can remain substantially unchanged in areas which matter the most. In fact, with the benefit of some teachings of Vedanta I actually became a greater seeker of pleasures and possessions as well as more adept at projecting my image as a person who was now knowledgeable about a rather esoteric topic. This can happen because Vedanta enhances our capacity for enjoyment by reducing many of our usual fears in the course of trying out new things; we can also draw false re-assurance from our presumption that its purity will be an antidote for anything else that we may do.

It is while I was seriously pursuing Vedanta that I also pursued a host of other things including learning to fly and to scuba-dive, embarking on a systematic exploration of fine-dining, beginning a collection of art, energetically visiting unusual travel destinations round the globe and cultivating a number of other hobbies like music, astronomy and sailing. And I did not do all this casually but with the full force of all my available resources. What have I learnt from these experiences? How do they fit in with the pursuit of Vedanta? Would I do anything differently the second time around, if I could turn the clock back?

Let me start by saying that to be born a human being with the ability to explore and experience our marvelous world is a privilege. The things in the world and our faculties which enable us to enjoy them are all naturally given to us. To attempt to go through life while ignoring what it offers is both a needless attempt to reform nature and the denial of a great gift to ourselves. The world out there not only caters to our basic physical and psychological needs but also nurtures our finer qualities like awe, gratitude and humility. In that sense, many pursuits and hobbies (especially those which re-connect us with the beauty and power of nature) are useful and enriching.

However, as we interact with the world, we must remember that our intelligence is also naturally given to us and we should not block its vital role of bringing in discrimination and balance into our lives. Intelligence requires us to partake of the world in moderation, to not let our equanimity be dependent on transient pleasures and to find greater purpose and meaning in our lives, beyond mere possessions, experiences and comparisons.

Someone who wants to seriously pursue Vedanta and derive real benefit from it has to not only refrain from obviously wrong or damaging pursuits but also needs to get to a point where otherwise innocuous or even desirable activities lose their hold over his mind. This is because all actions and experiences are centred on the body and mind, both of which need to be transcended if we are to discover our deeper reality. If we lead a life in which we continue to focus on things whose undue importance we are trying to reduce, the obvious result is confusion, contradictions and dilution of the effects of the teaching; we may as well spend our time in trying to fill water in a bucket with a big hole at its bottom. This, of course, does not mean that an earnest student of Vedanta can never sail a boat, look at stars or go scuba-diving; it is only the compulsive need to do such things (because one feels inadequate without them) and the devotion of excessive resources to their pursuit which detracts from Vedanta's journey.

The mistake which many of us make as we pursue Vedanta is to assume that all other activities are justified as long as they do not compromise ethics and are balanced with adequate time given to Vedanta. While such an approach is a good beginning, it does not remain valid or useful for too long. As we know from our own experience, all pursuits, attainments and experiences pall over time by the very nature of our mental make-up and by the fact that we inevitably make comparisons; ultimately, for such things to remain enjoyable, we are tempted to raise our stakes.

So, when I learnt flying I did not stop at flying simple, light aircraft but managed to get into high-performance fighters, high-altitude reconnaissance aircraft and airplanes equipped to provide a zero-gravity experience of a space-flight; and when I learnt diving I traversed the world from Palau in Micronesia, to the Galapagos

Islands in the Pacific and to the Ningaloo Reef in Western Australia, in search of extreme underwater experiences. The problem here is not with the exploration of a specific interest to its full extent but in a state of mind which drives us to relentlessly hunt for higher and even higher levels of similar experiences. If not kept within bounds, this escalation can consume inordinate amounts of time, focus and tranquility, all of which are required for the meaningful study of Vedanta.

Finally, a person committed only to 'eat, drink and be merry' may have occasional doubts about the long-term viability and meaning of his approach and may, some day, wake-up to the realization that there is more to life; on the other hand, a person who blends hedonism with Vedanta can be lulled into a false sense of complacence by apparently being on a path of spiritual growth and may never wake up to the fact that a wrong life-style and attitudes permit no more than baby-steps on Vedanta's path.

Some Practical Suggestions

In the light of all this, what should one actually do? The obvious answer, of course, is to work much more seriously on cultivating the qualities of mind and living which are a requisite for Vedanta. This would mean moderating frivolous pursuits, stopping the investment of time in image-building activities and superficial relationships and paying minimal attention to one's physical and economic well-being. Only such an approach is truly compatible with the teachings of Vedanta.

For many of us, this is easier said than done for a variety of reasons. Despite understanding the importance of greater rigour in our lives, we may just not be able to change ourselves because of insufficient commitment and motivation,[41] or because of the deep-rooted force of past habits and conditioning, or because of being inescapably surrounded by people whose agendas and thinking stifle our own growth. What are the options for those of us who find ourselves in this strait-jacket of our own making

---

41 The desire to seek the freedom offered by Vedanta is called *mumukshutvam* and tradition says that this needs to be as intense and urgent as the need to plunge into a river for someone whose hair is on fire!

or made by circumstances? Different people react differently to this predicament.

There are many people who do not see any contradiction between the study of Vedanta and an inappropriate way of living, just as many people who are regular about their periodic health-checks, continue to drink and smoke heavily. For such people, there is no problem because they enjoy their limited pursuit of Vedanta and the fact that they will not progress beyond a point is not a disturbing issue for them.

Some others, once they realise that Vedanta requires serious changes on their part, turn their backs on this subject; some of these people accept that they are not able to pay the price which Vedanta demands while others run down Vedanta to justify their staying away.

Then, of course, there are those who do see the problem in trying to simultaneously ride two horses and seek to resolve this by their own efforts and by guidance from others. In this context, some of the things which are useful are:

- Associating regularly with a proper teacher who can inspire and help.

- Creating a group of like-minded seekers permitting regular sharing of problems and the reinforcement of each other's zeal.

- Bringing in some ritual devotion and worship into one's daily life to create hope and to release negative emotions.

- Spending some time every day in the study of Vedanta by reading, writing or listening; regularity is invaluable in building up a critical mass of this knowledge.

- Meditating and contemplating daily to internalise Vedanta's insights; without taking time to develop a calm and focused mind and without deliberately re-visiting our thoughts and actions in light of Vedanta's teachings, it is almost impossible to make real progress.

In this process, one may be assailed by doubts and frustration because of no tangible progress may show for a long time, despite right intentions and effort. In such a situation, a few things which may be helpful to remember include:

- In Vedanta, no effort is ever wasted and all that we put into it bears fruit sometime or the other; often, it is just when chances of any change in us look bleak that chinks miraculously open in the dark clouds of our mind.

- The habits and conditioning we struggle against to become prepared for Vedanta are acquired over a lifetime and are almost visceral; it should not be surprising that a lot of effort, over a long period, should be needed to get over them.

- Vedanta is the search for the eternal and the boundless; the price we pay for it is only of the finite but our loss, if we give up, is infinite. Thus, despite its apparently heavy price, Vedanta's bargain is always in our favour.

- In Vedanta, as in everything else, we individuals can only make an honest effort towards something worthwhile; the results of our efforts are never entirely dependent on us because they are affected by a host of other people, factors and circumstances. After making our best effort, we should have faith, patience and the courage to accept their results. If the results are not initially encouraging, we must remember Vedanta's lesson: what we truly are always remains whole and unaffected even if our minds continue to be troubled by our apparent limitations.

Further, the full light of Vedanta does not necessarily dawn and stay in our minds as soon as we start leading exemplary lives. There are several examples of *sanyasis* who have not made real progress even after having renounced the usual format of living and having spent years in learning and practicing great discipline. Some of these people yet retain a significant amount of driving wants, negative emotions and insecure egos; they remain judgemental about others, carry a smug opinion of their own scholarship, penance and purity as well as have the need to be surrounded by followers and institutions deifying their names. In short, their minds remain turbulent and the teachings of Vedanta obviously do not work fully or constantly for them.

The fact is that desires are persistent and egos are versatile; they can flourish despite many efforts to moderate them. This is humorously brought out by a story about two wealthy philosophers of ancient Greece where one proclaims his giving up of all luxuries and goes about dressed in tattered clothes while the other continues to wear his fine robes. When they run into each other, the ascetic one scoffs at his richly dressed colleague by telling him "You call yourself a philosopher but I see nothing other than your ego in your expensive robes"; the other one smiles and says, "My friend, your ego shines even more brightly through the holes in your clothes"!

The point here is that being judgemental or being too taken up with superficial signs of dispassion is not called for. In this context, I have personally met a scholar of Vedanta who was actually convinced that using a ceiling-fan in the tropical summer was compatible with the pursuit of Vedanta but using an air-conditioner was not, merely because he had a fan but no air-conditioner. To come to such conclusions, which are based purely on our personal and subjective reference points, is obviously not justified.

The essence of discrimination and dispassion lies not so much in what we have as much as in the state of our minds; what is important is that pleasures, conveniences and possessions should not drive us or occupy the most significant portions of our minds. But we must also remember that using excessive force in suppressing our innate tendencies may to lead to contrary results; sustainable change within us has to come more by growth in maturity and understanding.

There is no general formula by which we can determine when we need to bring our willful effort to the forefront and when we should go along with the flow of our pre-conditioning. Being caught by the force of our desires and habits can be compared to being dragged away from the shore by a rip-current. Not doing anything will, of course, spell our doom but blindly fighting the current will not help because its direct force is likely to be far stronger than our best effort; the possibility of saving ourselves lies in not frittering away our strength in frenzied attempts when the current surges powerfully but in steadily swimming diagonally across its flow when it slackens a little, till we escape its clutches. How we actually accomplish this difficult task depends upon a combination of our strength, skill and luck.

APPENDIX

The Bhagavad Gita deals with desires, their consequences and ways of dealing with them in many of its chapters. Just as an example of the Gita's insights in this area, let us look at verses 62 and 63 from its second chapter:

dhyayato vishayanpumsah sangasteshupajayate
sangatsanjayate kamah kamat krodhobhijayate
krodhabhavati sammohah sammohat smritivibhramah
smritibrahmshad buddhinasho buddhinashat pranashyati

In a person who dwells upon objects, an attachment is born.
From attachment is born desire and from desire, anger is born.
Anger becomes delusion and from delusion, comes the loss
of memory.
Because of the loss of memory, the mind becomes incapacitated.
And when the mind is incapacitated, the person is destroyed.

This scriptural setting out of the process of a man's downfall is quite straight-forward but with some interesting subtleties.

The sequence starts with a person dwelling on objects. The problem is not in our noticing objects or in dealing with them; the problem begins by dwelling upon them to the extent that an attachment is born. Attachment is not simple affection or appreciation but a state where, without that particular object, there is a strong sense of lacking or a disturbing emptiness. From this attachment is born desire – desire to own, to be continuously associated with or to perpetuate; desire here is not that of having a goal in mind but of a pressing thirst or craving. Objects of attachment and desires, as we know, are endless and there is no way in which we can guarantee the continuous fulfilment of even a single desire. Because of frustrated desires, anger is born.

What happens after anger is born? Here, the verb used in the Gita changes from 'born' to 'becomes': anger becomes delusion ... etc. This change in language is deliberate, to denote the fact that once anger is born, the rest of the sequence quickly goes out of our hands. Thus, from anger automatically comes delusion (loss of discrimination) and from delusion comes loss of memory (of lessons we may have learnt from scriptures, teachers and from our own past experiences). This loss of memory is nothing other than the incapacitation of the mind, because whatever wisdom we may have accumulated is now no longer available to us. And what is a man without a mind? So with the incapacitation of the mind, the core of the person is itself destroyed. The person becomes like an animal acting helplessly on an impulse, without having the human freedom to make intelligent choices.

The point here is not that we should not have any wants or that all anger spells doom. The intended emphasis is on the need to moderate the strength of our desires. Anger is nothing but the reflected force of an obstructed desire and it is as powerful as the desire. Once anger is born, the other consequences necessarily follow and, if the anger is very powerful, these consequences can drive us to our own destruction. It is in this context that other parts of the Gita provide us with ways of intelligently handling our attachments and aversions, so that our desires are modulated and we can prevent excessive anger from poisoning our highest faculty.

Many other scriptures also talk about the same thing when they point out that we all have six major enemies which are listed as desires, anger, greed, delusion, pride and envy.[42] Such scriptural warnings remain valid because basic human nature has not substantially changed; therefore, even now, uncontrolled desires form the bed-rock of our negative qualities which have to be tackled with understanding, vigilance and a proper style of living.

In dealing with these issues, we not only face hurdles from our own make-up but also from the social system within which we live. One major factor which causes very significant distortions and imbalances across almost all societies today is undue emphasis on competitive success and, that too, defined almost entirely in financial terms; this relatively recent phenomenon is not directly mentioned in ancient texts for obvious reasons but is progressively affecting many lives.

---

42 The Sanskrit terms for these six enemies (*shadripu*) are: *kama, krodha, lobha, moha, mada* and *matsarya*.

To be and to feel successful certainly adds important dimensions to our lives and if success results in more money, it can be used to obtain leisure and security both of which are very desirable. But problems arise when success is sought to be achieved by sacrificing all other aspects of life at the altar of competition; these problems are compounded when money is sought for ostentatiously outshining others as well as for trying to prove (through fallacious logic) that one is somehow more intelligent and more refined merely because one has made more money. Some of the damaging issues which arise from such an orientation are:

- Excessive self-centredness with no genuine interest in anyone or anything unless he or it can contribute to success defined in this very narrow sense.

- Constant worry and fatigue because of ceaseless efforts to somehow reach a single goal.

- Fixation with reaching this chosen goal quickly, with no time or ability to enjoy the journey itself.

- Not valuing education which does not directly contribute to financial gain.[43]

- Elevation of public opinion to a high pedestal because success is considered desirable only when it generates public acclaim.[44]

---

43 This has long-term implications because narrow education denies us many forms of refined enjoyment and satisfaction which become available only when our minds are properly cultivated. Ironically, this lack of a fuller education leaves many successful people incapable of truly enjoying the leisure which they have worked so hard for.

44 In this process, people who consider themselves to be free and individualistic in fact become remarkably uniform and boring because they adopt the same ends and means to garner approval from the same audience. Examples of this blind conformity are seen even amongst the wealthy, who despite having the ability to carry off being individualistic, yet choose the same brands and styles of clothes, shoes and bags as well as very similar cars and yachts, completely in line with their peers and role-models.

- Development of narcissism or megalomania in those who believe they have outshone their neighbours in this game and, conversely, of diffidence or a persecution complex in those who have not been so fortunate.

One important reason why competitive success has assumed extraordinary importance is the erasure of traditional mechanisms to establish an identity and self-worth for an individual. In the past, the scope and intensity of competition for most individuals was moderated by a social set-up where people studied, worked, married and lived within the restrictions of a given geography, religion, caste and family background. Further, a sense of identity was established by strictly followed traditions such as wearing a sacred thread, dressing in a specific manner, going to a particular temple and following fixed norms regarding worship, food habits and so on.

With the disappearance of these forms, the modern individual has to establish his personal identity on a much more fluid and wider canvas; here, ethnic and cultural marks give way to branding which is more often than not reckoned in terms of the common denominator of spending power. Therefore, across the globe there is an increasing number of people who can see the relevance of an individual only in terms of the cost and the newness of baubles and accoutrements which he sports – it is the latest gadget we own, the model of the car we drive and the trendy restaurant where we are recognised which are now becoming the mark of our identity as well as of our worth.

While we cannot and need not turn back the clock of our social set-up, it is important for all of us to re-gain some perspective from time to time and restore balance in our frenzied chase of success defined purely in monetary terms. Our ultimate goal of abiding happiness cannot be achieved unless one is in natural harmony with the stream of life. Such harmony is not possible if one has a constant sense of being in an endless competition in an unforgiving world and is wracked by fractures and unresolved issues within one's self. Our desires, preferences and values have to be reformed and aligned to bring us peace and wholesomeness, despite our surroundings.

THAT IS WHOLE, THIS IS WHOLE

The Vedic Verse

This essay uses more Sanskrit terms and arguments compared to other essays but it gives a flavour of the way in which the core teachings of Vedanta are actually unfolded.

In the ancient teaching tradition of Vedanta, there is a certain order for listing the ten Upanishads which are usually studied. This list always begins with the *Isha* Upanishad which is prefaced[45] by the often recited verse or *mantra*: *"purnamadah purnamidam - - -"*. Therefore, for many students, this mantra becomes their very first introduction to the contents of the Upanishads. The five short lines of this mantra, and their translation, are:

purnamadah purnamidam	That is whole, this is whole.
purnat purnamudachyate	From that whole, comes this whole.
purnasya purnamadaya	Taking away whole from whole,
purnam eva avashishyate	Only whole remains.
om shanti shanti shanti	Om peace, peace, peace.

Cryptic? To say the least. Meaningful? Not on the face of it. In fact, a British scholar of colonial days had used this mantra as an example to support his view that the contents of the Upanishads were banal and riddled with contradictions. Yet, these few lines actually encapsulate some of the most important teachings of Vedanta. The key to unlocking the subtle meaning of this mantra lies in understanding the two pronouns, *adah* (that) and *idam* (this), in the first line itself.

That is Distant

We commonly use the pronoun *that* to refer to objects which are distant. Distance can be in terms of space, time or even knowledge. So, *that city* is distant in space from *this city* and *this birthday* is closer in time compared to *that birthday*. And we say, "I know nothing about *that subject*". In the case of this mantra, when it says "that is whole", it is referring to the wholeness of something which is away from us in terms of space,

---

45 like all the other Upanishads of the *shukla yajurveda*.

time or understanding. The mantra begins by declaring that such a distant entity is whole or complete when it says *"purnamadah"*.

This is Near

On the other hand, we use the pronoun *this* to refer to something which is close or known to us. In this mantra, *idam* or 'this' is used in its widest sense where it is not restricted to objects which happen to be close or known to us personally but to anybody. It thus refers to the entire world of objects, called *jagat* in Sanskrit. Jagat includes not only physical objects but also mental objects such as concepts, thoughts, memories, beliefs and products of imagination. Our own bodies, our personal sensations and our private thoughts are as much objects of our recognition as anything in the outside world and are, therefore, included in idam in this wide sense.

I Cannot Be This

But there is one thing which is very near to us and yet cannot be included in the definition of idam or 'this': our own consciousness or awareness. The entire world becomes apparent to us because of our consciousness but we cannot become aware of our consciousness in the way in which we become aware of other objects. To be able to objectify the consciousness by which everything is known to us, we would need another, deeper consciousness; we then get into an indefinite regression, till we accept a fundamental consciousness which is not an object of our awareness. This consciousness is the pure subject, the deepest meaning of the word "I", and is termed *atma* in Sanskrit. Atma is the only thing which cannot be included in idam or jagat because, as the ultimate subject, it can never become an object for our faculties to be aware of; unlike everything else, it can never be pointed out to or known as *this*.

Nothing We Know is Limitless

Let us go back to the mantra which says *purnamidam* or that this jagat is whole. 'Whole' means complete and implies a state where nothing further can be added; it is total fullness. Total fullness is the same as limitlessness because if a thing has limits, there has to be something outside its limits which could be added to it to make it fuller. What this mantra says flies in the face of our personal experience because nothing that we know in the world is full or limitless. Our own body and mind can always do with some additions: perhaps a little more hair on that balding patch, better memory, greater strength. The hybrid rose is beautiful to look at, but it would have been even better with some fragrance; the new car looks stunning in gleaming black but, by the very fact that it is black, it cannot be red, which colour I also like; being with my companion is bliss but this bliss would be more complete if I could be sure that his or her love for me will never wane. In fact everything in this jagat, far from being purnam, is always limited by space, by time and by its own characteristics.[46] Then, how can this Veda mantra say *purnamidam?* We have to either find a good explanation or condemn this statement as being false.

The Cause is Limitless

What this mantra actually means here is best understood by using a simple illustration such as when we say that "this is a sturdy shirt". What we mean by this statement is that the fabric, from which the shirt is made, is well-woven from strong yarn. We are not referring to the quality of the product or effect (the shirt); we are really referring to the quality of its cause (the fabric). In the same way, *purnamidam* does not refer to the wholeness of individual objects but to the wholeness of the cause of this entire creation.

Unlike the fabric of the shirt, the underlying cause of the world is not apparent to our senses because (as we will see later) it has no discernible attributes; therefore, it seems distant and is termed *adah*. The mantra states that this cause is purnam or whole and, because of that, its effect or jagat is also purnam or whole (like the shirt drawing its sturdiness from the sturdiness of its fabric). This is the only way in which limited entities can be whole. Thus, what the mantra actually says is that everything has a common, underlying cause which is limitless.

---

46 *desha kala vastu paricchinna.*

Mithya

How reasonable is it for us to accept such a cause? After all, the world of our experience is not a world of unity but of diversity, full of a stunning variety of objects. How can it have a common cause? And even if there is such a common cause, why should it be limitless? To understand this, we have to take another detour, to look at the way in which we understand all the things in the world.

We place everything we know in three distinct categories:

- Non-existent (*tuccham* in Sanskrit), such as a unicorn

- False (*anrtam*), such as the water in a mirage, and

- True (*satyam*), which is used as the residual category for all that is existent and not false.

Tuccham is absolute non-existence because it has no existence in any time-period: past, present or future. *Anrtam* appears to exist for a while, because of a defect in cognition, but disappears upon correct understanding. *Satyam* covers everything which is neither non-existent nor false. As we have no other category in which to place objects of our experience, everything has to be made to fit into one of these categories. But is this always a good and proper fit? Let us go back to our shirt and fabric illustration.

What is the category to which this shirt belongs? It exists and it is not false – I wear it and others admire it on me. Therefore, our conclusion is that the shirt is true or satyam. But then, what about the fabric? The feel of the shirt is the feel of the fabric and the weight of the shirt is the weight of the fabric. You cannot have a shirt without fabric; in fact, you cannot even imagine a shirt without necessarily imagining fabric. So, the fabric too is satyam. We thus have two apparent satyams - shirt and fabric. But this is an absurd conclusion because the shirt is not separate from the fabric and we cannot have one entity miraculously result in two independent things. However, because we cannot dismiss either the shirt or the fabric as non-existent or false, we are forced to categorise both of them as true.

In fact, between the fabric and the shirt, we give more reality to the shirt when we say "cotton shirt". Here, *shirt* is the noun or substantive and *cotton* is only the adjective or attribute. But, as we know, the fabric existed before the shirt and will exist even when the shirt is cut up into pieces. We can have fabric without a shirt but never a shirt without fabric. Therefore, if anything, the fabric is 'more real' than the shirt; it is the fabric which is actually the substantive while shirt is only a temporary attribute superimposed upon it. To be strictly accurate, we should be saying "shirty cotton" where *shirt* is only an attribute while *cotton* is properly stated as the substantive. The transient name and form of a shirt is then left in a sort of limbo: it is not true or satyam (because the fabric has occupied that category), it is not false or anrtam and it is not non-existent or tuccham.

This ontological problem is solved in Vedanta by having a unique category for the classification of things: *mithya*. Mithya refers to something which is completely dependent on something else and, therefore, has no real existence on its own. The shirt is experienced and has a form, utility and a separate name. However, the shirt has no substantial reality of its own because its substance is the fabric upon which the shirt is wholly dependent. Therefore, between the shirt and fabric, the shirt is mithya and the fabric is satyam. The fabric, in turn, depends upon yarn so it, too, is mithya; and the yarn is dependent on fibres and so on, ad infinitum.

Apart from physical objects, mithya also applies to concepts and sensations. A mental object like the idea of beauty is dependent on the idea of ugliness because such concepts can exist only in relation to their polar opposites: beauty & ugliness, fair & unfair or good & evil always arise in pairs which are inter-dependent. Therefore, they are mithya. Sensations, too, are mithya because they are entirely dependent upon a sensing subject: without the ears and the mind of a listener, a falling tree in a forest will create waves in the air but there will be no sound of its falling.

Thus, nothing we experience or know of in this world has completely independent existence. Everything has to be based on or thought of in terms of something else; everything, known or knowable, is mithya.

Mithya is Rooted in Satyam

If everything is a dependent reality, then everything is really an attribute (just as the shirt is an attribute on the underlying reality of the fabric). An endless chain of attributes cannot exist without ultimately being based on some substantive; we cannot have only adjectives and no noun. Such a final substantive is logically necessary and it must have independent reality; only such a reality can be truly called satyam.

What sort of attributes should this reality have? If we look at the example of a collection of clay objects, it is evident that to have the capacity to support various shapes (such as pots, jugs and plates), the clay itself has to be without its own intrinsic shape. In like manner, the cause of the entire jagat has to be free of any attributes and limitations of things in the jagat, which are all bound by attributes of space, time and specific characteristics. This satyam, without any such attributes to define and limit it, has to be truly and completely limitless – purnam. There can only be one limitless reality because multiple limitless things are a logical impossibility – each one would delimit the others. Therefore, satyam has to be non-dual (or *advaita* as it is termed in Sanskrit).

Because our senses and mind can only perceive or conceptualise objects and ideas which are defined by their specific characteristics in a space-time framework, nothing that we can be aware of, talk about or even think of is satyam. For an individual, mithya is of two types: purely subjective[47] (his own dreams, his individual mistakes such as seeing a snake in place of a rope or his personal notions such as money equals happiness) and objective[48] (seeing a mountain as a mountain). But, whether subjective or objective, everything with any attributes whatsoever is mithya. Thus mithya includes our own bodies and minds and, indeed, the entire creation; even our idea of God with limiting attributes of a specific form and a specific location (such as Krishna in Vaikuntha) is only mithya. It needs to be reiterated that mithya

---

47 *pratibhasika* or reflected.

48 *vyavaharika* or transactional.

here is not meant to convey any derogatory connotations - it simply refers to something limited by time, space & its own characteristics and dependent upon another object or upon the mind of the observer.

Incidentally, Vedanta too is part of mithya because it is in and of jagat and its words and concepts are limited things we can transact with. However, within mithya, Vedanta is *pavani* or uplifting. Vedanta's special position in the world is highlighted by comparison with a dream tiger. In this analogy dream, we are walking along a forest trail when suddenly a tiger emerges from the undergrowth and springs towards us with a roar. This tiger, even though in the dream, is enough to startle us into wakefulness. Vedanta is like that tiger; even though it is part of mithya, it can awaken us to absolute reality.

The basis of all mithya is this purnamadah, this attributeless satyam (also called *sat vastu* and *brahman*) which is the only reality. Brahman cannot be separate from its effect, the jagat, just as there is no separation between the clay and the pot; at the same time, brahman is not affected by the limitations of the various things in jagat just as the underlying clay remains essentially unaffected by the pot-shape presently superimposed upon it. The variety and plurality that we perceive in the jagat, has thus no effect on the real nature of its underlying cause.

To put it differently, there is brahman which is the cause of everything; everything that we can be aware of is mithya because it is dependent upon brahman. Mithya is nothing but brahman apparently limited by a name and form, just as a wave is nothing but water in a temporary form. Just as the essential content of the wave, which is water, will never change even when the wave breaks on the shore, the essential content of everything is always brahman which is purnam. Therefore, *purnamadah*: the cause, brahman, is whole or limitless, and *purnamidam*: the effect, jagat, being non-separate from brahman is also essentially whole or limitless.

There is Only Purnam

As we saw earlier, the only thing which we could not include within the term 'idam' or 'this' was our own consciousness, the subject *I* for whom everything else in the world is an object. If this consciousness or atma is not idam or *this*, the only other possibility is to classify it as adah or *that*. As *that* is brahman and brahman is limitless, atma can be 'included' in brahman only if both of these are really one and the same thing. What we have seen so far is that atma is consciousness and brahman is limitless existence. However, our consciousness has no limits because there is nothing which we cannot be conscious of and also because it has no attributes to define and delimit it; brahman, on the other hand, has to be conscious because it is the basis of an orderly creation whose inherent intelligence implies consciousness. Therefore, brahman and atma are one and the same: non-dual existence which is conscious and limitless. In fact, the conclusion we are led to is that the mantra is not pointing to an *adah* and an *idam* which are both purnam but only to purnam which we wrongly consider to be split as *adah* and *idam*.

Once this is understood, the other lines of the mantra become clear: *From that whole, comes this whole. Taking away whole from whole, only whole remains.* If we were to continue with our analogy of clay being satyam and clay-objects being mithya, then it is evident that all mithya comes only from satyam but even when mithya is not present i.e. when the forms of individual clay objects are obliterated, what remains is yet clay or satyam.

Even with this limited explanation, it becomes clear that this mantra sets out a startling vision of meta-physical reality which is expounded in the Upanishads. In its vision and scope, this short mantra is no less than a *mahavakya* (great statement) such as the famous *tat tvam asi*.

The purpose of such understanding is not mere intellectual speculation but the resolution of our false sense of limitation and consequent unhappiness. Once we are able to own up to the fact that we are not a limited body and mind which we take ourselves to be but are the boundless, unchanging and conscious reality which is the basis of all that exists, our agendas, our actions and their results lose any fundamental value and we are able to relax and fully enjoy the game of our lives.

In conclusion, it must be said that if the vision of reality brought out by this mantra seems difficult to relate to or accept, that is perfectly normal at this stage. The core of Vedanta holds out ideas which are dramatically unlike anything we have ever thought about until now and their implications are very far-reaching; a combination of preparedness, adequate time and a good guide are essential, if any of this is to effectively sink in. Therefore, this mantra, though capable of taking us to the ultimate understanding envisaged by Vedanta, remains for most of us just a great beginning of a great journey of discovery. Also, one major attraction of Vedanta is that even if we never get very enthusiastic about metaphysical discussions like this, it offers other insights through its preparatory teachings. These are related to our emotions, egos and life-styles; they are easier to deal with and of great immediate value. So, Vedanta adds value to our lives even when some of its more abstract and conceptual aspects are not quite our cup of tea.

SOME BIG QUESTIONS

Important teachings of Vedanta address us at three different levels of our lives:

- our day-to-day experiences,

- our intellects, and

- our intuitive or visionary aspects.

Vedanta does not initially challenge our common conclusion that we are independent individuals in a real world; instead, it emphasises dharma and postulates Ishwara as the creator of the universe we behold.

At an intellectual level, Vedanta provides arguments to support its insight that there is only a single and common truth behind the plurality that we perceive; it also refutes the counter-arguments of those who hold opposing views.

And at its highest level of insight, Vedanta does not enter into dialectics at all but encourages a direct apprehension of our inherent wholeness in a mind which is suitably cultivated, both emotionally and intellectually.

In this essay, four questions are raised: *Does God Exist? Is There Free Will? What is the Purpose of Life? Is There a Soul?* In discussing each of these questions, we will see what Vedanta has to say about them at the practical level and at its highest, insightful level; we will not dwell upon its intermediate, philosophical views because this will lead us into a maze of hair-splitting arguments.

DOES GOD EXIST?

To put this question in perspective, let us begin by listing the questions which are perhaps the most vital ones to us as human beings:

- Who am I?

- Why am I here?

- What is the nature of this world?

- Who is our creator?

Of these four questions, we seem to have ready answers to the first three; these answers are implied by the way we live our lives as individual body-mind organisms out to extract happiness from the world, which is reckoned to exist to cater to us. But the fourth question – about our creator – poses difficulties because we are unable to find a satisfactory answer.

A common way in which we deal with this difficulty is by side-stepping the question itself. Most of us seem quite happy to remain busy with our usual affairs without wasting time in figuring out the reality and relevance of God; this is despite the token obeisance we pay to him at events such as marriages and deaths as well as at festivals like Diwali or Christmas. However, built as we are, we cannot always escape from nagging doubts surrounding our creator and our relationship with him; often, such doubts and questions arise at inconvenient moments when we face reverses or the prospect of death.

I personally continue to be drawn into discussions on the subject of God's existence by even professed atheists,[49] especially if our conversation happens to veer to Vedanta. Often these conversations end with the questioner saying in some exasperation, "Just tell me in a simple 'yes' or 'no' whether God exists"! On the face of it, such a demand for a clear-cut

---

49 Atheists say that they do not believe in God. Such a statement seems to elevate them above a theist who believes in God, because 'belief' conveys lack of thinking. However, it may be fairer to say that atheists believe that there is no God. Both theists and atheists are believers who respectively accept and reject their own notions of God because God does not present himself to any of them for acceptance or rejection.

answer seems perfectly reasonable; it is only when we pause to understand the issues involved behind this apparently simple question that we begin to realise the difficulties in providing an equally simple answer.

To understand the problem in providing a straight 'yes' or 'no' answer, let us take some common situations out of our day-to-day experiences where also similar difficulties arise. For instance, if someone were to ask us whether our bachelor friend would make a good husband, we would not be able to give a fair answer unless we knew what exactly the questioner meant by a 'good husband' – for different people the weightage of factors like looks, race, wealth, or family-background can be so very different that a generalised answer would be useless. And, if we had to talk to a child about the importance of winning a tennis match, what we would say would depend upon the situation: before the match we may exhort the child to try his utmost to win but, after the child has lost, we may say with equal conviction that it was only a game and the winning or the losing of it was hardly relevant in the larger scheme of life.

Just as an unequivocal stand is not possible in these two instances without establishing some context, so it is with the question of God. Before we get into answers about God's existence, we first need clarity about what we mean by the term 'God'.

What Does God Mean?

Is he Krishna in Vaikunthloka? Is he our Father in Heaven? Is he Allah who made Mohammed his messenger? With so many religions holding out so many versions of the only God according to them, it is obvious that all of them cannot be right; in fact, if one leaves out one's personal beliefs, the most reasonable conclusion can only be that they are all likely to be equally wrong. Let us see why.

The God which popular religions hold out for us has certain common characteristics:

- He is supernatural in terms of his substance, form, powers, and location; he is beyond the observable and also beyond the usual laws of nature.

- He is almighty or omnipotent, all-knowing or omniscient and all-good or absolutely benevolent.

- He created the universe and continues to oversee its operations; he rewards merit and condones or punishes sin, answers prayers, wreaks miracles and knows our mind and its motivations.

- He is human-like, if not in appearance then at least in qualities such as being judgemental, having a goal or purpose behind his actions and having his own likes and dislikes.

God, the Designer

Traditionalists posit this super-natural God as the only possible explanation for the immensely complicated design and functioning of creation. The main justification for the presumed existence of such a God is the so-called 'argument by design'.[50] This argument says that when we see a watch, we necessarily infer an intelligent and capable watch-maker (because of the watch's complex make-up and obvious functionality); by the same logic, when we see something incredibly complex and functional like the human eye, a God with unlimited knowledge and powers who designed and constructed it, has to be inferred.

Modern scientific thinkers like Richard Dawkins say that postulating a 'designer' God, in the context of the complexity of living organisms, is unjustified because a more credible mechanism for explaining such complexity is available in the process of natural evolution. The theory of evolution was enunciated by Charles Darwin in the 1800s and establishes that complexity in organisms evolves, in very small incremental steps and over long periods of time, by natural selection. This process preserves and promotes naturally-occurring genetic variations at

---

50 Two other common arguments for the existence of the conventional God of western theists, not discussed here, are the First Cause Argument and the Ontological Argument; another facet to this perennial debate is provided by the so-called 'Pascal's Wager' which is not an argument for God's existence but tries to establish that if one had to take a gamble on whether God exists or not, it would be safer to go on the basis that he does.

the cellular level, which have the effect of providing an organism with even a tiny advantage in surviving and propagating itself compared to its peers. Over several generations, such variations get accentuated and pervade that species because individuals so endowed become more dominant.

Thus, a human eye, as we know it at present, may evoke a mighty God because of its amazing intricacy and functioning. But the assumption of such a master designer becomes redundant once we understand that the eye may have slowly evolved over millennia; this natural evolution could have started with a minor variation in the DNA of some cells of a pre-historic organism, making them partly translucent and receptive to variations in the level of light and thus providing to this organism some advantage over others in whom this random variation had not occurred.

Problem of Evil

Quite apart from the better explanation provided by the theory of evolution, the assumptions behind the God of religions also has other major problems. For instance, if this God is all-powerful, all-knowing and completely benevolent, why is there any evil in this world? A God who knows everything (the past, present and future) should have foreseen evil and should also see it now, as it exists. A truly benevolent God would not want us to suffer from this evil and an almighty God should be capable of eradicating evil. But, unfortunately, evil and its attendant pain still exist.

If one argues, as some do, that evil and pain were deliberately put in by God to test how we use our free-will (which is also God-given), the counter-argument is that he need not have given us a free-will or could have restricted it to more innocent matters like the freedom to choose chocolate over vanilla in our ice-creams flavours; in any event, a God who found it fit to give cancer to some children or a Hitler to Jews, merely to build-up characters and to test faith, would seem to be remarkably cruel and capricious instead of being kind and benevolent.

In this context, Hinduism brings in the *karma* theory to show that God is not callous or arbitrary because all that we reap is nothing other than the fruits of our own actions, either of this birth or of previous births; God is only the dispenser of our just desserts, without any judgement or partiality. Such an argument of course requires acceptance of our own previous births and this idea is not satisfactory for many of us. Further, even if one goes along with the theory of the actions of past births affecting us now, the question still remains about what caused a particular individual to commit his first wrong act, at the very beginning of his chain of births.

Source of Raw Materials

Another major problem with this God of religions is that if he is like a master-potter who created the universe in the way in which a potter creates a pot, then questions arise about the source of materials used by God to create. The potter gets his clay from around him. But, before God's creation, nothing at all would have been in existence and so there would be no materials lying around. In fact, there would not even be any time or space because these are concepts which arise only when there is an existing creation: space is the distance between two objects, time is the interval taken to traverse that distance and they both exist only with reference to created objects. Therefore, before creation, there would have been no material for God to use, there would have been no space for God himself to be located and there would have been no concept of time, without which it would be meaningless to talk of any 'before'.

Of course, proponents of religions who are fired by zealous devotion to their personal notion of God say that God's powers and his process of creation are supernatural and cannot be explained in terms of our usual and worldly understanding; such a view is obviously beyond any discussion and if someone is happy with the idea of an unknowable God producing something out of nothing from nowhere, then there is really nothing further which can be said to him. But if one pauses to think then, because of the explanation of evolution, because of the presence of evil and because of lack of a credible source of material prior to creation, the idea of the God of religions who designed, created and now runs this universe becomes difficult to understand or accept, unless one is willing to embrace him purely on faith.

Faith

What is wrong with faith as the basis for belief in God's existence? Faith is a wonderful thing but there are different types of faiths and all of them cannot be used in the same way. The earliest faith we all have is based on helplessness – for instance, as very young children, we had no option but to have faith in our grandmother's ability to take us across a busy road, not withstanding her cataracts and her wobbly legs! Here, we had no choice or decision to make.

The second type of faith is temporary faith pending our own knowledge – this is the faith we need when we enroll for, say, Vedanta classes where we have to start with the belief that there is something worth-while learning here and that the teacher is capable of imparting that knowledge. This type of faith is required initially but needs to get converted into knowledge-based conviction in due course.

And the third type of faith is where emotions remain the prime driver – for instance, the faith that our beloved will never stop loving us is, of course, emotional. Faith which makes us go along with the Gods of religions is of this third type, where the emotional content is very high. Such faith can lead to sublime emotions as well as submergence of our personal egos; however, it also comes along with issues which we need to be aware of.

To begin with, this faith is not something which we can choose to cultivate by using our will. One can choose to behave as if one has faith in God but whether genuine faith arises in one's heart or not, is entirely beyond one's volition.[51]

Then, the direction of one's faith here is most often dependent upon the accident of one's birth. So, whether one takes Krishna, Allah or the Holy Father as the ultimate truth depends largely upon whether one is born a Hindu, Muslim or Christian; again a Hindu may only accept either Shiva or Rama as the real God, depending upon his sub-sect within Hinduism. A God

---

51 It is interesting to note in this context that despite the emphasis on faith placed by Islam, verse 10:100 of the Quran starts by saying "No soul can believe, except by the will of Allah ..."

determined by the randomness of one's birth is not a very satisfactory explanation.

Further, faith in God driven by emotion and circumstances tends to shut out facts and reasoning which destabilise one's beliefs; this leads to prejudice and dogmatism and may even escalate to wanting the annihilation of those with contrary views. Finally, such faith is capable of being uprooted in the face of reverses. There are several instances of very devout people completely rejecting their own God when life delivers harsh blows like the loss of fortune, reputation or of a loved one; ironically, this is when they need this safety-net the most. Therefore, belief and faith in a God that one is culturally comfortable with and which is valuable in daily living, is not a substitute for a proper understanding of God. Because chance and emotional swings do not play a pivotal role in matters of knowledge, Vedanta teaches that God is something to be known and understood and not something to be just believed in or taken on faith.

Vedanta and Religious Gods

Despite Vedanta's emphasis on knowledge, it initially goes along with the faith-based Gods who, in the Hindu culture, are represented by deities like Shiva, Rama and Krishna. In fact, in the earlier portions of the Vedas, the deities which are mentioned are personifications of very basic natural forces such as fire and wind (*agni* and *vayu*). Many such personifications are imbued with qualities which we can relate to for worship and are often referred to as *bhagawan*[52] or *devata*[53]. Vedanta, however, does not stop here but goes on to a much wider understanding of divinity which it terms *Ishwara*. *Ishwara* is defined as *jagat nimitta upadana karanam* or as the combined intelligent (knowledgeable) and material cause of the world. This is not just

---

52 The word *bhagawan* refers to someone who has *bhaga* which the *puranas* define as the following six *shaktis* or powers in absolute measure: *aishwarya* (supremacy or overlordship), *virya* (capability or power), *yashas* (glory), *shri* (wealth), *jnana* (knowledge) and *vairagya* (dispassion).

53 Literally, the shining one.

a change in nomenclature[54] but a huge step forward in the proper understanding of God.

Ishwara

In Vedanta's vision, for an individual who sees himself as part of a real creation, there has to be a creator simply because no creation exists without a creator. But the Ishwara of Vedanta is not a remote person who mysteriously produces a universe from nothing and then supervises its workings based on his personal judgement of right and wrong. The Ishwara of Vedanta is both the material cause of creation (like the clay in the case of a pot) and its intelligent cause (like the knowledge and skill of the potter); Ishwara thus pervades the entire creation or is, in other words, immanent.

How can something be both the material and the knowledgeable cause at the same time? After all, in our experience the clay and the potter are always different. Vedanta gives an interesting example here. The example is that of a spider which not only has the knowledge and know-how for creating a web but also contains within itself the material for making it; the spider is both the material and the intelligent cause of its creation. But Vedanta then points out a problem with this analogy: the spider can walk away from his web which can continue to exist even after the spider goes away. So, the spider does not pervade his creation while, in Vedanta's understanding, Ishwara does. This illustration, therefore, is not enough.

Vedanta then moves on to another analogy which helps us to share its vision of Ishwara. This example is of us as dreamers. All objects in our dream world (both animate and inanimate) as well as all actions, results of such actions and attendant emotions occur within the order and the space-time framework of our dream; the entire existence and functioning of the dream is not separate from us because it is nothing but the projection of our own knowledge. We can therefore justifiably say that we pervade

---

54 The terms 'Ishwara' and 'bhagawan' when used by others, do not always carry the different sense in which they are used here because they are often also used synonymously.

our entire dream as its inseparable material and intelligent cause; in other words, we are immanent in our dream creation. Vedanta says that Ishwara's relationship with the world is similar to our relationship with our dream world.

Once Ishwara is understood to be a unique creator who is himself the material and the intelligence in creation, he necessarily becomes everything in the world; as the Isha Upanishad says, *ishavasyam idam sarvam* meaning all that is here is Ishwara. Thus, good & bad, high & low, sentient & insentient, virtue & evil and all other polarities are, in fact, nothing but manifestations of Ishwara; he is not only the substance of creation but also the laws which govern its functioning. It is in the light of this vision of Ishwara that there is no real division between the sacred and the secular in the Hindu culture; everything is sacred. This is why Ishwara can be worshipped in a pebble or in a betel-nut or in a lump of turmeric; this is why every person can be greeted with a respectful *namaste*; this is why our own body can be anointed with sandalwood paste and consecrated with a *tilak* or a *bindi*.[55]

This Ishwara also becomes the giver of the results of our actions,[56] not as a person sitting in judgement from heaven but as natural laws which produce specific consequences, in response to specific actions. At times, the working of these laws may not be apparent to us because a given result may be a product of a large number of actions and, that too, spread over a long period of time. But, these laws are never partial, arbitrary or fallible; therefore, all that happens (whether personally desirable for us or not) is nothing but the orderly working of Ishwara. This

---

55 While everything is Ishwara, not everything is worshipped because our emotions and conditioning make some things more conducive to worship (such as a pristine river emerging from a glacier) compared to others (such as the water in a sewer). In this context, people from other cultures find it peculiar that Hindus have traditionally protected and worshipped cows. But the fact is that all of us safeguard things which contribute to our economic well-being; many of us also venerate things whose attributes we admire. Cows became worthy of worship (in a culture where people were on the look-out for things to worship) because of their good qualities and economic importance: harmless creatures which use only grass and, in return, provide nourishing milk, fuel (from its dung) and bullocks whose power is vital for many activities in an agrarian society.

56 *karma phala data*.

understanding reduces pride in achievements and moderates anger or guilt upon failures because all results are consequences of laws which are not separate from Ishwara; there is also less scope for personal enmity because when someone impedes us, he too is an aspect of Ishwara and only a conduit for delivering an appropriate result to us.

How does this understanding of Ishwara reconcile with Darwin's theory of evolution? In Vedanta's view, there is no problem here at all. As we have already seen, Ishwara as the single cause of the universe is manifest not only as the objects in creation but also as the natural order or laws which govern them. The process of evolution is not different from other natural and orderly processes such as pro-creation or respiration which work in living things and convection or condensation which work in non-living things; thus, evolution connected with living organisms is also part and parcel of the much wider overall order which is Ishwara.

Going back to our dream analogy, we undoubtedly pervade our dream as its material and intelligent cause but our reality is much more than our dream world: we exist even without the dream but the dream cannot exist without us. We are therefore above and beyond our dream or are transcendent in relation to it. Similarly, in Vedanta's vision, Ishwara is also transcendent because while the world is entirely dependent on him, he is independent of the world.

This understanding of Ishwara as being both immanent and transcendent is beautifully expressed in a famous hymn called the *purusha suktam* from the Rig Veda which describes divinity as a person with a thousand heads, a thousand eyes and a thousand feet who pervades the earth in its entirety (symbolizing immanence) and then extends beyond it by ten fingers (symbolizing transcendence).

Pantheism

An understanding of Ishwara who is not limited or defined by anything (because he is everything) is labeled as pantheism by western philosophy and objected to, on two grounds. The first objection is that such a definition is so wide that it is tantamount to saying nothing at all about God – like a dinner invitation we may extend to someone saying *"Come any day, anytime"* which is vague enough to be no real invitation. The second objection is that if Ishwara is to be understood as the order which pervades the entire creation then one would have to worship, for example, the law of gravity, which is unlikely to be easy or useful.[57]

What needs to be pointed here is that there is no justification for our imposing our own definitions to come up with a personally convenient notion of God and then expect him to actually fall in line with it. God does not come and tell us that he will be found in a specific form at a given location, such as Krishna in Vaikuntha; God also does not promise us that if we pray hard enough, he will make our irresponsible son pass an examination. We may need a God based upon our own ideas and wants but this need not have any bearing on the real nature of Ishwara.

The problem here also is in a microcosm trying to understand the macrocosm of which it is a part. A single cell in our liver would have difficulty in understanding the liver itself and this difficulty would exponentially increase if this liver-cell tried to understand other organs and then the entire human-being. When we try to understand God, we tend to forget that we are just one of the billions of individuals on one planet in one solar system in one galaxy, trying to understand the order behind the unimaginable complexity and vastness of the universe, of which we happen to be an infinitesimal part. Or, to look at this in a different way, our trying to understand Ishwara is akin to an individual in our dream trying to understand us, the dreamers – the difficulty in doing this is obvious. Vedanta asks us to understand Ishwara as totality but this understanding does not make Ishwara available to us as a conveniently defined form with specific qualities which we may want to see.

---

57 As the famous British physicist, Stephen Hawking, said in a recent interview (on Channel 4 in June 2010), "If you like, you can call the laws of science 'God', but it wouldn't be a personal God that you could meet and ask questions."

Ishta Devata

What about worship? Human beings need an altar to look up to, to put their hopes and faith in and to feel connected with something larger. For this purpose, it is important to establish an emotional connection with God in a form and with qualities which one can relate to; here, Ishwara as the material and intelligent cause of everything would be too abstract and Ishwara as, say, the laws of thermo-dynamics would be too impersonal. This is where the Hindu tradition of an *ishta devata* or a favourite and personified form of bhagawan comes in. For the purpose of providing a symbolic representation of Ishwara, it does not matter which specific symbol is used as long as it does the job of invoking devotion, love, trust, humility and gratitude. An analogy here would be a country's flag which its citizens salute to express their sense of nation-hood, instead of revering every stone or structure around them. Such symbols derive their power from being consistently used over a long period of time.

For the purpose of worship, if more than one symbol is helpful in catering to needs of different individuals, a pantheon of deities is the answer. This is why Ishwara, for the purpose of worship, is presented in multiple forms such as Rama, Krishna, Shiva, Ganesha, Hanuman, Laxmi, Saraswati, Durga and so on. Each such personified depiction comes with stories which emphasise some particular moral ideas and qualities and are meant to engage different types of people with their personal orientations. These symbols are not originally important in themselves; but just as a flag has to be always honoured if it is to become an effective instrument for focusing national pride and patriotism, each representation of bhagawan also has to be continuously worshipped and revered once it is chosen and consecrated.

Not Polytheistic or Monotheistic

The Vedic religion, even though it sensibly offers a large number of deities for worship, is not polytheistic as it is popularly believed to be. Actually, at the level of proper understanding, there is nothing other than Ishwara or, to put it the other way around, everything is Ishwara; this takes Ishwara well beyond the ideas of polytheism (many gods) and even of monotheism (one god who is separate from the rest of creation). In this context, there is a story of a saint in western India who was found fast asleep on a temple floor with his feet touching the temple's idol; when woken and questioned about this desecration, he replied that he could not find any place to place his feet, where God was not. It is because of such an inclusive understanding of Ishwara that *sanyasis* (renunciates), who have opted out of the conventional mode of life based on discrimination and dispassion, are traditionally not required to visit temples and conduct ritual worship of symbolic representations of God.

For the rest of us, the fact that Ishwara is important to us in a personalised form for the purpose of worship should not lead us to expect that such a form will actually appear to cater to our sense of mystery or devotion. Even as we worship a specific and limited form of Ishwara, we must not forget that Ishwara is everywhere and everything; even we, the individual worshippers, are not separate from Ishwara. Finally, the purpose of worship is not to see magical visions but to cultivate a tranquil and collected state of mind which will ultimately aid us in learning the highest truths of Vedanta.

Brahman

Vedanta, of course, does not stop at Ishwara as the ultimate reality. Understanding Ishwara as both the intelligent and material cause of the world is a giant step forward from our usual ideas of God. However, any concept of a real creator and a real creation involves duality, even when the creation comes from nothing but the creator. For instance, yoghurt comes from nothing other than milk but, yet, these are two different things and remain so – this is why yoghurt cannot become milk again. In the terms of Vedanta, yoghurt is a *parinama* or an effect obtained by the actual conversion of its cause – milk – into something different.

In similar manner, if the ultimate reality underlying the entire creation actually got converted to produce this world, it would necessarily mean imparting attributes (and consequent limitations) to this reality and negating its non-dual nature.

However, Vedanta's arguments establish that ultimate reality has to be without any attributes or limitations of its own. Vedanta, therefore, goes on to explain that the world is not a real effect which involves a real change in its cause but just an appearance or a projection (*vivarta*) on the substratum of reality which itself never undergoes any change – like the sand which does not get wet even as it apparently becomes water in a mirage. Ishwara's creation is thus not real creation but an appearance which is only perceived to be real. Vedanta finally provides arguments to show that the true nature of the single reality, which appears to us as the world of diverse objects, is unchanging existence which is conscious and limitless; this reality is given the name of brahman.

As we saw earlier, a creator becomes necessary in the context of a creation – it is like the necessity of having to infer a watch-maker when a watch is seen. But what happens when the seeing itself is defective? If, in the twilight, we mistakenly see what we think is a snake in place of a real rope, do we have to infer this snake's parents? The answer is that till we continue to see the snake and take it as real, the inference of its parents necessarily comes along with its cognition; however, once the snake is recognised as a piece of rope, that snake's lineage also simultaneously disappears. When, with the teachings of Vedanta, the world is understood as not being absolutely and independently real but as *mithya*,[58] Ishwara also becomes part of the same mithya – an imagined snake can only have imagined parents and a mithya world can only have a mithya creator.

For most of us, our bodies and minds are real, our personalities are real, our pleasures and pains are real, other people and the rest of the world are real; for us, then, Ishwara too has to be real.

---

58 *Mithya* is a technical term of Vedanta used to refer to anything which is not real as it appears and is dependent on an underlying reality. Mithya includes both our subjective and objective perceptions: an imagined snake is mithya because its appearance is dependent on the rope which is mistakenly seen as a snake and a real chair is also mithya because it is dependent upon the wood from which it is made. In fact, everything in the world is mithya because everything depends upon something more basic than itself for its existence. Thus, a shirt depends upon fabric which, in turn, depends upon yarn and so on. This series of dependencies must end in something which exists on its own or independently; this ultimate and non-dependent existence is called brahman.

However, some of us are able to assimilate Vedanta's vision of *advaita* and understand that the truth of one's individuality and the truth of the rest of the world is a single conscious existence; then the whole universe and Ishwara (its creator) become mere projections of and within such a reality. This reality or brahman is the ultimate and the only truth, with everything else (without any exception) being only an appearance, shorn of intrinsic reality.

Does Vedanta Trivialise God?

This seems like a real issue in a scheme where bhagawan is a symbol and Ishwara is ultimately understood to be mithya. But, in fact, God is hallowed in Vedanta's tradition.

Starting with personified deities worshipped in temples, Vedanta never advocates questioning or de-stabilizing useful and comforting beliefs that people have in their chosen bhagawan. It is understood that temples and rituals fulfil vital psychological and social needs and also that many people just do not have the inclination to question the real nature of supernatural gods which are presented to them by their cultures. Further, it is not necessary to devalue something even after it is understood to be a symbol – for instance, as we salute a flag, our sense of respect for it is not compromised by our knowledge that it is a rectangular piece of cloth because what we are saluting is not cloth but nationhood.[59]

Coming next to an all-pervading and impersonal Ishwara, one may think that he becomes irrelevant as soon as he is understood as mithya, along with the rest of creation. Here, again, it is important not to jump to any such conclusion. As long as we take ourselves to be separate individuals living in a real world, we are ourselves part of mithya. And just as everything in a dream is absolutely real for a person in that dream, a mithya Ishwara is

---

59 Some people take pride in declaring that they do not go to temples or participate in any traditional worship because they are against rituals. However, the same people happily salute flags or stick candles in a birthday-cake and light them, as if these acts are not rituals. The fact is that rituals are part and parcel of every society and fulfil important psychological needs; they cannot be wholly dismissed as being irrational just because some specific rituals may not fit in with our individual and subjective ideas.

real for a person who continues to take himself and the world as being absolutely real. Further, the mithya status of the world is different from the mithya status of the snake seen in place of the rope. It is true that both the snake and the world are mithya in the sense that both are only projections on a real substratum – the rope is the locus of error in case of the snake and brahman in case of the world. However, there is an important difference between these two types of mithya: in the case of the imagined snake, as soon as the rope is recognised the snake disappears but, in the case of our individuality and the world, even after understanding brahman to be the underlying truth, our experience of duality does not change.

For a person with the knowledge of brahman, the world is still perceived and continues to function the way in which it always did and some sense of individuality also continues – even a sage of Vedanta will respond when his name is called. The situation here is like the sunset which we experience even after knowing that the sun neither rises and nor sets. Because the experience of duality is never erased till a person is alive, there is no question of Ishwara becoming redundant – a perceived world carries its own creator along with it. Also, till our body and mind continue to exist, there is always a possibility of our past conditioning resurfacing and undoing some benefits of Vedanta's knowledge; our emotions and egos continue to need processing and tempering till we continue to live and this is effectively achieved by worship.

To put the same thing in different words, Ishwara is the important way by which we continuously reduce the hold of duality in our lives to its minimum. It is for these reasons that Ishwara continues to play an important role even in a *jnani's* life – the great Shankara himself wrote beautiful poems extolling God even as he wrote monumental works of *advaita* which completely changed our understanding of God.

Back to the Beginning

So let us now come back to the original question with which we started: Does God exist? The answer is a resounding 'Yes' for the individual who is asking this question out of curiosity or concern;

in his very asking, he is declaring his evaluation of the world as being real and a real world must necessarily have a real creator.

What is the nature of this creator? He cannot be the all-knowing, all-mighty and all-good God in heaven because the evil and defects in creation do not support such a notion, because it is not possible to explain from what materials he made this creation and because the process of natural selection and evolution are enough to explain the complexity of living organisms within creation. In Vedanta's vision, this creator has to be consciousness itself because the world cannot be anything but the projection of knowledge which, in turn, can only be in consciousness; this is like our personal dream world which is created by a projection of our own consciousness. Such a 'creation' makes its creator both the material and the intelligent cause of that creation and this is the definition of Ishwara.

Once Ishwara is properly understood, he can still be installed on an altar, either as a personified or abstract symbol, for the purpose of worship and for catering to important psychological and social needs. On the other hand if, with the teachings of Vedanta, we are able to understand that our individuality and the world in which we live are only insubstantial projections of and within a single reality, then of course there is no real creator because there is no real creation. Ishwara, along with our own selves, thus gets resolved in the only and ultimate truth of existence which is changeless, boundless and conscious; however, because our perceived individuality persists till our death, our relationship with Ishwara yet continues through our entire life and brings us humility, love and compassion.

IS THERE FREE WILL?

We ask this question because we are not sure whether what happens to us is determined by our own choices or by destiny. This confusion is caused by our experiences where, at times, actions bring in the expected results while, at other times, unexpected results are produced due to matters outside our control. Such confusion is aggravated by religious teachings which exhort an individual to lead a moral life by the dint of his own choice and effort but then also maintain that nothing can happen unless God wants it to happen. It is therefore not surprising that a person wants to clearly know: *Who rules the roost? Destiny or freewill? God or I?*

Vedanta, in its practical approach, provides a variety of answers at different levels of understanding.

The Obvious Answer

At the level of the day-to-day life of an individual, the answer to this question is straight-forward: his life is largely run by his free-will. A few aspects of his life, like parentage or gender, are determined by destiny but all other aspects, such as career and life-style choices, are within his control. Such a practical approach validates our personal experience of being individuals empowered to make our own choice; it also provides a rational basis for setting-up the frame-work of civilised society. But just because something is conventionally accepted or practical, it does not necessarily make it the full truth. Thus, we say that the sun has set or that the foundation of our house is laid on level ground; these statements do not establish that the sun actually sets or that the earth is flat. We, therefore, need to examine whether the truth about free-will is different from the usual answer.

The reason for this examination goes beyond intellectual curiosity: an unfettered notion of free will can lead to damaging emotions such as excessive pride when things fall in line with our plans or guilt and anger when they do not.

A More Careful Look

If we carefully look at any action which we believe to be ours, we find that our action is only a response to either a mental happening (such as the arising of a desire or a memory) or to some external event. Mental movements occur spontaneously and have nothing to do with the operation of our will; external events obviously occur independent of our choice. Therefore, to begin with, the roots of all our actions lie in happenings outside our volition.

However, one can justifiably argue that while we may have no control over the internal and external inputs which are brought to our mind, we do have control over how we react to them; we are certainly responsible for the actions we choose to take in response to a given situation. Society supports this view – we are punished for the crimes we commit but not for crimes we thought of committing but then did not actually carry out. We now need to see how free is our will which apparently operates in matters where we elect to take action.

Our response to any situation has a lot to do with our upbringing and conditioning. An instance of this is seen when one person looks upon the ritual slaughter of an animal and distribution of its flesh for food as a holy duty while another finds the act of eating of even a sprouting bean to be unacceptable because it would mean ending the life of a living entity. These dramatically different choices are entirely the result of the family environment in which we grow up. Many of our 'free' choices are actually governed by the norms of the milieu in which we live.

But what about scenarios in which our cultural background may not play a pivotal role? What about a very determined businessman who nurtures a business through a long period of reverses till it prospers, when many others would have thrown in their towels much earlier? Are not this person's tenacity and intelligent foresight the products of his will-based choices? On the face of it, it would certainly seem so but let us look into this intelligence and tenacity a little deeper.

While people undoubtedly learn new things over time, the basic intelligence in a person remains the same, both when his business is faring poorly and when it prospers; it is very often changes in the external environment which transform his business prospects. It is our ego which makes us feel that our intelligence was the key for the turn in our fortune. Further, in qualities like tenacity and intelligence from which we draw pride because they are 'ours', it is difficult to see what role we, as individuals, actually played in the creation of these virtues. There is obviously no neighbourhood shop to which we could have gone and bought these things; there is no known mechanism within us which we can personally command to generate such useful aspects of our character. If such things were within our control, who would choose to be unintelligent or lacking in determination? It is actually impossible to figure out how personal traits can be so radically different, even amongst those sharing similar genes and upbringing. Whatever may be the source of such qualities (good or bad), one thing is clear: they come to us as given and there is no objective reason for us to draw personal pride or personal guilt from our strengths and weaknesses.

Because society needs to have a basis for operating, the sense of free-will which is experienced by all and the accompanying notion of personally cultivated qualities are used to dispense rewards and punishments;[60] however the truth is that both the saint and the psychopath are creations of nature, where the role of an individual "I" is only nominal. The desirable and the undesirable or virtue and vice are natural polarities which arise spontaneously. Therefore, while good and bad qualities arise in persons, there is really nothing personal about them.

This is not to suggest that we, as individuals, should not try to improve ourselves or continue to do wrong things. We happen to be self-conscious beings with in-built knowledge of right & wrong. A sense of being free agents with the power to choose is common to all of us and our very make-up does not permit us to ignore or deny that sense. Vedanta therefore advises us to be

---

60 At times, societies reward people not only for matters within their own choice but also for matters largely determined by destiny, such as physical beauty.

committed to using our free will for acting appropriately; but it also tells us that the actual results which are finally produced are a compound product depending upon a number of known and unknown factors, of which our effort is only one of the elements.

Once we have done whatever we think is right according to our judgement in a given situation, we should relax in the understanding that the outcome will be delivered by Ishwara (or by the totality of natural laws) and we should accept it with equanimity, without any driving sense of personal achievement or failure. It is in keeping with this understanding that Indian epics show the possibility of change and redemption even for confirmed evil-doers: Valmiki, who was a notorious robber, went on to become a respected sage and Ravana, who committed heinous crimes, is shown to have found a place in heaven after being killed by Rama in battle.

One other issue in the context of free will is the need for an explanation for the good or the bad fortune which befalls some of us, without being apparently related to our choices and actions. How do we account for the fact that someone is born blind in a destitute family while someone else is born with glowing health in a prosperous family? The traditional explanation provided here is the *karma* theory: if our known deeds cannot account for our lot in life then our condition is ascribed to deeds done by us in previous lives. While this explanation works for many, some of us are not comfortable with the concept of transmigration; further, even if transmigration is accepted, it does not explain why a particular person committed his first bad deed at the very beginning of his chain of births. Therefore, while the karma theory provides an explanation up to a point, it is not a total explanation.

The Ultimate Truth

Vedanta finally takes us to its highest vision to show that the question of free will and destiny is relevant only in the context of an individual who takes himself to be a real entity. When there is no sense of individuality, such as in deep sleep or in a moment of total contentment, this question itself does not arise. Vedanta says the truth is that the whole of creation has no absolute reality;[61] it is just a temporary appearance which comes and goes in time. The only truth is a single existence which is changeless, boundless and conscious, without any attributes or distinctions; all distinct things with attributes are projections which are non-separate from this reality, just as things in our personal dream-world are not separate from our own consciousness.[62] From this perspective, there is no real creation and no real individuals; here free-will and destiny have no real meaning. To ask about free-will or destiny is a bit like asking where the sun goes after it sets; once it is understood that the sun does not actually move, any question about the direction of its travel becomes redundant.

The Practical Approach

However, this final vision of Vedanta has to be handled with caution and not blindly applied at a level where practical experience calls for a different approach. All our thoughts, questions and actions take place at the level of a distinct individual with a sense of free-will who has to function within this world. At this level, no scripture or philosophy can ever take away our experience of free-will. Even if a person manages to convince himself that his life is like a long painting which has already been fully painted and is only being unrolled gradually, it is yet impossible to ignore the sense of personal choice we have in sitting down or standing up, in seeing a movie or reading a book, in doing something right or wrong. And valid experience cannot be and should not be denied: as Shankara put it, even if all the Vedas say that fire is cold, you should go by your own, contrary experience.

---

61 In Vedanta absolute reality is specifically defined as that which has unchanging existence in all time periods – the past, the present and the future; nothing in creation is absolutely real by this definition.

62 It should be clarified that when we use terms like 'our own consciousness', they should not lead to an understanding that there is our personal consciousness which projects our personal dream and there is another consciousness which projects the world. Our personal dreams, our sense of individual consciousness, our bodies & minds and the entire world arise in and are all based on the single, conscious truth which is the only reality.

Therefore, while we (as individuals within creation) have no absolute reality at the level of the highest truth, we have no option but to go along with the existence of our free will at the practical level. It would be patently wrong and damaging for anyone to presume that because everything always happens as it is supposed to, he can give up trying.

Just as a person who knows that the sun's motion is only apparent and is yet able to enjoy a beautiful sunset, we have to exercise our apparent free will by using our intelligence and determination. As a part of this set-up in which we find ourselves, we also have to accept the rewards and punishment of society consequent upon our choices. Wisdom does not lie in debating whether free will or destiny governs us; wisdom lies in using our sense of freedom and choice sensibly and, after having taken the action which seems most appropriate, wisdom lies in understanding that the actual result of our action will not depend on that action alone but on numerous factors related to other people and happenings. With this understanding, whatever that needs to be done is done without generating pride, guilt, regret, anger or enmity.

For someone on the path of growth shown by Vedanta, these negative emotions get further modulated because such a seeker's focus is neither ego-satisfaction nor sense-pleasure which is hoped to be derived from any action. He performs actions as a duty, consistent with the role that has been assigned to him by life; the objective behind his actions is not temporary pleasure but the processing of his ego and desires so that his mind is clear and steady enough to benefit from Vedanta's teachings. Because he is not committed to personal pleasure as his main objective, there is little scope for pride, anger and the like to arise. He thus uses his free will for his highest good, which he clearly understands to be the total release from any sense of limitation and compulsion, by using Vedanta's wisdom.

WHAT IS THE PURPOSE OF LIFE?

Is there really any real meaning to our lives? Is there a specific goal which we are here to achieve? Does it matter what we do or does it all end up in oblivion after we die? These are some of the vexing questions about our lives which occur to us, even if only occasionally.

Basic Needs and Obsessions

Let us start by recognizing that these questions will not get the attention of those of us who are denied basic needs or who suffer great pain. For people who are placed in a particularly distressing situation, the obtaining of essentials or the redressal of their painful condition naturally becomes the primary purpose of life. And others who are fortunate enough to have relatively normal lives can also become so besotted with something – be it the obtaining of the love of one person or of money or of fame – that it overcomes their entire minds; such a situation makes them lose all balance and the sole purpose of their lives then becomes the fulfilment of that one over-powering desire.[63]

Usual Pursuits

The rest of us, who are not so afflicted, spend our lives in the pursuits of security and pleasures, usually guided by ethics arising from a natural sense of right and wrong. Further, those of us with religious inclinations see our lives as a means to accumulate religious merit which, in turn, is expected to ensure our security and pleasures in this life as well as in the promised after-life. People who see these goals of obtaining security and pleasures within the limits of ethics and religion are termed *trivargi* in

---

63 Sanskrit has an apt word for such a person – *kamatma* – meaning someone in whom a desire has occupied the very core of his being.

Sanskrit and they form the pre-ponderant majority.[64] There is nothing inherently wrong in these goals except that they are never fully achieved: despite all our efforts, righteous or otherwise, we never have enough security and pleasures, our experience of happiness is never complete and our lives have only a limited span. Therefore, some people are not satisfied with such limited goals and look for a larger purpose to their lives.

Relationships

Within the pursuit of security and pleasure, developing a deep relationship with someone in whom we discover a special chemistry becomes a major plank of life for some of us. As this aspect is becoming increasingly important now, it is useful to understand the factors involved here.

It is true that communion with a kindred soul is a great blessing which fills life with zest, security and a deep sense of well-being. However, anything which makes us seek permanent happiness outside of our selves cannot be the final answer because anything which is external and comes to us in time will, for the same reasons, change or disappear in time. A truly good relationship is not between two incomplete, insecure individuals using each other for mutual comfort or for having a pleasant time; love and friendship deliver fully only when both parties use the blessing of their mutual support to find independent wholeness within their own selves. Great relationships are beautiful only when they are used to achieve a great purpose otherwise, at worst, they fester and, at best, they leave us short of our potential. When this is not understood, we become vulnerable to the role of others in our lives and we cause pain and turmoil as we desperately make and

---

64 It is interesting to note that there also existed in ancient India a well-known philosophy of pure materialism called *carvaka darshana* which accepted only the body and its sense pleasures as the be-all and end-all of life, without any place for ethics, religion or philosophy. Its approach is summarised in an old verse:

yavad jivet sukham jivet	Enjoy life while you are alive;
rinam krutva ghritam pibet	use ghee even by incurring debt (i.e. do not worry about any obligations);
bhasmi bhutasya dehasya	once the body is reduced to ashes,
punar agamanam kutaha	where is the question of any return?

break relationships on the wrong notion that they are complete ends in themselves.

In this context it should also be noted that the tremendous force of a great relationship between two people (especially of the opposite sex) ultimately rests not in the obvious physical and emotional gratification but arises from the temporary collapse of their ego boundaries. The sense of individuality of a person in love expands to include the other and this is why such a person may go through disproportionate effort and pain to bring even a little pleasure to his beloved – there is no sense of sacrifice or deprivation because the usual sense of separation or 'otherness' is absent. Unfortunately, with the passage of time, the magic which brings this fusion of two egos often wears out and individual egos again assume their own and rigid boundaries. On the other hand, the expansion of ego boundaries brought about by the proper assimilation of Vedanta, though less heady, is deeper and permanent because it is based upon proper understanding (as against an emotional upsurge) and includes everybody (as against just one other individual).

Self Knowledge

Vedanta offers a larger purpose to life for people who are not content with usual goals. Vedanta sets out this purpose in a number of different ways:

- The purpose of life is to gain freedom from our constant struggle to be totally and permanently happy; this has to be done not by the impossible task of trying to fulfil infinite desires but by discovering ourselves to be already complete, using Vedanta's teachings.

- The purpose of life is to really live – not a make-believe life based on delusions and mistakes (like the life of a person in an asylum who believes he is Alexander the Great) but a real life which is in harmony with the truth of ourselves; as this truth is not obvious or apparent, our purpose in life is to discover our own truth with appropriate effort.

- The purpose of any living being's life is to grow to its
  fullest and, as human beings, the purpose of our life is to
  grow to our full potential by using our unique faculty of
  thought to understand the true nature of ourselves and of
  the world in which we live.[65]

All these goals are just ways of expressing a single objective:
the recognition of our essence as being wholeness without
any boundaries or limitations. Vedanta calls this *moksha* and,
in its vision, this is the only meaningful purpose of our lives.
If we succeed in achieving it, all our problems and questions
become insignificant.

Why should our vital questions suddenly lose their force after
Vedanta's knowledge? The answer is quite simple. From our
own experience we know that in moments of deep happiness,
such questions just do not arise; for instance, we never ask
any questions immediately upon finding out that we have won
a huge lottery or when an infatuating person first reciprocates
our emotion. This is because our fundamental question is not
"What is the purpose of my life?" but it is "How can I be free of
unhappiness?". However, no transitory experience of happiness
deals with our question permanently because the experience itself
passes. Vedanta helps us to find permanent freedom from the
limitations of our bodies, minds and egos by making us see that
none of these adjuncts is our reality. Once the natural fullness of
our real self is apparent to us, such questions do not arise just as
they do not at the moment when we come into great wealth or
experience deep love. Further, because the proper recognition
of our own fullness brought about by Vedanta never wavers, such
questions never assume any significance even in the future.

---

65 In this context, a popular verse says:

ahara nidra bhaya maithunamcha	Eating, sleeping, fear and procreation
samanya etad pashubhir naranam	are common to animals and humans;
budhirhi tesham adhiko visheshaha	intellect or the power of reason is the extra
	and distinct human faculty;
budhyavihinah pashubhi samana	without intellect, humans would be as
	good as animals.

Only Real Questions Need Real Answers

Once we are able to assimilate Vedanta's vision that our individuality is like a transient wave in the ocean, then questions arising from a separate individual lose a large part of their relevance: from the perspective of a wave, there can be questions about its life-span and the purpose of its existence but, from the perspective of the water which is the truth behind all waves, there is no question because water never changes its essential quality, whether it is vapour in the clouds or rain or waves in the ocean.

Of course, even after the wisdom of Vedanta, the experience of our bodies, minds and the sense of individuality continue and questions about what goals we should pursue subsist till we live; however, such questions now remain as important as questions like "What is the purpose of the blueness of the sky?" or "What is the purpose of compassion?" Such questions do not need any real answer.

If we keep on struggling with questions about the purpose of life because our ego says there must be a purpose which provides a central role to our individual personality, we will miss life itself. The genuine purpose of life cannot be understood without the modulation of our ego and the moderation of our desires because, otherwise, our mind remains opaque to things which are more fundamental. When we fail to do this, we waste a great gift and end up drawing pain from our unique features of intelligence and self-awareness which, ironically, are designed to bring us total fulfilment.

IS THERE A SOUL?

Different Meanings

The word 'soul' holds a variety of meanings, depending upon the tradition from which it is drawn. The most common meaning of this word comes to us from the so-called Abrahamic religions which consist of Judaism, Christianity and Islam. The soul here is conceived to be the non-material essence of an individual which survives the death of his body and goes to heaven or hell for an eternal after-life. Vedanta's concept of a soul is different in important aspects.

In the Hindu tradition, too, the soul is reckoned to go to heaven or hell after a person's death, but only for a limited period of time. Further, while these other faiths believe that the soul has only a single human life, the Hindu view is that a soul has numerous cyclical lives which are human as well as non-human. Finally, the Abrahamic idea of a soul elevates it to the status of the ultimate reality of a person but Vedanta holds that it is unchanging and unmoving atma which is our reality.

Atma and Sukshma Sharira

In Vedanta's view, atma is the ultimate and conscious truth behind all existence; it is the only reality in which individuals and their souls appear and disappear. Atma lends its existence and sentience to individual bodies and minds but itself remains unaffected by their doings, much as our consciousness provides the basis for the existence and movement of figures in our dreams without being affected by their doings.

In the case of a human being, atma is like the sun and his individual consciousness is like the sun's reflection in a mirror. The physical body of a person is inert by itself; Vedanta says that associated with the physical body is a non-material or subtle body (*sukshma sharira*) – the soul – which is capable of reflecting the consciousness of atma. The sukshma sharira is also inert but because it reflects consciousness, it appears to be conscious just as a mirror seems to shine of its own. It is the nearest equivalent in Vedanta to the term 'soul'. It is this sukshma sharira which is reckoned to go to heaven or hell and also transmigrate to different lives on earth.[66]

Karma

The idea of a non-material body which transmigrates from life-form to life-form carries with it the idea of *karma*. The word *karma* literally means 'action' but in the context of a soul, it also refers to the consequences of actions; this reference is not only to direct and obvious consequences but more to subtle and indirect consequences. For instance, when envy makes us wish that our colleague would somehow lose the money he has just won in a lottery, our mere wish may not have any obvious consequence; however, according to the karma theory, our very wishing ill for someone is a karma (a volitional deed even if only mental) and each karma must necessarily produce its consequences, just as in physics where every action must produce a reaction. In this instance, our envy-based mental movement will produce a negative result in the form of something unpleasant happening to us, either in this life or in a future life. Each karma has to be enjoyed or suffered independently and there is no netting off – if one robs to give to charity, bad consequences will arise for that person due to the robbery and separate good consequences will arise because of his charity.

The karmas which are generated during a human being's life[67] may deliver a part of their consequences in the current life itself and the balance gets added to the stock of karmas which will be

---

66 Another term which is often used in this context is *jiva* and it refers to an embodied soul – a soul with an individual body and mind, an entity which takes itself to be mortal and limited. The soul is a part and parcel of the *jiva* and gives sentience to its associated body and mind.

67 In the Hindu scheme of things, a soul can earn merit or de-merit only when it has a human birth; in any other birth (such as an animal or insect) it can only enjoy or suffer consequences of its past human deeds. This is because merit or de-merit accrue only upon volitional actions and only human beings experience free-will and are, therefore, the only form of life capable of volitional action. This is why a human birth is called *yoga-yoni* (where one can accumulate good and bad deeds based upon one's own choice) while any other birth is called *bhoga-yoni* where one can only enjoy or suffer the consequences of past deeds but acquire no fresh merit or de-merit.

carried over to future lives. Once we die, some of the karmas accumulated around our soul come to the fore-front to trigger a new life; karmas which cause a new life are called *prarabhda* and they are only a small but active portion of our entire stock of latent karmas. Prarabhda determines which sort of body (human or animal or insect) a soul gets and also the basic framework of the new life: parents, gender, inclinations, attitudes and capabilities. Some of these factors (such as parents and gender) are fixed for a life-time while others (such as inclinations and attitudes) are capable of being modified by choices and actions during that life.

A soul's association with a new life starts at the moment of conception when a living embryo comes into being. If that life is human, the soul also accumulates fresh karmas based on its volitional actions. When a life-form exhausts its prarabhda by enjoying or suffering its effects, the soul breaks its association with that particular body. Just as a bucket from which water has been emptied no longer reflects the sun, a body without a soul no longer appears to be enlivened by consciousness. The body is then pronounced dead. After death, the soul is reckoned to go to heaven or hell for a period; it then again joins a new life-form on earth, depending upon which of its accumulated karmas come to the fore-front to become prarabhda. This cycle goes on endlessly because the stock of karmas pertaining to each soul is inexhaustibly large, arising from countless previous births.

This idea of a soul continuously transmigrating due to karmas raises several questions, of which two crucial ones are:

- If past karmas are the cause of a particular birth, how or why did the very first birth occur?

- If the stock of karmas is endless (because of an infinity of previous births), does every soul have to go through births and deaths for ever?

The First Birth

The answer which Vedanta initially provides to the question of the first birth is that creation is not a linear chain on which one can go backwards to trace the very first link; cycles of births and deaths are circles which are complete in themselves, without any specific beginning or end. It is, therefore, not appropriate to raise any questions about the first birth just as it is not appropriate to try and establish the beginning of a circle. This kind of answer yet leaves behind a number of doubts which can be cleared only by moving to a completely different perspective, which we will come to a little later.

How to Exhaust Infinite Karmas?

As far as the problem of nullifying the pressure of past karmas is concerned, Vedanta says that this infinite stock can never be exhausted by the limited number of actions and experiences which are possible in a life-time. This is why while Vedanta encourages ethics and religion, it never holds out rectitude and devotion as the ultimate solution for an individual who wants to escape an endless cycle of births and deaths.

In Vedanta's view, actions and their consequences accrue only to an individual who takes himself to be an independent doer and enjoyer of things. This sense of individual agency comes from an aspect of the mind called the *ahamkara* or the ego. When, with the benefit of Vedanta's knowledge, it is clearly understood that all that appears to exist is nothing but transient waves on the ocean of changeless truth, the focus on individual deeds and consequences evaporates and the ego loses its strength. Once it is fully assimilated that the apparently independent doer and enjoyer is only a passing notion, karmas cannot deliver consequences because, in a way, now there is no one at home to take delivery.

In a different analogy, we can think of the ego as a magnet and karmas as countless iron particles. Plucking away each particle from the magnet is an endless task but if the magnet itself can be de-magnetised then all the iron particles would instantly fall away on their own. Vedanta asks us to lead a balanced life without hankering for petty ego or sense satisfaction, to devote regular time to worship and meditation and strive to understand the ultimate truth of ourselves; all these are ways in which our driving sense of individuality can be made to lose its force (be de-magnetised) and cause karmas (the iron particles) to fall away.

Thus, it is not by good actions but only by Vedanta's knowledge that countless karmas can be finally nullified.

Karmas after the Dawning of Wisdom

What happens to a human being who has successfully imbibed Vedanta's wisdom? Vedanta says that the prarabhda karmas which brought about this person's current birth must run their course – they are like a bullet which has already been fired and cannot be called back. However, because this person's mind has been processed by full understanding of the truth, no new karmas accumulate around his soul and the whole load of his past karmas also disintegrates because the ego now lacks the hooks to hold them together. When a person who has achieved this state dies, there is no stock of karmas left; therefore no prarabhda karmas can arise to generate a new birth. Thus, the cycle of births and deaths breaks for that soul which itself dissipates, without any residual individual identity.

Karmas and Transmigration Are Not the Ultimate Truth

This entire theory of karma and souls which transmigrate is provided by Vedanta within the confines of our usual lives; here we take ourselves as real individuals who want explanations for the state of our lives and who are concerned about our future fate. From this perspective we want to know why, for instance, someone is born rich while someone else is born poor or why people who regularly do horrible things seem to enjoy comfortable lives while the good often suffer. The idea of a soul which accumulates and carries the consequences of its worldly deeds over different lives provides a good model within which such questions can be answered: someone is born rich because of his past good karmas and an evil person who may be enjoying himself at present (due to good karmas of his previous lives), will surely pay for his current misdeeds in some future life.

If one can accept and go by this model, it provides an incentive to remain good even without an immediate pay-off and gives comfort as well as hope to those going through difficult times. On the flip side, when the karma theory is misunderstood, it may encourage a sense of fatalism and apathy because our life may be seen to be governed by the inexorable force of prarabhda which cannot be halted. However, even the consequences of prarabhda can be moderated (or aggravated) to some extent by our choices in this life; further, all our volitional efforts will always bear fruit, if not in this life-time than in some future life. There is, therefore, never any suggestion that one should helplessly sit back and do nothing.[68]

As mentioned earlier, it is very important to remember that this entire model is valid only within a life taken to be absolutely real. However, in the highest vision of Vedanta, individuals and the world in which they live are not real as they appear; the only reality is atma or the single and unchanging existence which is conscious and limitless. The nearest we can come to understanding this situation in terms of a known experience is our personal dream where our consciousness (in the form of our thoughts) projects a very credible dream world, complete with animate and inanimate objects, births, deaths, choices, emotions, actions, consequences, time and space. Here, our single consciousness seems to become the many things which constitute our dream and, while the dream lasts, they appear as real as anything in our waking world.

An individual within our personal dream may wonder why he is born poor and hope that his present good deeds will give him a better life in the future; however, from the outside of our dream (i.e. from the perspective of our waking state) this person is not real at all and, therefore, his life and his questions have no relevance whatsoever. If this person in our dream were to ask about the reason for his first birth or how his soul acquired its first karma,

---

68 Interestingly, tradition says that if at all one wants to passively accept destiny (prarabdha), such acceptance should be limited to artha (earning money) and kama (fulfilling desires); however, one should always make great volitional effort in the matters of dharma (appropriate living) and moksha (getting rid of fundamental ignorance).

there is no good answer for him. But when the same question is looked at from outside of the dream, the answer becomes simple: for a dream to work, it has to spring up or be projected into existence as a complete set-up which includes individuals with their stock of accumulated karmas. This is necessary to explain the differing conditions of individuals within the dream and provide a frame-work for their actions and consequences.

Leaving aside the dream analogy, such an arrangement could be also understood by using the example of a popular board-game called Monopoly. This game starts with all players being given a certain amount of game-money as initial capital which, subsequently, can be added to or depleted only by the moves that the players make in the course of the game. The fact that the money earned or lost within the game is determined by a player's actions has no bearing on how each player 'earned' his initial capital; the starting money was not earned but had to be given to each player because, without this, the game itself could not have commenced.[69]

In similar fashion, if we are able to understand our lives as being akin to a dream or a game, then we will not look for the source of our first karma or raise questions about our first birth; these things are part of the initial set-up which makes the dream or the game possible. Our greater concern should be with waking up from the dream or ensuring that a game remains just a game, instead of endlessly agonizing over their details. And this is what the wisdom of Vedanta helps us to do in our own lives.

Non-acceptance of Vedanta

If we are not able to accept Vedanta's highest perspective (very often because we are not willing to deny the reality of our own

---

69 One could argue that in a game like Monopoly, each player is given an equal amount of starting capital while our starting karmas cannot be identical if they have to be the basis for our differing abilities and choices. Here, one must remember that no analogy should be stretched beyond its intent. Thus, a statement such as 'King Richard was lion-hearted' should stop with an idea of his bravery and not lead us to ask questions about Richard's tail and claws. The dream and the game examples are not and cannot be identical to our lives in all respects and are intended to illustrate only a limited point.

personality), then our next best option is to live our lives based on the karma theory; here we can do as much good (or as little harm) as possible in order to lead comfortable lives, even though we will not find a satisfactory answer here to all our questions. And, if we are not able to accept even the karma theory, then we will have to necessarily take our life as a random happening, where good and bad fortune comes to us arbitrarily and where our death is the final reality. This is a purely materialistic view of life (called *carvaka darshana* in the Indian tradition) and carries with it the risk of completely selfish and unregulated behaviour, along with the fear and hopelessness of facing ultimate oblivion.[70]

Vedanta's explanations about the soul (sukshma sharira) and karmas thus help to raise us from a mundane existence and create a bridge which we can use to cross-over to the shores of Vedanta's highest truth; this truth is beyond time and change and in which an individual, his soul and his deeds all subside.

---

70 People have found curious ways to console themselves when faced with their own mortality. An example is a rather well-known epitaph on an old grave (dating back to the 1400s) found in Florence which (translated) says to its beholders "*I was once that which you are, and what I am you also will be*"!

A SNAPSHOT OF THE TEACHINGS

A snapshot is a static and two-dimensional view, which can never fully reflect anything dynamic and multi-dimensional. Yet, there is no option for us but to use Vedanta's word-picture even as we know that such a picture cannot fully capture the live truth of ourselves.

To paraphrase what Adi Shankara had once said, millions of scriptures can be condensed into just half a verse: there is only one reality which supports the appearance of this world and you are not other than this reality yourself.[71] The core of Vedanta's teachings is based on the insight that everything, without any exception whatsoever, is this single reality. The rest of Vedanta's vast material only approaches and develops this cardinal truth in different ways, to prepare us to be receptive to it. If we could directly appropriate Vedanta's key revelation so that it became an integral part of our lives, instead of just an idea or a concept, there would be no real need for the rest of Vedanta's content; however, such miracles of instant assimilation do not happen often and most of us need sustained exposure to Vedanta's teachings to derive worthwhile benefit from them.

The Fundamental Problem

Why is Vedanta needed at all? After all, we do have families, careers, savings, health-care, amusements, ethics and religions to take care of our needs; many of us are also fortunate enough to live within open economic and political systems, with their attendant opportunities and benefits. All these factors provide us with a great deal of external freedom; yet, we are not free from the knowledge of our own mortality as well as an inexplicable urge for fullness, which persist despite our good fortune and achievements. No matter what we do and no matter whatever is done for us, we experience a sense of limitation centered on our own bodies and minds; we always remain with an inner incompleteness which forces us to change and augment ourselves in endless ways.

---

71 *slokardhena pravakshyami yad uktam granthakotibhih: brahma satyam jagan mithya jivo brahmaiva naparah.*

To overcome this internal pressure to be more than whatever we are now, requires constant efforts on our part. These efforts result in unpredictable levels of transitory successes or failures and generate pride or anger, fear and guilt. Further, this process of trying to become full and complete is endless because we never ever become entirely adequate or acceptable to ourselves, in our own judgment. Such ongoing dissatisfaction and anxiety is a universal and fundamental problem which is not solved by growing wealth or technology or evolving socio-economic systems.

Usual Goals Are Inadequate

The fact that we never stop wanting to be better and more does not mean that our ordinary efforts and achievements have no relevance – the Hindu tradition lists wealth (*artha*), pleasure (*kama*) and virtue (*dharma*) as the first three out of the four principal human goals. But Vedanta also points out their limitations: greed for wealth is like an insatiable fire which flares up with the fuel of further acquisition; the value of one's wealth can only be reckoned in terms of comparisons with the wealth of others, which always lead to insecurity and anxiety (and this applies to fame and power as well); pleasures not only depend upon situations and objects which change unpredictably but indulgence in them dulls the very faculties which provide us pleasurable experiences and our minds also get bored with their repetition; finally, even a large amount of virtue neither erases our sense of being small individuals nor shields us from the prospect of our inevitable death.

The Upanishads portray several individuals who discover such limitations of our usual attainments and possessions: the learned sage Narada (in the Chandogya Upanishad) finds in himself a mysterious sorrow and lacking, despite prodigal scholarship in all conventional fields of knowledge; a rather vain student Svetaketu (in the same Chandogya Upanishad) is chastened to find that his academic curriculum did not cover that special knowledge, by knowing which everything is as good as known; the wealthy wife Maitreyi is told (in the Brihadaranyaka Upanishad) that no amount of riches will make her immortal; the young prince Nachiketas (in the Katha Upanishad) has the discernment to say that pleasures and possessions are transient, sap the energy of our senses, leave us subject to death and are not, therefore, worth a great deal.

Discrimination is Vital

The realization that our usual efforts do not resolve the problem of an ongoing sense of inadequacy does not occur to everyone; most people therefore go through their lives without deviating from their common goals. However, a few people are able to discern that the real issue is not the temporary satisfaction of any specific want but addressing the urge for freedom from wants in general. As Vedanta points out, the core of every human quest is not the achievement of a particular goal in itself but release from the sense of limitation of any kind. This natural urge to be unlimited is specifically experienced by all of us in the form of three primary desires: to be free from death, ignorance and unhappiness, irrespective of time, place or set-up.[72]

To completely fulfil these desires would require us to exist for infinity, with infinite knowledge and with infinite happiness. Infinity implies both boundlessness and timelessness and it is obvious that all our usual efforts will not bring us to such a state. As the Mundaka Upanishad says, a wise person after examining the worldly gains obtained through actions, realises that the infinite cannot be achieved by finite action and thus becomes disenchanted and detached (with and from usual pursuits).

This realization is a crucial juncture; if we do not arrive at it, we will continue to make our normal efforts and, even after great attainments, yet remain wanting: always mortal, always ignorant and always less than fully happy because we always base our hopes and efforts on the tenuous, the limited and the temporary. All our external success will never bring us internal success, a lasting sense of peace and fulfilment which we all want but never get because we are unable to achieve the infinite.

---

72 There are a few people who are so fed-up with their lives that they contemplate suicide; this is not because of the absence of the desire to live but because they perceive no hope of experiencing happiness – an equally fundamental urge. If their personal misfortune is resolved, their natural urge to remain alive re-surfaces intact.

Is There a Solution?

Why should one assume that there is, in fact, anything which will take us to the infinite and bring us complete and permanent fulfilment? First, the answer here comes from our experience of nature itself, where there is no genuine need which does not have a corresponding means of its fulfilment – as an old saying goes, hunger pre-supposes bread. Our urge for the boundless and the eternal is universal and it is reasonable to assume that there is a way to cater to it. Second, we all experience total fulfilment which is not tainted by the prospect of our deaths, by our unanswered questions and by our pending desires; this happens every time we, for instance, are immersed in a sublime piece of music, or enthralled by natural beauty, or engrossed in play with a delightful child. These are of course brief experiences but, while they last, they give us a taste of the fullness and completeness which we intrinsically yearn for. And, last, for those of us for whom the Upanishads hold credibility, these scriptures repeatedly state that the attainment of complete and unchanging happiness is the highest human goal.

A Teacher is Necessary

What should we do next? How do we seek limitless and eternal happiness? Here, the Mundaka Upanishad makes a categorical statement: *'To know the infinite, he* (i.e. a person of wisdom) *should go with the appropriate attitude to a teacher who knows the teaching tradition and who himself is established in the infinite ... To the student who comes in the proper manner, whose mind is calm and who has self-control, the wise teacher should impart knowledge through which one knows the true and imperishable.'* Thus, the Upanishad not only tells us what to do but also sets out the crucial qualities of both a proper teacher and an eligible student.

The Infinite Cannot be Separate from Us

The teacher begins by imparting the initial understanding that if what is sought is boundless and timeless, it can neither be created by our actions, nor can it be ever away from us. This is because the *infinite* cannot be brought into being by finite action, the *timeless* has to exist in all periods of time and the *boundless* cannot exclude us, by the very meanings of these words. Therefore, our search has to be for something which is always and already with us. If we, the seekers, are seeking something which is not separate from us, then the seeker is in fact the sought and it is only lack of proper knowledge which keeps us apparently apart. Thus, our quest for infinity now changes from seeking something outside of us to gaining adequate understanding of our own self, which must already have what we want.

A parable here is about the quest for wealth by a young man who has been adopted by a poor family which found him as a child in a forest; this young man is actually the lost crown prince and what is needed by him is not any effort to get rich but just the knowledge of being the son of the king. In a similar manner, the Upanishads tell us that we only need true knowledge of our real nature, to claim the fullness which is already ours.

How Can I be Infinite?

We all know ourselves very well as mortal beings, limited in our knowledge, abilities and happiness. How can we, as such puny creatures, be the infinite? This leads us into an examination of who we really are. Upon proper inquiry, we find that our individual self which we always find wanting, is actually nothing but facets of our body and mind and of things associated with them. We spend our lives believing *"I am short", "I am sad", "I am hungry", "I am uneducated", "I am poor", "I am divorced"* and so on; but all these statements are only attributes of our bodies, the state of our minds, our attainments, our possessions and our relationships. In as much as these things are *'ours'*, they cannot be *'us'* as we are, in fact, the knowers of these things. After all, in a row of houses, when we recognise one house as being ours we do not conclude that we are that house; similarly, when amongst a multitude of bodies and minds we recognise one as ours, there is no reason for us to think that we are that body and mind. Behind the various objects and attributes by which we seek to define ourselves, there is a separate and constant knower to whom all that is known is apparent; Vedanta says that it is this knower who is the real "I".

The Cardinal Error

Despite the fact that our own reality is different from things which are known to us, we continuously make the mistake of a mix-up between the known and the knower. This error is apparent when we identify ourselves with the qualities of the known. While this confusion is natural and universal, it has great consequences. Once we align our identity with things which are limited, changing and transient, we automatically enter into a battle to seek more and to find something permanent, to cater to our natural urge to be free of any limitations. But this urge can never be fulfilled by our usual efforts because bodies, minds, attainments, possessions and relationships will always remain subject to their inherent limitations. If we need support for this fact, we only need to look at recent instances of exceptionally successful people doing pathetic or ridiculous things, driven by the notion that they are defined by their bodies: a renowned entertainer going through a life-time of painful surgeries to erase the marks of his racial characteristics and the president of a large country teetering on the tips of his toes during a group photo with other world leaders, to appear taller.

Vedanta tells us that the only real solution is to shift our focus from the known to the knower or, in other words, to the awareness or consciousness because of which things are known to us. This consciousness, which is the constant and final meaning of the word "I", is what we fundamentally are; Vedanta further says that this consciousness is also the eternal fullness which we so assiduously search for outside of us.

Consciousness or Atma

What is the nature of our consciousness? We have to bear in mind that the consciousness we are talking about here is not consciousness of anything specific but consciousness or awareness per se. Because such consciousness is not an object or a concept, it cannot be known by our sensory or intellectual processes. After all, to know consciousness in the usual way of knowing things we would need yet another level of consciousness and so on, till we stop at a basic consciousness which is not evident to any other consciousness but is self-evident. However, this does not mean that consciousness is completely unknown to us. Vedanta suggests that it is:

- Attributeless because it is consciousness which makes attributes known. If consciousness had attributes of its own, it would have imparted the same attributes to everything (just as the whole world appears yellow to a jaundiced eye) but we know different things having entirely different attributes.

- Changeless because it permits us to know change – just as the motion of a passing train is known only when we are stationary by-standers and not when we ourselves are on another moving train. Because changes in things are apparent to us, consciousness itself should be changeless.

- Limitless or boundless for two likely reasons. First, there is nothing which is outside of our consciousness: the past, present & future, the smallest sub-atomic particle and the largest galaxy are all within our consciousness. Our consciousness cannot be exceeded or negated by anything because everything (including the concept of unconsciousness) is within consciousness. Second, for things to have boundaries, they must have some attributes (a defined place in space and time and specific characteristics such as being heavy or being red). However, if we accept that consciousness does not have any attributes (for the reason mentioned a little earlier), it cannot have any boundaries or limitations. This, in turn, would also mean that consciousness is the ultimate fullness because nothing more can ever be added to something which is limitless.

Such infinite consciousness is our constant and inner-most truth, because of which we are awareful beings; this core reality of an individual is called *atma* in Sanskrit. Atma is existence which is changeless (*sat* in Sanskrit), conscious (or *chit*) and limitless (because it is limitless, it implies joy of fullness or *ananda*); the Upanishads therefore describe it as *sat chit ananda*. What we truly are is atma and not the temporary and limited characteristics of our bodies and minds, which we take ourselves to be. And this conclusion is not just of academic interest but it has a direct bearing on our usual struggle for happiness; if what we are is already changeless and boundless then our efforts to change and overcome limitations need not be so desperate or urgent.

Some Doubts

At this stage several doubts can arise:

- If I am truly changeless and boundless consciousness, there should be no change or need in me. However, the fact is that we all have needs and we also constantly experience change such as being joyful at one moment and sorrowful at another.

- If I am changeless and boundless consciousness, so is every other individual (by a similar process of logic) and so each one of us remains a competing pocket of consciousness, limited and bound by the presence of the other.

- The fact that I may be changeless and boundless consciousness does not explain the nature of the world I confront, the mystery of its creator and the method by which I should deal with its overwhelming scope and multiplicity.

You are That

Vedanta says that all these doubts and questions arise because of our mistaken idea that our bodies and minds are the truth of our identity. Correction of this wrong notion is facilitated by an analysis of probably the most famous single statement from the Upanishads: *tat tvam asi*. This *mahavakya* (a great statement) from the Chandogya Upanishad means *you are that*. The *you* here refers to an individual, the subject; the *that* refers to everything seen, known, imagined or conceptualised by the individual.[73] Thus, this statement enigmatically says that there is no essential difference between a small individual and the vast creation which he confronts.

73 As we will see a little later, there is a common cause for all the objects in the world and *that* actually refers to such a common cause of everything.

On the face of it, such an assertion of identity appears incredible and preposterous. But then, even in a simple equation, the identity of the two sides is not apparent unless each side is fully understood. Thus, for someone who does not know arithmetic, the equation 1.5 X (20-14)=6+3 may also seem incredible and for someone who does not know anything about astronomy, the statement that *'The Morning Star is the Evening Star'*[74] may seem meaningless. So, Vedanta tells that instead of dismissing the statement *You=That*, we should go beyond the obvious meanings of the words *you* and *that*, understand their implied meanings and see for ourselves their true identity.

You or tvam

Let us start with the *'you'* in the statement *you are that;* the *'you'* here refers to an individual, the one we mean when we say "I". We all use sentences frequently employing the pronoun "I" like "I am tall", "I am angry", "I am quick in understanding" or "I never take 'No' for an answer". In each of these statements, the "I" is supposed to refer to us, to our own selves. But how can we say anything about ourselves? As we have seen earlier, we can say these things only because we know them – we are the knowers and our physical and mental attributes are objects of our knowledge. The knower has to be different from anything which is known just as the eye has to be different from any object which is seen. The knower is not affected by the qualities of whatever that is known, just as our eyes do not become dirty when they see a pile of dirt; we (the knowers) cannot actually become tall just because our body is known to be tall or become angry because our mind is known to contain anger.

If this is so then why do we so readily take the qualities of our bodies and minds to be our qualities? After all, there must be some reason why we label ourselves to be brown when our skins are brown but do not call ourselves white when our shirts are white. If our skins and our shirts are both known objects which are different from us (the knowers), then why do we personally adopt the qualities of one of these objects and not

---

74 This statement refers to the planet Venus, which appears as a bright star at dusk in the west and also at dawn in the east, at certain times of the year.

of the other? The reasons for this are two-fold: The first is the special relationship we have with our own bodies and minds, which is very different from our relationship with other known objects. The second is the identity which we have with our senses because of which we come to know things.

We can begin with the special relationship we have with our minds. Our knowledge of the contents and state of our minds is very private and personal. For instance, while everyone can see that our shirt is white, only we know that envy is present in our mind and we can choose not to manifest this envy to anyone else. It is the proximity and intimacy of our mind which leads us to wrongly identify ourselves with its current state. Unlike our minds, our bodies can be seen by everyone else but because our sense of touch extends only to our skins, we have a special relationship with this boundary. It is for this reason that when someone touches our skin, we sense that we are being touched but this does not happen when someone irons our shirt. It is for the same reason that we do not consider the food on our table to be 'us' but, when that same food is eaten and integrated with our sensory apparatus by becoming our flesh and skin, it seems to become 'us'.

Coming to our senses in general, we consider our ability to know things as being our crucial ability. We know things because of our senses and because of our minds where the inputs of our senses are interpreted. Due to the fact that we strongly identify ourselves with our knowing capacities, the condition of our knowing apparatus seems to become our own condition. Thus, if our eyes cannot bring distant things into focus, we consider ourselves to be short-sighted and if the emotion of anger is present in our minds, we say we are angry.

However, even though we may label ourselves as being angry or intelligent or demanding, it is not that we are actually these states; if these states were our real nature, they would have remained constant just as sugar, which is actually sweet, always remains sweet. We, on the other hand, find ourselves experiencing peace and love instead of being angry at all times; or, till we have had our morning cup of tea, we may feel mentally dull; or, in the presence of someone whom we respect and look up to, we notice our egos becoming smaller and more flexible. Our mental states and the changes in them are known to us – we are not the mind but the knowers of the mind. The only reason why we take ourselves to be our minds is mere proximity. Just as a red flower placed next to a colourless crystal seems to make the crystal red, we, the knowers, seem to become the attributes of our minds which are known to us.

This association with things where there is a special and intimate relationship is natural. In fact, it is not restricted to our bodies and minds but extends to our roles and possessions which are also close to us. Therefore, we can go through our whole life saying "I am a doctor" when being a doctor is only one of the many roles we may play or, when the stock market crashes, we say "I am ruined" when, actually, we are ones who are aware of a monetary loss. Such identification is also greatly enhanced by our conditioning; for instance, a person may have been told from childhood that "You are pretty" or "You are clever" or "You are rich", thus promoting congruence of one's identity with the attributes of the body and mind as well as with other associated things.

If this confusion is natural and age-old, then what is the issue? How does it matter what our true nature is? As we have seen earlier, this matters a great deal because when we do not recognise our true nature, we go on to wrongly assume our bodies, minds, relationships and possessions to be our real identity. Having identified ourselves with such small, fallible and transient things, we spend our lives in search for the infallible and permanent. It is in this context that it is vital to understand from Vedanta that what we really are is boundless and changeless consciousness; our bodies, minds and other attributes are just things which are known, exactly like mountains, flowers and other people (which are also known to us but without the mistaken identification with our own selves).

That or tat

Granting that we are actually consciousness or awareness in our essence, what about our bodies and minds as well as the mountains, flowers and other people that are known to us? What is their nature? This is where we come to the other side of the equation, to the word *tat* or *that*, to the world which is apparent to our consciousness.

Vedanta tells us that we know the world through the operation of our senses, through the attributes of objects in the world (such as being soft, red, or fragrant) and through the conditioning loaded in our minds. Let us look at each of these three factors and the impact they have on our evaluation of the reality of the world:

- Because we only experience the world through our senses, we never *directly* cognise anything in it; whatever we perceive is only a mental interpretation of the signals received by our sense organs. This results in our understanding of the world being affected by the state of our sense organs and the condition of our minds. For instance, we may see a fuzzy person if our eyes are defective and we may see nothing at all (even as our eyes pick up the required visual signals) if our mind is fully pre-occupied with other thoughts and concerns. If our eyes had been naturally endowed with a higher level of magnification of, say, that of an electron microscope, we would have not seen a person at all but only vast swathes of emptiness with a few atomic particles floating around, and our conclusion about the real nature of this person would then have been formed by such a perception. And we cannot even imagine what kind of 'seeing' experience we would have had if, like bats, we had been equipped with echo-location as a means of finding our way around, instead of sight. Of course, our senses are vital for living in this world and they provide a common platform from which we can communicate and co-operate with other human beings; however, we need to bear in mind that just because our perceptions are practically useful, we should not conclude that they disclose reality in the total sense of that word. What we perceive and take to be fully real are, in fact, only facets or perspectives, as limited by our senses and our minds.

• Again, we conclude that a number of real things exist in the world because of their unique qualities. Thus, a chair is a chair and a flower is a flower because of their specific attributes and forms to which we give a special name. But each individual object can be reduced to something more basic and more real[75] and when this is done, the special attributes and form of the object itself are lost. Thus, a chair is nothing but several pieces of wood but none of these pieces themselves have the element of 'chairness' in them; a flower can be separated into a stem, petals and stamens, none of which are flowers. In fact, the basis of any object is something which does not have the special attributes of that object. If we progressively follow the process of reducing each object to its more basic elements and thereby shedding some attributes, Vedanta suggests that we will end up with a ground reality which is without any attributes at all. However, because a thing without attributes cannot be sensed by us, this reality remains unknown. We therefore end up wrongly taking objects with attributes as real, even though each such object is insubstantial: for instance, there is no substance called 'pot' because it is clay which is the substance here.

• Things become apparent to us as discrete objects based upon the conditioning loaded into our mind. Someone who has no idea of the constellation Orion will only see a random sprinkling of stars in the night sky; for someone else, with prior exposure to astronomy, Orion will clearly stand out. So, is Orion really out there or in our minds? And such cognition is not restricted to imagined patterns like a constellation of stars; an adult clearly recognises a clay pot as a pot only due to prior conditioning and, for an infant, this object would be no different from any lump of clay and would trigger no recognition of a pot. Giving a name to a particular form is subjective, depending upon our notions of utility and conventions. For instance, we

---

75 The cause is more real than the effect because while the cause does not need the effect, the effect cannot exist without the cause — you cannot have a pot without clay but clay can exist without being a pot.

do not give a name to all possible shapes of clay but we
call a certain shape a saucer because of its utility to us;
and the shape of a swastika is recognised only in certain
cultures, merely out of local convention. The fact is that
all objects which we call 'real' become so only because of
ideas in our minds.

The purpose of saying all this is not to deny the empirical reality
of the world or of our practical need to inter-act with the objects
in it. The world is real enough in terms of our experience of it:
it is stable, it is continuous and we can see and touch it. But just
because we experience it, we should not automatically conclude
that it independently exists just as we experience it. Vedanta wants
us to remember that the things we take to be objectively real are
actually affected by our subjectivity and the limitations of our
senses and minds; it also tries to make us appreciate that there is
a greater common and impartite truth behind the multiplicity of
things which we assume to be absolutely real.

Why should this truth behind everything be single and partless
when the experienced world is one of variety and plurality?
As we saw earlier, all objects in the world consist of attributes,
based on a substantive. Thus, a shirt is an attribute whose
substantive is fabric but the fabric, in turn, is actually just
another attribute whose substantive is yarn and so on. Anything
we know and speak of can be reduced to a more elementary
reality. An endless chain of attributes alone cannot logically
exist, without ultimately resting in a substantive. Further, the
fact that each object can be reduced to something which does
not have the attributes of the original object (such as the fabric
having no 'shirtness'), means that we should finally end up with
a substantive reality with no attributes.[76]

Anything without attributes has to be changeless and boundless
because changes and boundaries are always with reference to

---

76 As the Brihadaranyaka Upanishad expresses it (in verse 3-8-8):"....it is neither
gross nor subtle, neither short nor long, neither red nor oily ....has neither taste
nor odour... without measure, without interior and without exterior."

the attributes of a particular object.[77] Also, anything boundless has to be a singularity because two boundless things are not possible by definition. Finally, because a thing without attributes cannot be known or have any parts or components, one cannot meaningfully talk of its coming into being or of its destruction and it is, therefore, outside the bounds of time. Thus, we are led to an absolute reality which is non-dual (*advaita*), changeless (*nirvikalpa*), boundless (*ananta*) and timeless (*nitya*).

But there yet remains something more which can be said about this ground reality. The world we perceive and deal with is an orderly world which functions in accordance with specific laws; even disruptive or destructive events (such as the death of massive stars, hurricanes in our planet's atmosphere or the outbreak of a disease) all follow the relevant laws of physics, chemistry and biology. There is, in fact, nothing random or disorderly in creation; even when things appear to be so, it is only because we have, as yet, not been able to discern the appropriate underlying laws for that particular phenomenon. A universe which is orderly and functional has to involve intelligence and this is apparent at all levels: at the sub-atomic level, at the level of our bodies and minds and the level of heavenly bodies. Where does this intelligence reside?

There are some traditional schools of thought which hold out this intelligent principle (called *purusha*) as an independent reality which is separate from creation's insentient and material cause (called *prakriti*). Vedanta, however, rejects any such duality and asserts that there is only a single, eternal, boundless and changeless basis to this world and the intelligence displayed in it is an integral aspect of this reality.[78] Because knowledge or

---

77 The reference here is not only to physical attributes but also to the attributes of time as well as of opposites. Thus a given thought, which does not have any physical boundary, is limited by time because it is there in one moment and not there in the next; an abstract concept of say, justice, is limited by the opposite concept of injustice, without which the concept of justice itself cannot arise.

78 This is also in keeping with an established principle of Western logic which says that where more than one explanation is equally possible, the explanation involving the least number of entities should be chosen; this principle is popularly known as Occam's razor.

intelligence is only compatible with a conscious entity, this reality cannot be inert but has to be conscious. This is also supported by the fact that when individual objects are properly investigated, they prove to be only ideas in our mind (like the constellation Orion or a pot which appear only for someone for whom these ideas are already loaded in his mind); ideas are nothing but waves in awareness or consciousness, which is their truth.

This ultimate and irreducible reality is named *brahman* by the Upanishads which describe it as *satyam* (independent and unchanging existence) *jnanam* (knowledge or intelligence) *anantam* (limitless or boundless); it is the only real existence upon which all other apparent existence depends.

Tat and *Tvam* are the Same

By an analysis of the words 'you' (*tvam*) and 'that' (*tat*), we come to the conclusion that 'you' refers not to an individual's body and mind but to the underlying unchanging, boundless consciousness because of which things become known to us. 'That' refers not to the variety of objects in the world which are witnessed by us but to their underlying truth which is also unchanging, boundless and conscious. On the face of it, these two realities appear to be separate: one is behind the individual (the subject) and the other is behind the world experienced by the individual (objects). However, the Upanishads go on to say that the reality of the individual and the reality of the world are not two separate entities but just one existence.

That consciousness is an undivided whole, even though it is experienced by people individually, is supported by the fact that neither does anyone ever know of consciousness other than his own and nor does any individual's consciousness have distinguishing attributes as a result of which it can be segregated it from any other consciousness. The oneness of the consciousness which is at the core of individuals and the consciousness which is the basis of the rest of the world is derived from the fact that they are both boundless. If these two boundless realities were different, it would be a contradiction in terms – if there is a separate, second entity then the first entity cannot be boundless because the other entity would have to be outside its bounds. The limitless consciousness experienced by an individual as his own being and the limitless existence deduced to be the basis of the world, has to be the same, undivided reality.

Thus, Vedanta leads us to its great perspective where we are not individual bodies and minds with a core of consciousness who perceive and deal with the world; the truth in which all bodies and minds as well other objects of the world appear is single and unbroken.

This identity between the truth of ourselves and the truth behind everything which appears before us is not of some passing or speculative interest. If we are able to accept, feel and own up to our true nature, it fundamentally resolves our struggle for happiness because our truth is the truth of everything and we are not limited by or separated from anything at all; the differences and limitations which are perceived are only superficial and unreal, arising from the mistaken identification with our bodies and minds.

Existence and Consciousness Are Not Adjectives

The fact that atma (our individual reality) and brahman (the truth behind the world) are one and the same is sometimes obscured by the convention of highlighting different aspects of these two synonymous terms. When we talk of atma, it is the consciousness facet of this single reality which is emphasised because we primarily experience ourselves as conscious knowers. However, because existence is the obvious feature of the world, it is this aspect which is brought to the forefront when the same reality is discussed as the basis of the world. Such usage should not lead us to believe that either consciousness or unchanging existence is the primary quality of this reality.

The Upanishads describe reality as *sat chit ananda* in case of atma and *satyam jnanam anantam* in case of brahman. These three words in each of the two descriptions are, in the technical terms of grammar, in apposition; this means that they are placed with one another as explanatory equivalents without implying any different syntactic relationship such as one of these terms being a noun and the others being adjectives. Changelessness, limitlessness and consciousness are the very nature of the same reality without any of these words being adjectives, just as liquidity and wetness are the very nature of water and not just adjectives. However, depending upon the situation, any one aspect of the same reality may appear to be more prominent. If, for instance, we were out in a boat on choppy seas, water's liquid nature would be more apparent to us but if were caught in a sudden rain-shower during our evening walk, water's wetness would seem more evident. Similarly, existence and consciousness appear more prominent in brahman and atma respectively but both are one: existence which is conscious or consciousness which exists.

Dream Analogy

That the basis for all that exists is a single reality is a concept which is difficult to understand and accept but we may find some help from a comparison with a common experience which we all have – the experience of a dream. While our dream is on, we are a participating individual within it and we inter-act with other people and things in the dream's frame-work of time and space. But the entire dream, consisting of subject and objects, time and space, emotions and concepts, is nothing but our own thought projection, a movement or play of our own consciousness. Because our dream is short and we wake up from it, we dismiss it as a 'mere dream' and gloss over the fact that, while the dream was on, there was no break, contradiction or reason within it which would make us doubt its reality. Thus, our dream experience shows how it is possible for our single consciousness to apparently create a whole and viable world of a subject and objects.

Nothing is Completely Unreal

Are our waking or 'real' lives as unreal as our dreams? Vedanta sees any perceived reality as having two levels or grades:

- A completely individual perception which includes errors (such as seeing a snake in place of a rope) and other projections of the mind (such as our personal dreams or our looking upon another person as being noble just because he is wealthy). Such purely personal perception is termed *pratibhasika* or reflected.

- An objective 'waking-world' perception where we see mountains, flowers and other individuals as they are, as does everyone else. This common, empirical cognition is called *vyahavarika* or transactional.

However, underlying individual projections and common experiences is the only true reality, the basis for all that appears to exist, and this is called *parmarthika* or the ultimate. And Vedanta's attempt is to take us to the ultimate, from which perspective both the subjective and the transactional lose their apparent reality.

It is not Vedanta's contention that our errors, dreams and waking-experiences are without any basis. All of them are founded upon a single, conscious reality. Everything and anything which exists, even as an illusion, draws its existence from this reality which is all that actually exists. But when we take the things we perceive to be absolutely real, we make an error because we forget the underlying truth of changeless and boundless consciousness, without which no existence is sustainable. To some extent, this is like not seeing the gold because we are so taken up by the design of the ornaments or being so mesmerised by the action on a movie screen so that we forget that it is only a play of light. This error occurs because ultimate reality is without any attributes and, therefore, its wholeness remains beyond the ambit of our senses; our senses can only capture its limited facets and, that too, only by our minds superimposing temporary forms and names.

Of course, even the senses and minds which do this are also not separate from this conscious reality. So, for an individual, everything that he beholds (other individuals, objects, illusions, errors and 'real' experiences) are all a projection or play of consciousness, within consciousness, by consciousness. If one were to express this in the language of a theatrical production, consciousness is simultaneously the script-writer, the director, the actor and the audience. In fact, in the ultimate analysis, that which we call 'creation' should be more accurately termed 'projection' because reality never undergoes any actual transformation – it only *appears* to be split as subject and objects. Vedanta, therefore, is neither objective realism (where the world is reckoned to have completely independent reality) nor subjective idealism (where nothing other than the observing subject is real) because, in Vedanta's vision, the division between subject and objects itself is not real.

Vedanta is Unsettling

This, of course, sounds incredulous because it is so alien to our common notion of perceived multiplicity being real. But then conclusions based on common experiences do not have a track-record of perfect reliability: at various times we, as a race, were convinced that the world was flat, that the earth was the centre of the universe and that (in some cultures) it was legitimate to keep a section of fellow human-beings in slavery. Again, there are several aspects of modern physics (such as gravity distorting space-time or the same thing being simultaneously a particle and a wave) which we cannot easily understand or relate to. We, therefore, should not summarily dismiss Vedanta's insights, just because they appear strange or uncomfortable.

Unfortunately, we are so conditioned to look upon the world and our own individuality as being absolutely real and are also so driven by our desires, that we have difficulty in internalizing Vedanta's fundamental teaching that all existence is singular. Fully accepting such a proposition would mean reducing our world to a secondary level of reality and making us into insubstantial figures playing a role which has no fundamental relevance; it would also render insignificant our desires and our related efforts to fulfil them. Even as we may grudgingly nod our heads in response to Vedanta's explanations, our stubborn individuality refuses to let go of its self-generated importance and our desires continue to hold us in their strong flow.

By showing our personalities and our world to be projections of and within consciousness, Vedanta tries to give us freedom *from* our bodies and minds; however, our egos try to use Vedanta for freedom *for* the body and mind, because disassociation from these adjuncts is very difficult. This is why the dream analogy does not go home easily and we persist in trying to find purpose, satisfaction and answers within our world which we continue to take to be absolutely and independently real.

How Does One Appear to Become Many?

In our exploration of Vedanta's teachings so far, we have tried to use reason and logic to the extent we can. However, the truth is that the words of Vedanta are only a limited attempt to establish and describe an all-encompassing reality which is actually beyond arguments. Lectures are delivered and books are written on this subject only because they are initially helpful but they cannot take us all the way. In fact, if we carefully examine any aspect of Vedanta's core teachings, they only tell us what we are not, without trying to define and capture what we actually are.[79] Even the apparently positive statements such as atma being *sat chit ananda* are not complete definitions even though they appear to be so.[80]

It is important to remind ourselves here that Vedanta does not hold itself out as the repository for answers to all possible questions. If we, for instance, expect Vedanta to prove by positive and irrefutable arguments that objects and the subject are both one and the same, we will be disappointed. If we ask Vedanta why is there any movement at all in the single reality behind all existence which gives rise to the projection of plurality, we may be given an explanation of *maya* (a mysterious power) or *lila* (divine play) but both of these are not much of explanations in terms of strict logic.

---

[79] In this context, the Upanishads use the term *neti neti* meaning 'not this, not this' and thus signify that we can only know what is unreal but cannot define the real.

[80] All our wrong notions can be reduced to three basic mistakes: we see ourselves as mortal, ignorant and unhappy (or limited). It is only to counter these three mistakes that reality is described as *sat* or changeless existence (which denies our notion of being mortal), *chit* or pure awareness (which counters our notion of being ignorant) and *ananda* or joy of fullness (which negates our conclusion of being unhappy). This description is not meant to define but to help us where our understanding is most fundamentally flawed.

Vedanta has a lot of supporting reasons to substantiate its insights but, finally, it is not an explanation but a remedy for the endless struggle of individuals trying to overcome mortality and the other limitations of their bodies and minds. Reality itself has no problems, asks no questions and wants no answers. We experience this every time we are truly happy. When we obtain a much-wanted thing or when we are fully immersed in an absorbing experience, all our questions and doubts momentarily vanish. We, at such instances, don't want to know the meaning and purpose of our lives or worry about how long we will live or regret not having acted upon that stock-market tip. This is because some experiences temporarily manage to still our wanting, questioning and worrying minds and all that then remains is the pure and conscious reality which is naturally fulfilled. While these experiences are temporary, fullness is actually our natural state which Vedanta helps us to discover and stay in. However, Vedanta cannot take us to our goal of abiding happiness by only an intellectual process of arguments and logic, because no process can 'take' us to the fullness which is already ours by our very nature.

This is why even after everything that can be clarified in Vedanta has been clarified, there yet remains something inexpressible; this can only be experienced directly, beyond the realm of words and concepts. To fully benefit from Vedanta, we certainly need our intellectual prowess, effort and discipline; but we also need initial faith in the words of the Upanishads, till our personal experience makes Vedanta's insights into our own. The culmination of Vedanta is not just a mass of information about a thing which we need to understand but, ultimately, an abiding and live experience of our own wholeness.

The Role of the Mind

If Vedanta does not have complete explanations supported by strict logic, what is the role of our minds in this pursuit? The Upanishads themselves seem to say contradictory things here. For instance, the Kena Upanishad says that ultimate reality cannot be comprehended by the mind[81] while the Katha Upanishad says

---

81 Kena Upanishad (1.6): *yanmanasa na manute.*

that it is to be perceived by the mind alone.[82] Such confusing statements are made because while our minds and intelligence are necessary in our pursuit, they cannot ensure that we will reach our goal within a predictable time-frame. Our minds are needed to obtain clear and firm knowledge that "I" cannot be synonymous with our body and mind and also to understand the nature of the substratum underlying the world which we behold. Our intelligence is further needed to lead balanced lives, in keeping with natural laws, so that our minds remain free of turmoil caused by contradictions, greed, anger, fear, insecurity and egotism. But the transformation within us, which brings total peace and fulfilment from the realization of the oneness of the subject and objects, finally comes to us and pervades our very being without being tied to a time-bound process.

If this is so then why so much concern with gaining the knowledge of Vedanta and leading an ethical and religious life to modulate and reform aspects of our mind? A useful analogy here is of the mind with a bucket of water and of reality with the sun whose image we want to see in the water. If the bucket is covered, the sun's image will not be seen and if the water is murky or if the water is in agitation, the sun's image will seem to be accordingly affected. In terms of Vedanta, our self-ignorance is the covering (*avarana*) which blankets our mind; our driving desires, negative emotions and misapprehensions are the dirt (*mala*) which make the mind murky; our habitual and fevered mental activity is the agitation (*vikshepa*) which disturbs our mental peace and stillness. We have to remove ignorance through Vedanta's knowledge; we have to free our mind of compulsive likes, dislikes and undesirable emotions through a life focused on duty rather than on personal pleasure and recognition (*karma yoga*); we have to bring tranquility to our mind by regular worship and devotion (*upasana*).[83] Only then does the mind become capable of reflecting pure and conscious existence without any impediment or distortion. As the famous Sufi saint Sheikh

---

82 Katha Upanishad (2.1.11): *manasaivedamaptavyam.*

83 There are some traditions which seek to still the mind by using practices of intense meditation but these are not permanent solutions in themselves, unless one's goal is to go through life in a state of suspended animation.

Abdulla Ansari (also known as Pir-e-Herat) said, *"The noblest inspiration and awareness comes suddenly, but only to he whose mind is tuned to receive it"*. Once the mind is properly prepared, there is no specific effort required for this reflection to occur because it happens on its own; the effort required is only in mental preparation.

Therefore, it is said that the same mind is both the cause of our notion of bondage as well as of liberation; pure consciousness is not evident in an unprepared mind and leads to a false sense of limitation, but it becomes self-evident in a prepared mind, without needing any other sensory or intellectual process, and 'restores' our natural freedom which was only apparently lost. In some ways, our mind can be compared to a thief; by being carefully watched, the thief does not give us anything new but our attention stops him from robbing us.

Another related question which often occurs in the context of the mind is that if, as Vedanta says, our reality is not our body and mind then why be concerned with them at all? The answer is that to get to our reality, we have to go beyond both the body and the mind; however, an unhealthy body and mind will not permit us to transcend them because they will continuously demand our attention by their aches, wants and complaints.

It is in order to develop a healthy body-mind complex that the *asanas, pranayam* and *dhyana* of yoga, the tenets of *dharma* and the attitude of *karma yoga* form such an important and integral part of the pursuit of Vedanta. Most of us also first need to experience the world and achieve a degree of success in our usual goals. This is because, barring an exceptional few who seem to be born with discrimination and dispassion, we need to accumulate a range and depth of experiences before we are able to see their limitations. Similarly, success needs to be tasted and a healthy ego needs to develop before we can begin the work of sublimating that ego. However, of all these matters, it is dharma and the associated devotion to Ishwara which play a pivotal role in the pursuit of Vedanta.

Dharma and Ishwara

We find Vedanta unsettling because the force of our desires do not permit us to go beyond the obvious multiplicity of the world which we continuously experience.

Our desires draw a lot of their force from wrong ways of life and wrong attitudes. Dharma helps us here by providing injunctions and suggestions which encourage us to lead a life not ruled by personal subjectivity; the life-style suggested by dharma also softens the ego and promotes attitudes such as compassion, humility and veneration of knowledge which are required for Vedanta.

However, even after our emotions, desires and egos are processed by a life of balance and rectitude, we yet continue to perceive the multiplicity of the world. Ishwara, as the creator of everything, comes in here to minimise the effects of this apparent multiplicity on our minds. Just as we feel closer to our siblings compared to other people because of common parents, a common creator for all of us reduces our sense of separation with others. Because Ishwara is the creator of not only human beings but of all the animate and inanimate objects in creation, nothing is separated from Ishwara; therefore, everything (including animals, trees and rivers) is related to us and deserves our respect and consideration. Finally, when Ishwara is understood not only as the material substance of the world but also as its inherent natural laws, such understanding leads to a reduction of pride, guilt, anger and enmity; this is because it now becomes clear that nothing (good or bad) can happen except in accordance with the order which is Ishwara.

Without dharma and Ishwara in our lives, our preparation for Vedanta is not complete and it becomes almost impossible for our driven and divided minds to directly apprehend our intrinsic wholeness which is what Vedanta wants to show us. Of course, once the vision of Vedanta is fully imbibed then Ishwara loses some of his meaning because he is now understood as the apparent cause of a dream-like creation; however, at the level of daily living and emotions, Ishwara yet always continues to be beneficial.

Deliverance

How does the wisdom of Vedanta benefit us? Let us remind ourselves of the problem which makes us explore Vedanta in the first place. Our basic problem is one of ignorance. Ignorance of the real nature of our self makes us assume the natural limitations of our body and mind to be our own. Identification with these limitations creates in us a sense of inadequacy and wanting. Tremendous attempts are then made by us in all directions – pleasures, possessions, relationships, attainments and so on – to feel adequate.[84]

However, till our dying day, these attempts to become adequate and acceptable in our own perception, never fully succeed – our bodies and minds continue to remain limited by their very nature. (Attempts to find acceptance and approval from other people also do not succeed because once we find our own selves to be unacceptable, we find other people to be equally unacceptable. This happens both because we see their own body-mind limitations and also because it seems good for our own mental health to find defects in others. So trying to find approval from those whom we don't fully approve of and who, in turn, don't fully approve of us, does not take us too far.)

When Vedanta works for us and we discover ourselves to be naturally full and complete, all our desires lose their motive force; we are no more dependent on the fulfilment of desires because we are now at one with our very own nature which is already full. All our fears (including those of loss of life, wealth, fame and companionships), which are the flip-side of our desires, also lose their sting. All our questions and doubts about the meaning of our lives and the nature of our world lose their relevance. We are at peace not only with our present but also with the past and the future. As Sextus the Pythagorean (ca 300 BCE) said, "*A wise man is always similar to himself*" and a true vedantin has complete self-acceptance, without any lingering doubts or reservations.

---

84 Self-ignorance, because of which we conclude that we are small and vulnerable, leads to desires targeted at overcoming these limitations and then to actions to fulfil such desires. This triad of ignorance, desires and actions is termed *avidya kama karma* in Sanskrit.

Of course, even after self-knowledge, our bodies and minds continue and many of their past propensities remain: our joints still ache in winter, we still prefer tea over coffee and our conversational disapproval of a political party's agenda may remain intact. However, all these things happen at the surface, without affecting the basic fullness and equilibrium we have discovered. Negative emotions in response to an appropriate situation can also arise in a person who has discovered his truth: a flash of anger upon seeing someone being brutally victimised, natural regret upon an untimely death or a touch of annoyance with deliberate tardiness or carelessness. But these are now spontaneous outcomes which come up but do not get extended in time (in the form of brooding, sulking, and feeling hostile, guilty or victimised).

Things continue to happen in and around us but, because our falsely limited "I" sense has vanished, happenings cannot draw extra fuel from our personality. We become uninvolved witnesses to events around our own bodies and minds as much as we are witnesses to happenings around unconnected things. Because our bodies and minds are programmed to protect themselves, we will still look both ways before we cross a road but the prospect of ultimate and inevitable death holds no fear; we will instinctively try to keep ourselves better informed but will remain steady in the knowledge that our reality is pure awareness which makes even our ignorance known to us; we will not go out of our way to court unpleasant circumstances but will never judge ourselves as lacking or inadequate when things are not in line with our preferences.

The knowledge that everything is in and of one limitless, changeless, conscious existence, makes us care-free and yet not callous. While we now have no driving agenda of our own, we see others suffering needlessly from an illegitimate problem; these others are not essentially different from us because we all are manifestations within one truth. Our sense of connectedness and empathy makes us naturally reach out and help in whichever way we can. Very often, this flow of help emerges in the form of teaching because only Vedanta's knowledge can solve the human problem at its fundamental level. Vedanta, despite its focus on self-knowledge, does not divide and isolate but brings out life's unity and inter-relatedness, by showing that there is only one self which is the self of all.

When the knowledge of Vedanta blesses us with its full vision, the freedom (called *moksha*) which we obtain is so complete that we are free to enjoy the use of our limited bodies and minds as they live out their destiny; just as a blind-fold put on during the game of blind man's bluff has no real impact on the player, the limitations of our physical and mental attributes do not affect us where it matters. Our lives, our personalities, our agendas and our achievements as well as our failures no longer need to be taken so grimly or with so much self-importance. Living becomes a privilege and a game; we can see and participate in its ups and downs without the compelling need to bend it and twist it to fall in line with any personal notions. Without these pressures, leading an objectively appropriate life and being non-competitive as well as compassionate to others, comes naturally. Thus, not only is the seeker released from his false notions of inadequacy but also those around him benefit from his wisdom, compassion and example.

Finally

The teachings of Vedanta, even in their peripheral and initial aspects are very valuable and go a long way in answering some of our questions, reducing many of our internal pressures and giving us hope for the resolution of our constant struggle to be other than what we are. However, no amount of teaching can ensure the abidance of our mind in a state of undisturbed oneness (*akhandakara vritti*), which is the ultimate fruit of Vedanta. To live a life of total peace and contentment, connected with all in a state of love and compassion, needs both time and that 'x'-factor which may be called fortune or grace, in addition to exposure to Vedanta's teachings. We, as individuals, can and should make efforts to cultivate proper values, adopt an appropriate way of living and devote ourselves to the teachings of Vedanta; beyond this we can only hope and pray that the wisdom of Vedanta will bless us by clearing the obstacles in our minds and hearts which appear to keep us away from the only truth, which is ironically never separate from us.

RATIONALITY OR MYSTICISM?

Vedanta is dismissed by some people as being inappropriate for thinking minds because it is considered to be mystical and, therefore, irrational. This conclusion needs to be examined a little further.

Rationality means using reason so that our conclusions are based on due process of thought, validated by logic. Mysticism, on the other hand, is arriving at an understanding of a thing beyond perceptual or intellectual grasp, by direct experience. The ability to reason is undoubtedly our unique gift but this does not mean that we should narrow down our minds to the point where we reject every thing unless it is <u>directly and fully</u> proved by reason. And 'mystical' does not always mean something mysterious or offensive to reason.

A distorted understanding of the terms 'rationality' and 'mysticism' makes it difficult for some of us to be open to Vedanta's teachings. Vedanta's ultimate insight is that there is only one reality which actually exists. It is true that this reality is trans-sensory; this also makes it trans-logical because the starting point of logical processes is sensory data. Therefore, Vedanta cannot provide answers to all our possible questions. However, whatever Vedanta says neither contradicts logic nor goes against our valid experiences. Further, Vedanta's promise has never been to be the grand theory of every thing; it is only meant to provide a remedy for our personal problem of endlessly seeking fulfilment, by helping us to recognise our own inherent wholeness.

It is important to look at this issue squarely because some of us have disdain for things which cannot be made to fit into our ideas of rationality and logic. And I say this out of personal experience, having spent several frustrating years in trying to fit Vedanta into my own notions of reason.

Traditional Texts

The source texts of Vedanta - the Upanishads - do not contain many structured arguments because they are mainly a record of scattered insights by ancient seers (*rishis*), without any attempt to consolidate and defend such insights. These scriptures, called *shruti*, are not always helpful if we are looking for arguments and logic to prove what they say.

The next level of traditional scriptures, called *smriti,* includes the epic poem, the Maharbharata. The Mahabharata contains a section of 700 verses famously known as the Bhagavada Gita, which is one of the primary texts for studying Vedanta. The Gita states great metaphysical truths, but it also does not employ detailed reasoning and a significant part of its content covers lifestyle and attitudinal issues.

One important primary scripture of Vedanta which does give importance to systemization and logic is called the Brahma Sutras; it is a collection of aphorisms written by Badarayana Vyasa and is almost always studied with the aid of a monumental commentary written upon it by Adi Shankaracharya. While this commentary contains intricate arguments based on logic, it is not initially very helpful for a modern student of Vedanta. This is so due to three main reasons.

The first issue here is that the Brahma Sutras and Shankaracharya's commentary assume full knowledge of the contents of all the important Upanishads. However, for someone who is not intimately familiar with individual statements in the Upanishads, the arguments used here (based on such an assumption) are not completely meaningful.

Then, a significant part of the Brahma Sutras and the commentary are addressed to traditionalists who accept the Vedas as the primary means of knowledge in their sphere. With such an orientation, the Brahma Sutras take various important statements in the Upanishads as settled facts and restrict their arguments to showing how only a particular conclusion can fit in and reconcile a variety of such statements.[85] But this does not work if one questions the truth of the Upanishad statements themselves.

---

85 Using this approach, statements in the Upanishads such as 'everything is brahman' (*sarvam khalu idam brahman*) and 'brahman is non-dual' (*ekam advitiyam*) can be used to establish that the perceived world of plurality cannot have absolute reality – only a projected world which is a transient apparition can fit in, once both these statements are accepted as being true.

Finally, while a portion of the Brahma Sutras and the attendant commentary are addressed to people outside the vedic fold, they mainly refute the ancient contentions of Buddhists and Jains and do not deal with the problems of a modern student. A modern student often has a perspective called material realism where perceived physical objects are taken as being absolutely and independently real and where consciousness is considered to be a by-product of physical reality. The contents of the Brahma Sutras provide only limited help for someone with such an orientation.

With this background, let us see how we can approach the issue of Vedanta being considered irrational and therefore not worth exploring. Let us begin by first examining whether it is actually true that we believe things only when they are fully proved.

Iron-clad Proof

The fact is that we accept many things without full proof. The well-known American philosopher, Thomas Nagel, gives an example of this when he points out that we cannot actually prove that other people's senses provide them with an experience identical to that provided by our own senses, even though we regularly assume that this is so. For instance, it is not possible to prove that the input of your ears provide you with what I call a sound experience – perhaps your brain interprets the electrical signals from your ears so that it creates in your mind what for me would be an experience of sight. Even though this sounds absurd, it need not be that far-fetched; after all, bats 'see' by processing reflections of sound.

If one wants to take this even further, there is no way of completely disproving the possibility that our individual brain is the only thing in creation and that the whole world is just its projection. Maybe, what we call our real or waking-world is just like a very long dream which does not exist outside of us. One may intuitively feel and say that this is nonsense but can one actually prove that such a sceptical view of reality (called *solipsism*) is wrong?

The point of saying all this is not to suggest that sensory experiences for different individuals are actually different or that all that exists is a single brain; the limited point here is that everything cannot be and need not be completely proved to its last degree.

Let us now move away from these extreme scenarios and go to one of the more common ways in which we use logic. This logical process is called induction and it involves using specific facts to arrive at a general conclusion. So, if you have always chosen to drink white wine on the past several occasions that you have come to my house, I conclude that you will do this the next time as well and plan accordingly. But my conclusion may not be necessarily true – you may now prefer red wine or you may have stopped drinking wine altogether. Conclusions based on past data only show a strong probability but do not provide conclusive proof: based on such inductive logic, it was once taken as a settled fact that all swans are white, till black swans were first seen in Australia in the 17th century and proved this long-held conclusion to be wrong. Inductive logic can never provide infallible proof but that does not stop us from using it, with practical benefit, in our daily lives.

We also accept some very important generalised conclusions as being self-evident truths, without requiring any proof for their veracity. Such truths, which are not only taken for granted but are also used as a basis for deducing other truths, are called axioms. The ancient Greek mathematician, Euclid, stated 'The whole is greater than the part' as an example of an axiom; another example of an axiom is the common conclusion that a thing cannot be true and false at the same time. Axioms appear to be proven facts only because we define some words in a way which leads us to a given conclusion.

We accept conclusions based on inductive logic and axioms only because they are <u>nearly</u> indubitable or because there is <u>no equally plausible</u> way to explain known facts and experiences. We should bear this in mind as we look at Vedanta's insights: here, too, we should not get too fixated on looking for conclusive proof if there is no other and better explanation for some of the fundamental issues that Vedanta deals with.

Leaving aside logic and axioms, we seem to be happy to accept some things just because they come from a source which we judge as being credible. Thus, most of us accept the 'Big Bang' theory as an explanation for the origin of our universe because it is considered to be scientific. However, this theory starts by saying that the entire universe was compressed into a tiny kernel which suddenly exploded some 15 billion years ago and expanded into our universe. This theory does not explain the crucial point of how that primordial ball (called 'ylem') came into existence and, yet, we seem to be happy with this 'explanation' of creation.

Rationality in Our Lives

Let us now turn towards the basis of our tendency to ask for conclusive proof: our assumption that we are entirely rational beings. If we are always rational then we should be living in a manner which maximises our own welfare and also leave behind a world capable of catering to the happiness of our children and grand-children. But do we regularly do this? The way many of us abuse our bodies and minds (with wrong food or with drink, drugs and superficial amusements) does not show great regard for our own well-being.

And our economic and social systems regularly promote excessive consumption and waste, upsetting the long-term equilibrium of our planet. This becomes evident when one sees some of the most advanced economies of the world actually wasting up to half of the food that they produce or when lauded architects in hot & arid countries design houses with glass walls and rain-showers, leading to mindless over-consumption of electricity and water. While our innovative skills may yet save us from the full consequences of such abuse (or pull us back from what in an aeroplane would be called an irrecoverable spin), such brinkmanship with the only planet we have as home can hardly be classified as being rational.

In a different example, the well-known American economist, Joseph Stiglitz, says that a rational economic system is supposed to reward persons according to the contribution that they make to society. He then points out that our system actually pays more to bankers, whose short-sighted and greedy behaviour has jeopardised global economy on several occasions, than the remuneration paid to Norman Borlaug – a man whose agricultural innovations saved millions of human beings from starvation and who has left behind a legacy equalled by only a few in our entire history.

It is difficult, therefore, to assert that our societies and systems are consistently rational.

In our own, personal lives we end up falling in love with individuals whose ability to truly enhance our lives cannot always stand up to logical scrutiny; we tread softly in the presence of a dead body and handle it with reverential gentleness though pure reason tells us that dead bodies do not hear or feel anything; we chase possessions and experiences as if they will bring us lasting fulfilment despite our personal experience (often of several decades) to the contrary; we encourage our children to undergo narrow education which will generate quick monetary returns, in the completely unreasonable hope that money will somehow bring them peace and fulfilment even though it did not do so for us; we often firmly believe that our personal religion or philosophy has the monopoly on truth. And, as Yudhishtira said in the Mahabharata, the greatest wonder in the world is that though human-beings know that everyone dies, all live as if there is no death for them personally!

All this should make us pause before confidently asserting that we are entirely rational and logical in all aspects of life.

Brahman Can Never Be a Known Object

Let us now change tracks and look at a basic reason why, when it comes to the great truth postulated by Vedanta, it is impossible to get the kind of proof we can get in other areas. Vedanta says that behind the apparent multiplicity of seen objects, there is only one common reality which is brahman. According to Vedanta, brahman is the only thing which actually exists and everything else which seems to exist is only a temporary form without substance. In terms of a simile, brahman is like water while individual things in the world are like waves, spray, surf and foam: all nothing but water in their essential nature. Now, if an individual wave wanted to understand water, it would not be able do this because to understand something you have to have a knower-known relationship with it. But how can the wave stand separate from water and become its knower? The wave is nothing but water through and through; it is not possible for it to distance itself from water so that water becomes an object capable of making itself known to the wave.

Similarly, we as individuals can never actually know brahman as a separate object if brahman is the reality of everything including ourselves. And in this sense it can be called mystical because it is finally available to us only as a direct experience of our own reality, and not as a sensory or conceptual object. Brahman is actually our own being which becomes self-evident once we have shed wrong ideas about ourselves.

There Is Supporting Logic

While Vedanta cannot make brahman available for us to know in the usual sense of knowing, it does not ask us to take its insight purely on faith. Vedanta uses our own experiences and reasoning to lead us to the conclusion that both atma and brahman are unchanging, unlimited and conscious. Vedanta then says that they are not actually two different things which happen to have the same characteristics but one and the same thing which merely appears to be divided as subject and objects. There is some logical justification to this great unity brought out by Vedanta. If atma and brahman are both deduced to be limitless then two limitless or boundless things are not possible by definition – for a second thing to exist independently, it would have to be outside the boundary of the first thing but then, because of something else being outside its limits, the first thing would stop being limitless.

Also, there is a well-established principle of thinking (known as Occam's razor) which says that if two explanations are equally possible in a given situation, then the least complicated explanation (or the explanation involving the least number of entities) should be chosen. It is simpler and more convincing to accept one self-evident existence because more than one real thing would generate a greater need to find the creator of this multiplicity (such a creator not having been seen by us so far) as well as to discover the purpose behind his creation (for which we have yet to find discernible meaning).

All this supports Vedanta's insight of only one and undifferentiated existence which only appears as multiplicity without undergoing any real changes itself; only this explanation which declares the world to be *mithya* (or without primary reality) solves the problem of making sense of the world and its maker – by making the problem itself to be of no real consequence.

How Was the Single Reality Created?

How did this only reality come into being? As this reality is conscious and we ourselves are nothing other than that consciousness, we can never answer this question, just as a figure in our dream can never understand its own source. However, the existence of consciousness cannot be denied because we experience ourselves as conscious beings; what can be denied is the existence of any other reality because this will raise more questions than it answers.

Another thing which we should bear in mind as we ask about the cause of brahman is that our question itself may contain an invalid assumption. If, for instance, an 'yes' or 'no' answer was required from us to the question, *"Have you stopped beating your wife?"*, we would have difficulty with either one of these answers because the framing of the question itself is defective. When we ask a question about brahman's cause, we are assuming that time, space and the cause-effect framework which apply in the created world will also apply to brahman, the very basis of creation. However, there is no justification for such an assumption and, without this assumption, the question itself does not stand.

What If Vedanta Is Wrong?

But despite all that has been said so far, it is very difficult for us to accept that the entire world is a mere appearance or dream-like, without any intrinsic reality. After all, a dream is personal and internal to us; it is dependent on us and does not really affect us. The world, on the other hand, is experienced by us as being independent and very capable of affecting us. These are real and serious issues which need convincing answers. Advanced texts of Vedanta[86] do go into these questions in great detail but it is not appropriate in this introductory book to consider their lengthy (and, at time, torturous) arguments and counter-arguments. Here, we will restrict ourselves to a limited aspect of this issue: if Vedanta's key insight is not true but just a clever idea put forward without any real basis then we should have a better alternative explanation for our lives and the world.

And the most obvious alternate view we have is to take the world and ourselves as real: we are real individuals who have to extract maximum joy from the real world which confronts us in the form of a multitude of real living and non-living objects. The most comfortable thing about such a view, of course, is that it tallies with our experience. But such a 'real' world has huge questions and insoluble problems built into it, even if we choose to gloss over them in our day-to-day lives. Let us look at some major ones.

Creator

A real creation must have a creator because our common-sense and experience demand such a creator. As we saw a little earlier, the 'big bang' theory of science is not of help here because it does not explain the source of the ball of compressed matter or energy with which it starts and nor does it explain the source of intelligent natural laws which have been in operation since the beginning of the universe. Evolution by natural selection is restricted to living things and it, too, does not explain the source of the initial material or of the intelligent order built into the evolutionary process itself. The god of religions, accepted by many as the creator, is based on faith and this cannot be called an explanation; and, in any case, such a god leads to a host of other questions such as the source of materials needed for creation and the reason for the pain & evil in it.

A more advanced view within Hinduism tries to deal with these

---

86 Such as the Mandukya Upanishad along with Gaudpada's *karika* and Shankara's *bhashya*.

problems by holding out god as the combined material and intelligent cause of the universe; but this then leads to questions about the real nature of such a god who must necessarily lose his special attributes if he himself becomes the trouble-prone and transitory things of the world. Thus, one major problem with our idea of a real world is our inability to explain its creation in a credible manner.

Reality

Leaving aside questions surrounding the world's creator, let us look at what we mean when we say the world is real. What constitutes 'real'? We consider a dream to be unreal, even though we experience it as being completely real while it lasts. Why? Because it lasts for a short time. On the other hand, we see our lives as real because they last for many decades. But this is not an objective reason - we are just using an arbitrary time-period to determine reality. And of course time itself is not always objective – we can have somebody experience years of his life during a few minutes of his dream and, even in our waking state, time flies in a pleasant situation but crawls in an unpleasant one.

Then, another critical feature of reality or the truth is its consistency. Therefore, we call a man who keeps on changing his word as being untrue; or, to take a different instance, we know that heat is not the real property of water because, unlike wetness, it does not subsist – hot water loses its warmth even if it is kept in an insulated flask. Just as water never loses its wetness because wetness is its true property, a thing should not change or lose its real characteristics at any time (past, present or the future). If existence is the real property of things, they should retain unchanging existence. But nothing in this world is constant or consistent over a length of time; things do not exist before they come into being, they undergoe continuous changes in the short period that they remain in existence and finally disappear into permanent oblivion. Therefore, nothing we know can be called real in its strict sense.

One other vital test we apply to objects we call real is their substantiality. Thus, we classify our own image in a mirror as unreal because that image has no substance – if we reach out to touch that image, all that we will actually touch will be the mirror. Now let us apply this test to an object like a pot which we consider to be real. Does the pot we see really exist? The pot has no substance of its own – its weight and feel is that of clay and, if clay is removed, this pot will also vanish. Thus, within this example, the real substance is clay and not the pot. 'Pot' is only a name given to an insubstantial and temporary form, based upon utility and convention. And the substance of the pot - clay - itself has no intrinsic 'potness', which is why it can also become a saucer.

Then where did this pot come from? Vedanta says there is no real pot - it is just an idea and it only appears for someone who has that idea already loaded on to his mind. And this applies to all objects and can be extended backwards to their constituents indefinitely. Thus our shirt is an idea upon the reality of fabric; but the reality of fabric is yarn and the reality of yarn is fibres and so on. This makes all 'real' objects into non-substantial ideas which can be reduced to a deeper and a yet deeper cause without reaching a fundamentally real substance.

One final issue with our idea of reality is that if we ourselves and the objects we behold are real then we should be able to logically establish the separation between ourselves and these objects; we must be able to point out the boundary where we, the subjects, come to an end and a separate object begins. Where is our boundary as a subject? Is our body, bounded by our skin, that boundary? But the body and skin are known to us – they are objects in our perception. What we are looking for is our own boundary – the boundary of us as subjects. But all we can ever find are objects and never the subject. And without a well-defined subject, it is difficult to assert that the subject and objects are actually the independent realities which they appear to be.

Happiness

If the world is real as it appears to be, we will also have to accept that some of our most fundamental problems and questions have no real answers. We will never find convincing reasons for some peoples' unfortunate fates or discover the real purpose of our lives. We will never solve the mystery of our creator and his creation. And we will never come to the end of our compelling but endless search for happiness. As we know, manipulating the world to extract happiness does not always work and, even when it does, such happiness does not last. Faith in god and religion may provide respite but it is not unshakeable and it also does not resolve our sense of being insignificant, ignorant and mortal. Saying that death is our final destination and we should systematically make merry before it catches up with us, leads to number of disturbing physical and psychological issues.

Vedanta's vision of *advaita* or a singular wholeness does not solve all these problems at the level at which they arise; instead, it dissolves them by raising our perspective so that we stop taking our individuality and the world to be independently real. Our questions then cease to be the critical matters which they appear to be from the stand-point of duality.

Credible Sources

A completely different type of reasoning which should make us pause before dismissing Vedanta's views as unfounded is connected with Vedanta's source. Vedanta comes to us from mankind's oldest scriptures which are not ascribed to any one person who could be propagating his own fancies. Further, the earlier parts of the Vedas which deal with more conventional things contain remarkable facts which were 'discovered' by modern science much after the Vedas were compiled. For instance, the Krishna Yajur Veda clearly talks about the sun's light comprising of seven separate wave-bands represented by its chariot of seven horses. That visible light can be refracted into a spectrum of seven colours was first recorded in modern science by Isaac Newton only in the 17th century CE. Even more surprisingly, the same Veda goes on to talk about an eighth band of light which is available only in the high mountains and is harmful to us – now known to us as UV radiation. In a similar vein, other ancient scriptures use time-space as a single noun (*deshakala*) much before Einstein pronounced these concepts as being inter-related, by calling them a 'time-space continuum'; the planet Jupiter which is now known to be the biggest and heaviest of all planets has always been called *Guru* meaning 'heavy'. None of this in any way proves Vedanta's insights; it only makes us pause to think whether these ancient scriptures can be readily judged as being wrong in their most vital insight.

Apart from the Vedas, if one reads the works of Shankaracharya, his brilliance, his conviction and his penetrating analysis ring with truth. This is supported in more recent times by the statements of sages like Ramana Maharishi and Nisargadatta Maharaj; the example of their own lives and the testimony of those who actually met these sages leave no doubt that they experienced the great wholeness which is at the heart of Vedanta. Such evidence cannot be readily ignored.

Proof of the Pudding

Finally, there are many things in our lives which need to be actually experienced by us before they make sense. If, for instance, someone came to us and said that he was in possession of a few strands of metal using which he could stop time and also resolve all our desires, we would either label him a rogue or pity him for his deranged mind. However, when we go to a music concert and a Ravi Shankar plucks the metal strings of his sitar to produce a haunting Raga Yaman, time does stand still for those of us for whom this music strikes a personal chord and our desires do stop bothering us for the time being. If we have never been affected by sublime music, it may be impossible to understand how a succession of sounds in specific frequencies can sublate our minds, where the sense of time and our desires reside. Music is not only notes, octaves and the structure of a raga; the real heart of music is the fusing of the listener with that music. This is not something which can be analysed or interpreted by using our reason. Similarly, Vedanta does not stop at the limits of knowledge set by our intellects but goes beyond to re-connect us with our natural integrity and wholeness.[87]

87 It needs to be clarified here that the consequences of Vedanta are very different from the consequences of being lost in music or meditation. Such experiences are temporary states of 'no mind' where our individuality is absent and where we cannot undertake any other mental or physical activity. Vedanta does not seek to shut down our mind but only to change our understanding so that physical and mental events lose their ability to disturb us.

Ultimately, as the old saying goes, the proof of the pudding lies in the eating. In this context, a contemporary teacher of Vedanta tells a story of a blind man who underwent a newly developed surgical procedure for restoring his sight. When his bandages were about to be removed after the surgery, he stops his doctors from doing so unless they can confirm that he will definitely be able to see; this is because, in case surgery had not worked, he did not want to face the disappointment of finding that he is still blind. But the only real proof of our eye-sight is in our own seeing – no one else's testimony or any form of reasoning can prove that we can see. And if one decides not to open one's eyes till full proof is available, the only consequence will be that one will continue to remain blind.

We all try to arrive at our goal of unbroken happiness by accepting duality as real and then manipulating it to serve our agenda. Some of us come to the conclusion that this does not work for us fully or permanently and that we are not willing to live with half-hearted and temporary solutions. At this stage Vedanta comes along to say that there is a solution, that this solution is knowledge-based and that Vedanta is a unique and independent means for this knowledge. A specific means of knowledge can only prove its efficacy by being actually employed in its own sphere; we know our eyes work only if we open them and they bring us knowledge of colours and forms. In the same manner, Vedanta needs to be actually employed by us before passing any judgement based on conjecture.

Why Don't More People Take to Vedanta?

If Vedanta is so clear and beneficial, it should lead to many more people embracing it. But this is not so today and nor was it so in the past. Vedanta draws relatively few people towards it for a number of reasons. To begin with, a person has to accept that the world cannot bring the total and permanent happiness that one is seeking. He also has to believe that there is a real solution to this problem which can be addressed by Vedanta's wisdom. However, most people are not disillusioned even though all their experiences of joy have been limited and transitory; many make do with their lives of alternating pleasure and pain in the belief that there can be no other life; even those looking for a solution find it difficult to give Vedanta a fair chance by according it initial faith.

A very important requirement of Vedanta is a proper style of life with appropriate conduct and attitudes; many are not willing to put enough effort in this direction or deny themselves temporary pleasures and security, often obtained in manner not consistent with Vedanta's requirements. Many others are scared of giving Vedanta a proper trial: scared to face the possibility that years of effort in their lives so far may have been misdirected, scared of alienation from friends and family. Finally, the highest truths of Vedanta are radical, subtle and intuitive; it is not surprising that we have difficulty in imbibing wisdom which seeks to obliterate the apparently fundamental difference between the observer and what he observes.

But all these difficulties can be gradually overcome if we pursue Vedanta with patience, diligence and initial faith along with the blessing of having a good teacher. Also, the great advantage of Vedanta is that even if we are not fully eligible and even if we do not find the perfect teacher, it yet offers a lot of beneficial insights in its initial content. Finally, the beauty and strength of the Hindu tradition is the number of options it offers to help us; if Vedanta and its extraordinary vision of a singular reality do not work for us, there are other view-points such as *visisht advaita* and *dvaita* which are less demanding because they accept duality and theism to a smaller or larger extent. While these approaches do not solve the fundamental problem which Vedanta does, they yet make our lives more balanced and rewarding. But whichever route we choose to personally follow, we should not jump to hasty conclusions about the lack of rationality in Vedanta which, in fact, is one of the most rigorously developed knowledge-based traditions in the world.

WHAT MAKES VEDANTA UNIQUE?

Vedanta is very different from any religion or philosophy in vital aspects and this is what makes it so rewarding. The key insights of Vedanta are similar to the vision of other bodies of wisdom such as Taoism, Sufism and some facets of Christianity. These streams of thought also speak of a single ground reality (the brahman of Vedanta) and they often do this in language which is strikingly similar to that used in the Upanishads.[88] Despite this commonality, Vedanta remains very different from all of these.

In the Mainstream

Vedanta in India has been in the mainstream of the country's culture and its vision of unity has had a deep and lasting impact on society's attitudes and customs. For instance, it is because of the vision of Vedanta that most people in India, even now, will avoid touching money or books with their feet and will bow to another person in reverential greeting with folded hands (namaste) – divinity is seen everywhere because nothing is considered to be separate from God. In other cultures, such appreciation of non-duality has been restricted to an outside fringe of visionaries who have often been looked upon as heretics; many of them, such as the Sufi saint Mansoor Hallaj[89] and the Christian mystic Meister Eckhart, have been persecuted for daring to speak of a great oneness. On the other hand, because of the wide-spread acceptance of a unity behind all apparent diversity, traditional Hindu culture has largely remained tolerant, with the ability to accept and assimilate many different influences. It has also kept this culture free of proselytizing zeal and provided resilience in adverse circumstances.

Another very significant outcome of Vedanta's vision of non-duality or oneness has been the resulting attitude to all elements

---

88 Some aspects of Buddhism, especially the mahayana branch, also share a similar flavour but this is not surprising given that Buddhism was born and brought up in vedic India.

89 He famously said 'an-ul haq' meaning 'I am him' and was executed for this great insight of oneness with God, which was considered blasphemous by conformist Muslims.

of creation, including the non-human. The Abrahamic faiths, for instance, consider only human beings to be made in God's image and treat the rest of the world (animals, plants, water, air and minerals) as being made for our exploitation. In the vision of Vedanta, on the other hand, nothing is separate from Ishwara who pervades every single thing as both its material and intelligent cause. Without getting into the rationale behind this, there is no doubt that such an understanding obliterates any essential difference between things in the world. People are, of course, superficially different from each other and they need to make use of nature's resources for their existence and development. But the vision of inter-connected oneness does provide for mutual consideration and dignity in human inter-actions as well as for gratitude and moderation when making use of natural bounty.

Further, Vedanta's insight that peace and fulfilment are every one's natural state reduces emphasis on escalating consumption which is often but wrongly considered to be the the only path to happiness. While the effect of this wisdom may be waning fast in India today, it was very apparent in history when this culture found no need to colonise and exploit other countries despite having dominant economic power.[90] And we can still see its effects in a persisting tendency to moderate consumption and avoid waste.[91] The fallacy that growing consumption always represents progress is only now becoming clear to a world which is facing the real costs and consequences of over-consumption and the mindless exploitation of nature.

No Cult Figure

Most philosophical streams of thought, especially those related to a religion, are based up on the views of an individual proponent who becomes a sacred cult-figure for that particular tradition. In contrast, Vedanta is not founded upon the words of any one person, even though many of its teachers are respected and even worshipped; the source of this wisdom is acknowledged to be the

90 From the days of the Mauryan empire to the time of Akbar, India's GDP ranged between 33% and 20% of the world's total GDP.

91 In economic terms, this attitude of moderation becomes evident in a remarkably high ratio of national savings to national income, even now.

Vedas, which do not owe their existence to any identified person. Vedanta, therefore, does not have the belief-based dogmatism which is more common in traditions relying on the words of a single human being.

No Devil or Satan

Most major world religions have a concept of a powerful devil or Satan, a dark force which is constantly pitted against the divine goodness of God. The Hindu religion also talks of good and evil but the *asuras* and *rakshasahs* of Hindu mythology are never shown as being close to Ishwara in terms of their power. And, at the philosophical level, Vedanta refutes any fundamental duality and holds that everything is just a manifestation of one boundless and changeless consciousness; good and bad or sin and salvation are, therefore, mere notions at a secondary level, with no basic consequence. Because of this vision Vedanta does not stop at preaching the virtues of goodness but goes on to a more elevated perspective where a fundamental wholeness eclipses the importance of all polarities, including good and bad. Vedanta, of course, recognises the importance of goodness but only as a means of gaining such a perspective and not as an end in itself.

No Postponement of Solution

Some major cultures have a concept of 'original sin' which apparently taints all of us from birth and from which we are supposed to need salvation by divine intervention in the hereinafter. In Vedanta's view, our problems of limitations and bondage appear only because of wrong understanding and their solution lies in proper knowledge which will show us the fullness and freedom that are already ours, here and now. We do not have to wait for a messiah and death to find bliss in heaven; we only need to correct our wrong thinking to find the final solution right away. The immediacy of the solution by knowledge offered by Vedanta is unique.

Insights into the Human Mind

Vedanta fully confronts the realities of our minds and its teachings cover not only with pure knowledge but also practical ways to deal with troublesome aspects of our egos and emotions. Vedanta's deep understanding of our mental make-up comes out in several of its teachings.

Personal Happiness is the Goal

Unlike Vedanta, there seems to be no traditional teaching in other cultures which unequivocally proclaims that whatever we do is for the sake of our own selves.[92] This may sound cynical or false because we like to believe that we undertake 'selfless' work such as making sacrifices for our families, giving to charities and contributing our efforts to public causes. However, the fact is that we do all of this only because we like ourselves when doing what we believe in. In all that we do, our motivation is the same: we want to feel good.[93] There is, of course, a difference in the make-up of a person who feels good in doing self-centred things as against someone who draws fulfilment from service to others; yet, both these types of people are seeking the same sense of personal fulfilment, a 'feel good' within themselves. Only Vedanta states this honestly and explicitly and, by doing this, helps us on our way to a more fundamental solution to the problem of finding happiness, beyond remaining mere 'do-gooders'.

Three Primary Desires

Another area of our minds where Vedanta brings in unique insight is when it states that all our desires have their roots in just three basic urges: to remain in existence, to be fully aware and to experience fullness.[94] Our wanting to be alive is, of course, our most primeval drive. However, just being alive is not enough because we want to be alive not in a coma but with awareness; this is expressed in our daily need to always know and to be kept informed – we avidly wait for the 9 O'clock news, try to ferret out secrets or take art appreciation classes. But even awareful existence is not enough for us without an experience of fullness, which is more commonly described as being happy. We want to

---

92 *atmanastu kamaya sarvam priyam bhavati* - - - - - Brihadaranyaka Upanishad.

93 At times, some of these activities help to fill up our time or create a certain public image of ourselves which, in turn, makes us feel good.

94 *Sat, chit* and *ananda*.

be happy in all time periods, in all locations and in all situations. By summarizing the multitude of our desires and attendant actions under just these three basic urges, Vedanta makes it much easier to see that they can never be properly addressed. These three underlying wants can be fully satisfied only when we become immortal, all-knowing and limitlessly happy but our usual efforts will never take us to such a state. This understanding is critical if we are to turn to a profoundly different solution which Vedanta offers.

Happiness Comes from Within

Yet another exceptional revelation of Vedanta challenges our common belief that happiness comes from possessions, attainment, experiences, relationships and many other things outside of us. Vedanta tells us that the actual locus of happiness is within us; this is evident in situations where we experience happiness without obtaining anything or resolving any need, such as when confronted with the magnificence of nature or in the company of a delightful infant. We, of course, also experience happiness when we take delivery of a much wanted car or when someone whose approval we crave responds appropriately; it, therefore, seems that this happiness comes from the car or from the other person. Vedanta, however, explains that desire for a particular object or for someone's approval first causes waves of turbulence in the mind which subside when that specific desire is met. What happens when a desire is fulfilled is not the import of happiness from outside but only that our inherent fullness becomes apparent because it is now not obstructed by the agitations of a wanting mind. Being struck by nature's magnificence or getting absorbed in a child also leads to an abeyance of mental movements and the consequent unimpaired experience of our already fulfilled reality. Unfortunately, these experiences of fullness are temporary because our mind soon picks up another desire and again breaks our peaceful stillness. This startling revelation leads us to the conclusion that we do not really need anything outside of us to be happy. Such insight is critical and immensely useful because it invites us to handle our minds better and also to get to know our own true nature, instead of constantly chasing external sources which can provide only fleeting experiences of happiness.

Dharma and Karma Yoga

Vedanta also incorporates wise ways of processing our emotions and our personalities into its teachings. The background to the pursuit of Vedanta is a life of dharma which emphasises duties over rights, promotes ethical living and elevates devotion and worship to a central place in daily life; it also contains mechanisms designed to nurture our psychological needs while providing for sublimation of their excesses. Vedanta itself holds out *karma-yoga* as a way of life for a serious seeker. Vedanta's teachings here make it clear that the outcome of our actions is affected by a whole lot of factors beyond our own actions; they also tell us that the personal enjoyment of the fruits of one's actions can never be a valid goal for a true seeker of the freedom promised by Vedanta. Both these teachings are meant to tone down emotional swings and reduce the role of our egos. This entire approach is based upon the clear understanding that emotions, desires, egos and habits cannot be dealt with by the use of rationality and will-power alone but need gradual refinement by mechanisms built into our daily lives.

Teaching Methods

Another remarkable feature about Vedanta is a superbly-structured teaching methodology which has evolved over the ages. While Vedanta's insights are shared by other cultures, Vedanta's teaching methods put it on a different plane in terms of its ability to transfer wisdom to qualified seekers. The basic teaching method of Vedanta is to disclose its more radical truths only gradually, instead of knocking off all the props of a student's beliefs and notions in one go. Further, Vedanta divides its teaching process into three distinct phases which makes it easier for us to assimilate its wisdom into our daily lives. Finally, unlike many other cultures, Vedanta recognises that the words of its scriptures have to be skillfully wielded by a teacher who is not only familiar with their contents but also with tried and tested teaching techniques and, most important, who himself lives in accord with the truth he is teaching. The crucial role given to a personal teacher in this tradition is one of the reasons why the teachings of Vedanta continue to remain vibrant and relevant, despite the passage of centuries.

God or Ishwara

Because most of us need God to provide an initial explanation for the universe as well as to provide an altar for devotion, Vedanta goes along with the concept of God but in a remarkably different and graded manner. The vedic religion first offers a whole host of divine beings representing nature and its forces such as the sun, the moon, rivers, trees, fire and wind. At the next level, divinity is condensed into the three primary aspects of the universe which are creation, sustenance and dissolution; each of these aspects is represented in figurative form as Brahma (the creator), Vishnu (the preserver) and Mahesh (the dissolver) so that they can be placed on an altar.

Vedanta then goes further and, for a more evolved seeker, combines all these three aspects into a single reality called *Ishwara* who is held out as being the combined material and intelligent cause of the universe. Ishwara is non-separate from everything, just as all individual waves are non-separate from the ocean. Without getting into the arguments for this vision, let us just note here that such understanding dissolves the usual division between the sacred and the secular which is present in most other cultures.

Amazing as this vision of an all-inclusive Ishwara is, Vedanta does not stop here. At its highest level, it brings out the understanding that such a creator has limited relevance when the world itself is understood as being without intrinsic reality. This extra-ordinary understanding of Vedanta may seem disturbing and difficult to deal with but it is in keeping with Vedanta's unique and consistent vision of non-duality.

Independent Means of Knowledge

All learning is based on the proper use of valid means of knowledge. All systems of thought accept perception (knowledge brought in by the sense organs) and inference (knowledge brought in by use of mental faculties) as the primary means of knowledge. However, Vedanta is different in that it includes scriptural words also as a valid means of knowledge. Vedanta does not do this out of devotion or blind faith but because the usual means of knowledge like perception and inference, which are operated and used by an individual, cannot be used for obtaining knowledge of the individual himself. When we obtain our usual knowledge, we say "I saw it with my own eyes" or "I have figured it out". Here, there is an "I" who sees or figures but, when it comes to self-knowledge, who will use what means of knowledge to know the "I" itself? This special knowledge is available only from the testimony of scriptures when employed by a properly qualified teacher for the benefit of an eligible student. The analogy used here is of the eyes and a mirror: eyes, which normally cannot be used for seeing themselves, are able to do this with a mirror and the words of Vedanta act like a mirror for obtaining self-knowledge, when used appropriately. Such understanding and use of Vedanta as an independent and authoritative means of knowledge has important bearing on a student's attitude and approach in the process of learning.

Criticism

Vedanta's vision and approach are, of course, not free of criticism. The most important negative issues in the context of Vedanta revolve around its apparent lack of emphasis on morality and humanity, the elitist and condescending attitude in many of its proponents, the deficiencies in logically proving key areas of its vision and the sense of indifference and fatalism which Vedanta is thought to generate.

- There is no doubt that Vedanta's source scriptures do not provide a convenient list of Do's and Don'ts; further, by their emphasis on self-knowledge for solving an individual's problem, they seem to display lack of concern for an individual's obligation to humanity as a whole. Such criticism, which may appear valid when seen in isolation, loses its force when placed in proper context. The fact is that no scripture or teaching can place equal emphasis on all aspects of human life and can only highlight some specific areas which it targets. In the traditional scheme of things, the knowledge of Vedanta was not to be disseminated to any passer-by with cursory interest; it was meant to be carefully unfolded to an *adhikari* or an eligible person equipped with certain qualities of head and heart. An ethical life, evaporation of self-centred drives, compassion for others and disenchantment with usual goals were already assumed to be in place, before a student got to Vedanta's threshold.[95] Because of this, there was no need for vedantic texts to labour this aspect again. Vedanta therefore focuses on self-inquiry, not because ethics and humanity are unimportant but because its intention is to take its students to a different and unexplored realm.

Things have obviously changed since the original scheme of Vedanta was put in place and now a student would be short-sighted and a teacher would be irresponsible if deficient ethics and lack of concern about fellow-beings are left un-addressed. It must also be remembered that while Vedanta does not directly address issues like poverty and disease, it makes for a more caring and peaceful society if its wisdom is properly imbibed and reflected, especially by opinion-makers and role-models.[96]

- Vedanta's breadth of vision, which comes from its

---

95 In this context, it is relevant to note that the very first Brahma Sutra (the Brahma Sutras being an orderly condensation of Vedanta's teachings into 555 cryptic aphorisms) is *athato brahmajignasa* which means 'Now, therefore, the enquiry into brahman'; the 'now' and 'therefore' indicate that before a person approaches Vedanta, he would have already led a life of dharma and accumulated qualities required for the effective pursuit of Vedanta.

96 It should be pointed out here that other societies which display more care and civility often restrict these virtues to their own borders and, that too, in times of security and abundance. Highly civilised societies have no compunctions in supporting economic and political policies which consume irreplaceable natural assets at prodigal rates or prop up repressive regimes in other countries, for their own, short-term interests; their veneer of civilised behavior, even on home grounds, quickly slips when people there have to face occasional shortages or danger.

raised perspective, also becomes a unique problem in the hands of the neophyte and the dogmatic scholar. Because Vedanta's key-stone of *advaita* (or non-duality) admits no distinctions or compartments at its highest level, many Vedantins go around with an elitist air bordering on arrogance, because 'their' Vedanta includes and transcends everything. Further, because Vedanta emphasises knowledge and proper understanding, some students of Vedanta seem to take upon themselves the roles of reformers and saviours for the 'poor' others who are wasting their lives in chasing the bauble of money or are driven by fragile egos and sloppy emotions.

Actually, the tradition of Vedanta is for a proper student to not even discuss what he is learning except with fellow-students or with those who specifically ask out of genuine interest. It is also not in keeping with Vedanta's spirit to believe that its students knows everything better and are infallible. The real spirit and the consequences of Vedanta's teachings are not in becoming supercilious and patronizing but in becoming humble and quiet in the knowledge that the truth is beyond all words, concepts and distinctions. It is only when this true spirit is not imbibed that the world is seen as categorised between 'we, vedantins' and 'others'.

• Vedanta is often seen as a fashionable pastime for the idle rich who form cults around charismatic and extravagant gurus. A few things need to be kept in mind here so that objectivity is not lost. To begin with, Vedanta has been of great benefit to all qualified students irrespective of their backgrounds. So, from Adi Shankara (a poor Brahmin) in the past to Nisargadatta Maharaj (a non-Brahmin *bidi* vendor) in contemporary times, a variety of people have not only found their highest personal good in Vedanta but have also become sources of inspiration and learning for countless others.

Having said this, it must also be said that some human endeavours do require a cultivated mind and unpressured time which may not be readily available to those struggling for survival. But then this is true not only for Vedanta but for fine arts and for pure science as well; however, we value art-forms, support museums and fund scientific research because we know that all disciplines ultimately benefit society at large, even if the benefit comes indirectly and much later. Finally, the badge of Vedanta is undoubtedly misused by some but this is a comment on the general human capacity to be manipulative as well as gullible which is not restricted to Vedanta.

- Vedanta's source texts – the Upanishads – are written in a manner which makes orderly comprehension difficult; in fact, if one tries to read these texts without the guidance of a good teacher, one may be left with disjointed and contradictory ideas and not obtain anything of benefit. Subsequent texts and teachers try and bring order and logic to bear upon this material but, ultimately, the highest reaches of Vedanta cannot be accessed with logic alone. Reliance upon only dialectics to understand why and how an attributeless, unchanging and motionless brahman supports a projection of world of plurality, does not produce answers which are infallible in terms of pure logic. For many of us, this becomes a big stumbling block and we are not able to accept or assimilate Vedanta's vision because all of it cannot be made to follow a series of rational steps.

It requires good guidance, considerable time and a certain mental orientation to overcome this hurdle. It is only then that it begins to get clear that there are logical reasons why all of Vedanta's insights cannot be established by logic, that nothing in its vision contradicts logic and also that other views lead to even greater logical difficulties. Further, once the wisdom of Vedanta begins to take root in a student's mind, the propensity of the mind to throw up and be agitated by its own endless questions is itself reduced as one becomes relaxed and contented in the discovery of one's own, inherent fullness.

The promise of Vedanta is not in finding answers to all possible questions but in finding abiding peace in the face of unanswered questions. Vedanta does not achieve this happy state by stunning our minds or conditioning them to ignore logical questions but by exposing us to the highest truth. In some ways, Vedanta is like the re-assuring walk to the pop-corn machine in the cinema's foyer, after one is frightened by a particularly scary sequence in a movie; the movie's horror story does not change as a result of this walk outside but its scare-value drastically reduces, because of a different perspective.

- Vedanta teaches an inherent wholeness and completeness of everything[97] and also refers to the role of past deeds (*karma*) in our lives, and thus seems to promote inertia and fatalism throughout society. This is a common and serious criticism leveled at Vedanta and apparently validated by apathy exhibited by many sections of Indian society towards inefficiency and corruption as well as indifference to individual human suffering and indignity. To deposit this entire load of real problems at Vedanta's door-step is not quite justified.

Some of these issues have their genesis in an inappropriate style of governance, going back to days of colonial rule. This has then been aggravated with a misplaced ideological emphasis on state management of large swathes of the economy; such experiments, as we now know, have led to similar economic and social problems in socialistic economies round the world, where Vedanta has had no role to play.

Neither Vedanta's vision of oneness nor its reference to the role of past deeds in our lives contains any suggestion that an individual has no discretion over his actions or that no one needs to do anything to improve his personal condition as well as the state of society as a whole.

---

97 For instance, the well-known Ishavasya Upanishad is prefaced by a *shanti mantra* which starts with *purnam adah purnam idam* and thus points out to the intrinsic wholeness of everything, without any exceptions.

What Vedanta encourages is graceful acceptance of the actual results after appropriate action has been taken; it also asks us to move away from personal enjoyment and ego-satisfaction as the primary motivations behind our actions. This, in no way, implies that indifference, fatalism and apathy are appropriate.

Of course, the teachings of Vedanta can be used to justify laziness and exploitation in the hands of those who have not understood its true spirit but then such misuse is possible with almost anything. A life-saving drug can become a fatal weapon in the hands of the wrong person and the benefits of democracy can be nullified by a coterie of conniving politicians; such facts are not indictments of the drug or of democracy but only a sign of their inappropriate usage.

To Sum Up

Despite societal changes and a host of contrary views, Vedanta continues to hold a special place in the history of mankind's highest thoughts. Because of its unique features it provides meaning and freedom to its students around the world; in its home environment it continues to support a framework which moderates the attitude of significant portions of society and provides a surprising level of resilience and tolerance even in difficult situations. With the waning of the importance of traditional values and social structures, with greater emphasis on individual rights and with unfettered options of consumption and anodyne amusements, we today sorely need the balanced and practical wisdom of Vedanta, to nurture us in a way in which only Vedanta can.

THE ELOQUENT NATARAJA

Most ancient Indian artforms are steeped in the vision of Vedanta and depicts something or the other out of its teachings. The Nataraja stands out as an icon which conveys a complex set of Vedantic messages in a very beautiful and effective manner.

Nataraja (literally, the King of Dance) is the name given to a particular form of a dancing Shiva. The Nataraja image reached the zenith of its development between the tenth and twelfth centuries CE, in bronze sculptures of the Chola kingdom in southern India. In the words of the curator of New York's Metropolitan Museum of Art, "*If a single icon had to be chosen to represent the extraordinarily rich and complex cultural heritage of India, the Shiva Nataraja might well be the most remunerative candidate. It is such a brilliant iconographic invention that it comes as close to being a summation of the genius of the Indian people as any single icon can.*" Such a gush of praise for the Nataraja is fully deserved because this artistic form is not only a venerated object of worship, but is also the embodiment of several vital messages that are presented in an exceptionally intelligent and elegant manner.

The Actual Figure

The typical Nataraja is an upright figure with four arms, like many Indian gods who are shown with added arms to symbolise their extraordinary powers. The Nataraja's two upper hands carry a drum and a flame, respectively. His lower right arm makes a protective hand gesture while the other points towards his left leg which is raised off the ground. His right leg is firmly planted on a demonic dwarf, pinning him to the ground. His face is completely serene, almost mask-like. A vertical third eye is etched in the centre of the forehead. The head-gear is elaborate and bears a crescent moon. Locks of hair fly along both sides of his face; one of these locks contains a small, feminine figure. His left ear-lobe is adorned with an intricate round ear-ring but the right one either has a simpler ear-ring or is empty; there is also ornamentation around the neck, waist, arms and legs. There is a cobra entwined around his lower right arm and often there are more snakes on the Nataraja's body. The whole figure is encircled by an arch of flames.

Two different ear-rings, a feminite figure and the crescent moon are clearly visible.

The sculpture is designed on two different vertical planes, which become obvious if the whole figure is looked at sideways. The body of the Nataraja along with his two upper arms and his grounded right leg are all on the inner plane, while the two lower arms and the raised left leg project outwards, forming the second and outer plane. This is significant to note because, as we will see later, it is symbolic of an important message.

The *murti* is on two vertical planes

A Work of Art

The most obvious and secular attraction of the Nataraja is, of course, artistic. Bronze Natarajas have been traditionally made by the lost wax process (*cire perdue* is the often-used French term), which makes each sculpture unique.[98] A well-made Nataraja, in the classical Chola style, exhibits perfect proportions and cohesive fluidity; it balances a sense of power and movement in Shiva's body with a remarkably still face; the figure has finely crafted ornamentation. A good example of a

---

98 In this technique, a fully detailed figure is carved from a block of wax. Because wax is soft and malleable, graceful shapes and intricate designs are possible. The wax statue is then covered with a paste of fine clay which is allowed to harden; further coats of coarser clay paste are layered for strength. Holes and channels are provided in the clay to serve as run-offs for the wax which melts when the hardened mould is heated and to permit the pouring of molten metal into the now hollow mould. After the poured metal solidifies, the clay mould is broken open and the idol is finished by scouring, filing and etching. In this process, because the initial wax sculpture melts and the clay mould is broken, each final sculpture is the only one of its kind.

Nataraja sculpture, especially a sizeable one that has been used in religious ceremonies, has undeniable presence and immediate impact; such sculptures are much sought after by museums and collectors worldwide. However, the Nataraja has a much deeper message than simply its aesthetic beauty.

Religious Idol

As in the case of most traditional art forms, the primary purpose of the Nataraja *murti* (idol) was religious. The very conceptualization of an individual work was preceded by performance of rituals and meditation by the sculptor, seeking divine inspiration. During the sculpting process, the artist led an ordained life of purity and followed rules regarding the composition of materials to be used as well as the proportions, gestures and adornments of the figure.[99]

The deliberately unfinished eyes of the idol were formally completed and 'opened' at the time of its installation in a temple. Upon this sanctification, everyone (including the sculptor himself) no more saw a man-made work, but the live embodiment of Maheshwara (the Great Lord) himself. Whether or not this scheme of things imbued the murti with extraordinary powers is a moot point; what is without doubt is that the common acknowledgement of divinity in such an idol and out-pouring of devotion towards it by people over the years, brought into being a powerful altar of worship for those with the appropriate cultural orientation.[100]

At a raw emotional level, the Nataraja evokes awe in a devotee by the great energy of his dance and by his control over frightening creatures such as the cobra and the dwarf demon; the richness of his ornamentation adds to his majesty. Shiva's limitless power is also exhibited by the moon being a mere bauble for his head-gear. At the same time, the devotee draws comfort from the Lord's remarkably serene face and the benign gesture of his right

---

99 These rules are mainly found in the *silpasara* section of the *agamas*, which are ancient texts dealing with (amongst other things) the process of conceptualisation, construction and worship of different representations of divinity.

100 The most prominent example of a Nataraja as the primary deity in a major temple is at Chidambaram, in the state of Tamil Nadu in southern India.

hand; his left hand, which points to the raised leg, re-assuringly invites the devotee to seek shelter at the mighty Lord's feet.

On A Deeper Plane

On a more interpretive level, the Nataraja contains several important lessons, including the core message of *advaita Vedanta* (the most prominent of the six traditional schools of Indian philosophy).[101] These lessons are reflected in the figure's remarkable iconography.

The Five Elements

One of the preliminary teachings of Vedanta states that the entire universe consists of five fundamental elements, or the *pancha mahabhutas*. These five are reckoned to be space, air, fire, water and earth.[102]

It should be noted here that that the ultimate intention of Vedanta is not to explain the ingredients of creation; it is only to address our initial curiosity that Vedanta offers the pancha mahabhutas as a possible model. The Nataraja faithfully presents these five elements:

- Earth is depicted by the very material of the idol – be it metal or stone.

- Water is represented by the small feminine figure in the Nataraja's flying locks of hair – this figure is the river goddess Ganga.[103]

- Fire is shown by the flame in one hand of the murti, as well as by the flames circling the entire figure.

- Air or wind is indicated by his flying locks of hair.

- Space is rather cleverly implied by the *damaru* – a drum which produces sound. Because sound is only heard

---

101 It needs to be clarified here that the Nataraja, being of much later conception, finds no mention in Vedanta's source scripture, the Vedas.

102 Known as *akasha, vayu, agni, apa* and *prithvi* in Sanskrit.

103 Based on a story of how its torrential waters were first cushioned by Shiva's hair, as this mighty river descended from heaven to earth.

after it is propagated through space (as waves), the drum here becomes a symbol for space.

In order to complete the showing of the entire universe, the crescent moon adorning the Nataraja's head-gear represents all the heavenly bodies.

Cyclic Creation

The Nataraja also displays the cyclic nature of creation which Hindu scriptures present as going through alternating phases of appearance, continuance, and disappearance:[104]

- Creation is conveyed by the creative energy of the dancer's movement. The drum, too, stands for creation; it signifies the sound of the primordial *Om* which, according to the scriptures, marks the beginning of creation.

- The serene face of the Nataraja, his protective hand gesture and his holding of inimical forces in check (symbolised by the demon underfoot), all suggest the orderly and peaceful continuation of the universe; this aspect is further reinforced by the lower left hand of the idol which resembles an elephant's trunk (*gaja hasta mudra*) and thus refers to the elephant-headed god Ganesha,[105] regarded as the remover of obstacles in our lives.

- The flames and the supra-normal third eye[106] stand for destruction.

This simultaneous display of the three states of creation,

104 Known as *shrishti*, *sthiti* and *samhara*. Each of these three phases is associated with an attribute of godhood which, for the purpose of worship, is personified as Brahma, Vishnu and Mahesh.

105 The background to Ganesha's appearance is a characteristically dramatic Shiva story where, in a fit rage, he lops off the head of his own son. Then, to make peace with his anguished wife – Parvati – he brings their dead son back to life by giving him the head of the nearest available living creature, which happened to be a passing elephant.

106 According to a well-known story, an annoyed Shiva reduced Kama (the god of love who had the temerity to disturb Shiva's meditation) to ashes by merely opening his third eye to release rays of destructive energy.

maintenance and dissolution also signifies that they are all part of a single, unified event; the surrounding ring of flames shows that the whole process is an ongoing cycle.

The imagery here also represents both time and timelessness, to tie in with Shiva's description as *kala* as well as *mahakala*. The rhythm of the drum and the dance stands for the beat of ordinary time. However, the drum is held by the Nataraja and the dance is contained within him; so he, as the wielder of time, is himself beyond time.

How to Lead Life

But it is not enough for us to just be a passive part of this cycle and contentedly worship a mysterious higher power; something further is necessary to lead a full life. An important message in this context is conveyed by the two separate vertical planes of the Nataraja murti. The basic idol, with the two upper arms and the leg on the ground, represents our earth-bound life. The advice which the Nataraja provides in relation to our ordinary life is to keep our ego and wrong notions in check; this is conveyed by the firmly pinned down dwarf-demon called Apasmara, who represents our negative qualities. To overcome our baser facets is a very demanding task; this is portrayed by the masterly skill of the Nataraja as he dances while standing on just one leg and, that too, on a writhing demon.

But, while it is important as well as difficult to lead an intelligently regulated life (called a life of dharma), it is yet not enough for our full growth and development. This is why the second plane of the Nataraja idol (which consists of the two lower arms and the lifted left leg), draws our attention to the leg raised high above the ground. The purpose here is to point out that there is a further and loftier level of our existence, beyond the material.[107] This

---

107 It is significant here that it is the left foot of the Nataraja that is raised and not the right one. The Nataraja figure combines both the male and female aspects in itself, as shown by its feminine left ear-ring and its masculine right ear-ring. The left side of the Nataraja is the feminine side and, traditionally, feminity is always associated with the material cause of creation (as against the intelligent cause which is associated with masculinity). The raised left foot, therefore, signifies getting away from materiality.

is the level of our transcendental or spiritual aspects, where we need to seek a deeper understanding of ourselves, of the world and its creator.

The Nataraja murti goes on to tell us that to obtain such understanding requires not only modulation of our ego but also discrimination, an ability to see beyond the obvious and dedicated effort. The control of ego, as mentioned earlier, is shown by the subjugated dwarf-demon. Discrimination is portrayed by the hand which resembles an elephant's trunk – the elephant is considered to be wisest of all animals and its trunk is a powerful yet sensitive instrument of discernment; further, the third eye of the Nataraja symbolises (quite apart from its destructive aspect) the special faculty of insight. One or more cobras wrapped around the Nataraja stand for coiled energy latent within us (called *kundalini* in the scriptures of *yoga* and *tantra*), which needs to be harnessed in this effort. The objective of this effort is to discover the infinite and the eternal which, according to Vedanta, is the ultimate goal for all of us.

Ishwara, the Creator

One possible starting point for our journey to discover the infinite and the eternal is an enquiry into the nature of the creator of the universe. Any creation implies a creator. Our usual experience of any creation (of, say, a pot) is that its intelligent cause (the potter) is different from its material cause (the clay). However, Vedanta explains that there can never be any separation between the creator of the entire universe and his creation because this ultimate creator, called Ishwara, is both the intelligent and the material cause of the world. While this may sound fantastic and unlike anything that we know, a comparison with a dream may provide a helpful analogy: in our own dreams, all objects (sentient and insentient) as well as events and concepts (including those of time and space) are nothing but our own consciousness – we are both the intelligent and material causes of our dream creations.

Expanding on and justifying Vedanta's understanding of the creator in this fashion is outside our scope here. However, what is indisputable is that the Nataraja's dance does a beautiful job of portraying the creator as not being separate from creation. The analogy used here is of the dancer and his dance. Dance is not random movements but involves intelligent order; dance is the creation of a conscious dancer; in fact, dance is nothing but the dancer as it exists only in and through him. The dancer, on the other hand, is completely independent and exists even when he is not dancing. The Nataraja's dance thus symbolises creation to be dependent on and subsumed by its intelligent creator, Ishwara, who himself is entirely independent. It also shows that, like the dancer having full knowledge of the dance, this creator has all possible knowledge and power to be able to generate and pervade the entire universe.[108]

It is because of such a vision of Ishwara that there is no division between the secular and sacred in the Hindu tradition – everything is Ishwara. This is why we can venerate and anoint our own bodies (with a *tilak* or *bindi*), do *namaste* to anyone we meet and worship Ishwara even in a betel-nut or a river-stone or a lump of turmeric. And this remarkable understanding, that there is really nothing but Ishwara, is brilliantly brought out by the Nataraja's dance which symbolises our universe.

Yet another thing which the Nataraja portrays here is Ishwara's power to veil reality. We can get so captivated by the movement of a dance and so engrossed in its enjoyment that we begin to look upon the dance as an independent thing in itself and lose sight of the fact that it is nothing but just an aspect of the dancer; similarly our fascination with the world obscures Ishwara, and makes us miss this underlying reality.[109]

Advaita or Non-Duality

Vedanta does not stop at Ishwara but goes on to say that there is an ultimate reality which goes beyond both Ishwara and his creation. A frequently used metaphor in this context is that of the ocean and its waves. Waves emerge from, have their being in and finally recede into the ocean; this makes the ocean akin to the

---

108 Ishwara is also called *sarvajna, sarvashaktiman, sarvavyapi.*

109 In the case of Ishwara, the ability to veil the real nature of the world is called *maya* while the activity of Shiva, which creates an illusion, is called *tirobhava.*

Ishwara of the world of waves. However, there is a greater truth which includes and transcends both waves and the ocean and this truth is water. Similarly, from the stand-point of an individual human being, there is an all-powerful, all-knowing, all-pervading Ishwara, but there is a common truth behind both the entire creation and Ishwara; this truth is called brahman or atma. The same reality underlying everything has far-reaching implications because it makes everything identical in essence; it makes even Ishwara only superficially different from us. While we will not get into an examination of Vedanta's justification for such a radical view, we should note that this insight of a single and common truth being all that really exists is Vedanta's core teaching.

Vedanta further says that despite things in creation having so many attributes, the reality underlying all of them is without any attributes, just as water itself has no shape even though waves do. The Nataraja highlights this singular nature of brahman by the display of opposing attributes which, in effect, cancel out each other: creation against destruction (the dance and drum versus the flame), male against female (the female ear with its round ear-ring versus the male one), action against inaction (the dance and flying locks of hair versus the serene, immobile face).

Advaita Vedanta goes on to say that while this non-dual reality has no transient attributes, it has the essential nature of being existent, conscious and limitless,[110] just as wetness and sweetness are the essential nature of water and sugar, respectively. Existence, consciousness and limitlessness are known as *sat, chit* and *ananta* in Sanskrit; because limitlessness implies fullness, the associated word *ananda* (the joy of fullness) is also used instead of *ananta*. The Nataraja murti displays all these three aspects of the fundamental reality by its own existence (*sat*), by posing movement (which denotes consciousness or *chit*) and by its fulfilled face and dance[111] (standing for joy or *ananda*). The

---

110 Brahman or atma has to be basic existence, from which this entire creation draws its existence; it has to be pure consciousness because it is the sole cause of an intelligent and orderly universe; it has to be limitless because limits come out of attributes, but the cause of all attributes itself cannot have any attributes.

111 Called the *ananda tandava*.

Nataraja's ananda is intrinsic and not dependent on any external object; this is shown by his raised left foot and his hooded eyes, both of which stand for withdrawal from the material world. The Nataraja thus eloquently tells us of brahman or atma, the truth of everything, the abiding and limitless consciousness which we all really are.

The result of the full and proper understanding of this message is not ordinary – it leads to complete fearlessness (*abhaya*) and liberation or *moksha* from ignorance, illusion and the sense of being helplessly caught in the changing cycles of the universe. Such is the promise of the Nataraja's raised foot, the dancing defiance of the negative force of gravity, a symbol of Shiva's grace (*anugraha*), a symbol of release. This, then, is the magnificent Nataraja, he who is also called *Maheshwara* (the Great Lord) and *Shiva* (the auspicious one), and we bow to him – *om namah shivaya*.

HOW DO I STUDY VEDANTA?

'Doing' Vedanta is somewhat like 'doing' swimming. You have to learn swimming by getting into the water; Vedanta is learnt by actually living life in keeping with its vision.

Vedanta gives us new understanding that the reality of the world and of our own selves is not as absolute as it appears to be. To be of real value, this understanding has to become the constant back-drop to all our thoughts and actions. This is similar to the way in which our understanding of a friend's mental make-up is always available to us, even if sub-consciously, to filter and calibrate whatever he says. But the difficulty in Vedanta's case is that its ultimate vision goes against our well-entrenched conclusions and seems counter-intuitive. The ingrained tendency to go along with our seat-of-the-pants feeling is very strong; therefore our emotions and reactions may continue unchanged despite our exposure to Vedanta's teachings. (This human tendency is also evident in a number of air-crashes caused by a pilot flying in blind conditions and taking action based on the false information from his senses, despite rigorous training which teaches him to rely on his instruments.) So one of the biggest challenges in Vedanta is to unlearn our habitual patterns of thoughts and reactions.

The process of gaining Vedanta's vision itself is quite straight-forward and does not involve miracles or mysteries (like awakening the *kundalini* and other esoteric practices). All that is needed for an eligible student is to go to a proper teacher, put in the required effort for clearly understanding that vision and then internalise it so that it becomes his own. Difficulties arise when one or more of these elements are not properly in place. If at all there is any mystery or miracle here, it is only in why some people turn to Vedanta while others, despite similar backgrounds and experiences, do not.

Teachers commence the process of imparting Vedanta's knowledge by using different starting points. Thus, teaching may begin with an analysis of our search for happiness, or a discussion on the nature of God, or an understanding of what we really are, or an evaluation of the world which confronts us. The actual starting point of our exploration of Vedanta does not matter because everything is inter-related and so once we pick up any strand, it will lead to the unravelling of its whole fabric.

PREPARATION

A student of Vedanta is not just any seeker of knowledge. He has to be someone who has already come to the conclusion that no amount of possessions, experiences and achievements can satisfy his perennial sense of lacking which he now wants to tackle at its very root. This seeking of freedom from the sense of wanting in general, as against trying to cope with each individual want, is what converts a person into a *mumukshu* (a seeker of *moksha* or freedom). But this is not all. The student of Vedanta has also to be convinced that no actions (not even ethical or religious actions such as honest work, charity and prayer) will deal with his fundamental problem which can be solved with proper knowledge alone. Such a seeker of knowledge is the real student of Vedanta.

This student needs certain personal qualities to be eligible for drawing benefit from Vedanta.[112] It is important to understand what makes a person eligible because, without adequate preparation, no amount of mere study will bring proper results. On the other hand, attempts to become eligible should not become a misguided battle towards absolute control over all physical and emotional needs or frantic efforts towards total ethical perfection. Let us look at the traditional list of four attributes which make a person eligible for employing Vedanta as a means of knowledge. This list is to be found, among other places, in verse 17 of the *Vivekachudamani* (a beautiful introductory text attributed to Shankara) which says:

> He alone is considered qualified to enquire into the absolute reality, who has discrimination, detachment, a collection of certain qualities beginning with a settled mind and a burning desire for liberation.[113]

---

112 The Sanskrit word for eligibility or entitlement is *adhikaritvam* and an eligible person is called an *adhikari*.

113 *vivekino viraktasya shamadigunashalin mumukshorevhi brahmajignyasayogyata matah.*

We can now briefly look at what is said about each of these four qualifications:

- Discrimination is explained as proper understanding of the eternal and the time-bound.[114] In practice, because no one knows anything truly eternal, all we can do is to clearly understand that everything that we have worked for or achieved so far is time-bound or non-eternal.

- Detachment is lack of a driving desire to enjoy the rewards of our actions, either here or in the hereinafter.[115] Detachment should not be taken to mean only physical renunciation or outward asceticism; it is a state which follows discrimination, when we stop imposing a false value on an object or a situation. Detachment does not mean, for instance, that we should convince ourselves that money has no value; but it does mean that we should not look to money as the means of dealing with our sense of insecurity because money cannot provide a permanent solution if our own nature is insecure.

- The next item on the list is actually a collection of six qualities beginning with *shama*:

  Shama is a description of a settled state of mind, coming out of an acceptance of one's own body and mind as well as by properly managing one's likes and dislikes; it is a product of maturity. With *shama*, our mind is under our control as we pursue Vedanta, instead of it being controlled by situations, people, likes and dislikes.

  Dama is will-based regulation of the senses and reactions which is needed till *shama* develops. In a situation capable of provoking anger, the absence of anger would be *shama* but the restraint of one's speech or hand, once anger has arisen, would be *dama*.

  Uparati has connotations of love or enjoyment. We, as students, may be intellectually clear about the value

---

114 *nityanitya vastu viveka.*

115 *ihamutraphalabhoga viraga.*

of our pursuit but, yet, may be emotionally distant. By practice and association there is need to develop a love for spirituality so that other pursuits automatically lose their hold, the mind does not lean on external objects for its joy and, consequently, the usually strong sense of *me* and *mine* begins to dissipate.

Titiksha is the capacity to endure. It is the ability to put up with unpleasant situations and people, patiently and with equanimity. This can only come from objectivity (based on the understanding that all lives must face pairs of opposites like success and failure or the pleasant and the unpleasant) and from the conviction that the only goal worth pursuing is the goal of knowledge of the self.

Shraddha is often translated as *faith* but it is not just faith in the sense of blind belief. *Shraddha* here means trust in the words of the teacher and of the scriptures pending discovery of the truth by the student himself. What is required is the ability to give the teachings and the teacher the benefit of doubt and the suspension of prejudice, cynicism and scepticism until what is being taught irreconcilably contradicts our valid experiences or outrages our other means of knowledge.

Samadhan is the ability to concentrate upon a given subject for an appropriate length of time. To understand and assimilate the teachings of Vedanta requires a mind which can hold experiences and complex ideas and be absorbed in study and understanding. This ability requires a certain amount of intellectual development as well as emotional tranquility.

• We now come to the fourth and last item on our main list which is a fervent desire for liberation or *moksha*. We have already talked about a *mumukshu* as being a spiritual seeker who wants to tackle his perennial sense of lacking and wanting. For an eligible student of Vedanta, moksha should not be just one of his many desires but the pre-dominant desire. The desire for liberation may start as a simple, manageable desire (like initial thirst) but, in time, has to become intense and over-powering, like a burning thirst. Someone who is not consumed by a longing for the ultimate answer is not likely to penetrate to the heart of Vedanta.

We had earlier said that without all the qualities which we have just seen, there would be no eligibility and that, without this, the teachings of Vedanta will not work — not having the required qualifications does not make the pursuit of Vedanta merely difficult but almost meaningless. On the other hand, we had also said that becoming eligible does not mean an impractical attempt at total objectivity and control. All that is required at the initial stage is to develop a structure of personal values, possessions and ego boundaries which is realistic and appropriate for launching on the path of spiritual growth. These qualities then need to keep on growing throughout the learning process.

One reason why the question of eligibility is repeatedly emphasised in Vedanta is not only because some minimum criteria are necessary but also to ensure that there is no false conclusion in the matter of Vedanta being an independent means of knowledge. If Vedanta is a proper means of knowledge, it *must* work by dispelling self-ignorance in every seeker. However, this of course does not always happen; then the immediate and, perhaps, defensive reaction may be that Vedanta's vision is false. This is where the issue of eligibility becomes important — Vedanta is a means of knowledge for an *eligible* seeker and when it does not work it is because there is need to improve eligibility.

How does a student know whether he has enough eligibility to start the pursuit of Vedanta? The answer is simple and practical. If a person has taken even some interest in Vedanta then there is already an element of eligibility. If he continues to pursue Vedanta and some of its teachings begin to take root and actually start working for him, even in small measure, then this is a sign of growing eligibility.

Let us now take a look at a few other matters connected with the topic of the student. One prevailing notion about Vedanta is that people only turn to it due to great physical or emotional pain or due to major reverses like the total loss of a fortune or of a reputation. It is true that suffering is a trigger which can prompt a turn to Vedanta. But often a surfeit of comforts and apparent security also act as a trigger; this is because for some people the contradiction in continuing to feel unfulfilled amidst plenty provokes questions outside the structure of their usual ideas and conclusions.

On the other hand, great misfortunes and great good fortune can also be major obstacles on the path of Vedanta. A person who has gone through extreme suffering is likely to look for quick comfort and instant fixes rather than permanent redemption; his reservoir of resources like energy, patience and tenacity is likely to have been depleted and his emotions may be charged with anger, bitterness, hostility and general negativity. Such a person would need a lot care and compassion along with sufficient time with the preparatory teachings of Vedanta to restore balance to his mind; without this preparation, the ultimate message of Vedanta cannot strike home. Similarly, a person who has achieved an exceptional degree of conventional success may have, in that process, developed an aggressive and exploitative approach to everything; success tends to inflate and strengthen the ego. Such a state is obviously not very conducive to learning where receptivity and humility are necessary.

However, all these are generalizations based on possible tendencies and, like all generalizations, they need not apply to any one specific instance. Human minds are very complex and can change unpredictably; individuals can learn and achieve things which defy usual expectations. While probabilities are useful as guides, they should not be taken as foregone conclusions. People become students of Vedanta for a variety of reasons and progress at widely differing rates in their pursuit.

With this, let us now turn to the teacher without whom our study of Vedanta cannot be undertaken. While we look at the teacher, we will also indirectly look at a few more qualities required of the student in relation to the teacher.

THE TEACHER

In the entire scheme of Vedanta, the teacher undoubtedly has the pivotal role. Without the appropriate teacher, this wisdom and its teaching methodology are likely to remain sterile even for an eligible student; the words of the Upanishads become a means of self-knowledge *only* when wielded by the right teacher. Why is this so? What is so special about a teacher of Vedanta?

But before we go further, let us start using the Sanskrit word *guru* instead of the word *teacher*. This word has a number of different meanings but we will go with the most commonly accepted variant which is *remover of darkness*. The title *guru* has now passed into common parlance not only in relation to traditional Indian art-forms (such as music and dance) but in almost any field of endeavour (and so we have marketing gurus, management gurus and the like). However, students of Vedanta are interested in the removal of only one kind of darkness and this is the ignorance covering the true nature of their own selves. Therefore, in the context of Vedanta, a guru is described as or as someone who unfolds the meaning of the great sentences of the Upanishads.[116]

Let us go back to the questions which we raised about the guru. Why is he indispensable and so special? The answer lies both in the nature of the subject on which he is expected to throw light and the complex relationship he needs to establish and maintain with the student.

The self is the consciousness reality which is the basis of all knowing and the invariable presence in all experiences. Other teachers have to teach about objects, places, events, relationships, emotions, and concepts all of which can be considered as objects in the sense that they are all separate from the consciousness or the cognitivity of the student. The guru's peculiar task is to focus on consciousness itself, because of which the student experiences and understands anything. The difficulty here is obvious because how is the student's consciousness to be made conscious of consciousness?

---

116 *mahavakya updesha karta.*

A different kind of difficulty arises from the fact that the guru cannot solve the student's problem at the level at which the problem arises. The problem of the student is that his body and mind are mortal, ignorant and limited and no guru can make these immortal, all-knowing and unlimited. The freedom provided by Vedanta is not *for* the individual but *from* the individual. The guru has to provide initial reassurance by saying that the problem has a solution but, ultimately, the guru has to lead the student to the conclusion that the very notion of bondage and limitation, which has launched the student on the path of self-knowledge, is illegitimate. The guru has to solve a problem which had no real existence to begin with!

The Upanishads and other traditional texts, which contain knowledge of the self, are written in an archaic language and style. Sanskrit is not the easiest of languages to learn and interpret. Further, even in Sanskrit, the message of the Upanishads is not put forth in an organised and sequential manner. Many statements in the Upanishads are, on the face of it, ambiguous and even contradictory. They were never designed to be read as a structured course but contain vignettes of sublime insights which become meaningful only when unfolded by a teacher who has personally discovered the truth of such insights for himself.

The problem of apparently-known words used in the Upanishads and other texts is also considerable. Words like *eternal, infinite, immortal* and *all-pervading* are often used. Because these words are included in our vocabulary, it is assumed that their meanings are obvious; however, none of us actually has any clear and direct understanding of their meanings. This is not very surprising — for instance none of us has ever known or experienced anything truly eternal and so when we use this word we may have an idea of something which stretches over aeons of time but are not able to really relate to timelessness. It is for this reason that when we are taught about the self by less than a proper guru, we think we have understood that the atma is eternal and all-pervading and yet wonder when and where we will actually find the atma. There, of course, cannot be any *when* or *where* about the eternal and the all-pervading.

A guru has to repeatedly make it clear during the teaching process that what is being discussed is not some remote object but the very essence of the student as he is, here and now. If the guru is not competent and careful, then the student will automatically employ the usual process of subject-object division where the atma is treated as an object to be known by the student. Once this happens, any teaching about the atma loses its true relevance and becomes a further layer of mere information which will reinforce the fundamental problem instead of resolving it.

Yet another unusual feature of the process of vedantic teaching is the fact that the guru has to not only impart the actual teachings but also simultaneously guide the student in the effort to improve his eligibility for benefitting from these teachings. Both these processes have to go on side-by-side. Here the guru has to judge the conditioning and capacity of the student. Students come to learn with different levels of intellectual and emotional preparedness; each student also has his unique collection of wrong notions and conditioning. Emotional maturity requires healing and discharge of pent-up issues in the conscious and the sub-conscious mind; it also requires learning to deal with life without a further build-up of unwanted emotions.

The guru's work in this area can cover religion, God, family, work, money, friends, relationships, disease, death, fears, hopes and ambitions. A guru needs to be a person who can play the role of a father and a friend, a priest and a psychologist, a man of the world and a philosopher if he is to guide the student to maturity and objectivity. In this process, the student's many questions need to be answered and he has to be provided with prescriptions and practices; often, the answers provided to an individual student, and prescriptions and practices suggested for him, may have nothing to do with the actual teachings of Vedanta but more to do with the particular mind-set and conditioning of that student.

And the guru's task does not end with just exposing the student to the entire teachings because, even after that, it is possible for the new understanding not to have too much practical effect in the student's daily life. The weight of age-old conditioning and the deep grooves of past thinking modes may lead to the continuation of the student's fundamental problem. Redemption and deliverance may require extended further effort, guided by the guru, for de-conditioning and for full absorption of the teachings in every aspect of living.

There is another and rather curious but relevant aspect of the guru which we should look at while we are on the topic of his importance. This has to do with being in the live, physical presence of a true guru. By some inexplicable process and in some unfathomable way, just being in the guru's presence brings about a certain settlement in the state of the student's mind and creates openness, receptivity and hope. The words of the Upanishads assume a different kind of liveliness and relevance when they are personally explained by the guru; the ring of truth in the teachings is heard and felt instinctively and unambiguously in his presence. The tranquility, the quiet conviction, the healing and the wholeness felt in association with the guru is a joy and blessing which needs to be actually experienced because, like love, it defies description or explanations. Without this special touch, the teachings of Vedanta can remain inert and be ineffective beyond pandering to idle or scholarly curiosity.

Having seen some of the reasons because of which the guru is indispensable, we can now look at what the Upanishads say about a proper guru. The Mundaka Upanishad states:

— Let him (the student), *in order to obtain the knowledge of the eternal, take sacrificial fuel in his hands and approach that teacher alone who is well-versed in the vedas and is established in* (committed to) *brahman.*[117]

The prepared and eligible student is asked to go with the attitude of humility and service (denoted by the phrase *take sacrificial fuel in his hands*) to a guru who is not only well-versed in the vedas but who is also committed to only brahman. Why these two qualifications for the guru? Is it not possible for a person to have self-knowledge and teach it without knowing the vedas? On

---

117 Verse I ii 12: ---- *tadvignyanartham sa gurumevabhighacchet .*
samitpanih shrotriyam brahmanishtham.

the other hand, why does a guru who knows the vedas have to be established or absorbed in brahman?

There is no doubt that there have been and there will continue to be some persons who have resolved their self-ignorance without reading the vedas. The experiences and words of many such persons have an uncanny similarity with the contents of the Upanishads even though they may have never been exposed to them. Quite a few persons with such wisdom become well-known and are proclaimed as gurus by their associates and admirers. As long as people seeking liberation promised by Vedanta look upon such accomplished men as symbols for reverence and inspiration, there is no difficulty. However, an average student of Vedanta is not likely to achieve systematic removal of his self-ignorance by only relying on teachings derived from such persons. This is because the traditional teachings not only contain great truths but also contain equally important methods and well-established processes and practices for guiding students on the path of learning. This entire teaching tradition has evolved over centuries; it is handed over from generation to generation in an unbroken line (termed *parampara*) of traditional teachers of Vedanta. A guru who is not well-versed in this teaching tradition is unlikely to be able to effectively unfold this knowledge for the usual student. Hence, the injunction is to go to a proper guru.

Why the requirement that the guru should be committed to only brahman? The crux of Vedanta's teaching is that there is only one reality, called brahman or atma, which is all that really exists. A person who has truly absorbed this teaching can never have any commitment to anything else because, to him, everything in creation is only a shadow of the reality of brahman. The guru certainly plays his role in the game of life and living — he lives, teaches, works and plays and, in many ways, appears to be no different than many of us. However, beneath these superficial appearances, no situations, actions or results of actions (including the success or failure of his teaching) can really affect him. If the guru has other commitments and has his own personal agenda to fulfil, then he too is in the process of becoming, of feeling a lack and of making efforts to overcome that limitation. If this is so then he has not understood his own nature as being already fulfilled and is thus as ignorant as his students, even though he may have memorised the contents of all the Upanishads. Such a guru can, of course, pass on the words of Vedanta to his students but, because he does not feel and actually live the teachings himself, he will never be able to communicate the true and first-hand spirit of the teachings.

Apart from these traditional qualifications of a guru, there are a few other considerations which are relevant. Let us begin with a mundane but practical consideration of the language in which the teaching is conducted. What matters here is not only the basic language in which the guru teaches (say, English) but also his expression, idiom and fluency. English can be used in an outmoded and dead manner; it can also be skillfully used in a lively and contemporary fashion to convey proper meaning in a manner relevant to current times. In this context, the cultural orientation of the guru may also affect students considerably. Many modern students could be put off at the very outset if the guru adopts a pompously formal and distant style; in the same vein, a guru who discourages questions and dialogue is not likely to be effective today because we are no longer willing to receive and accept even true knowledge in the format of a sermon, no matter how fervently and eloquently preached.

Another very important matter which the guru needs to periodically clarify during the process of teaching is the fact that while the Upanishads are the unique means of self-knowledge, they are not the ultimate authority in respect of their other contents. The Upanishads not only contain material regarding the true nature of our own self but also a lot of other interspersed material dealing with matters like the process of creation of this universe, the working of the *karma* theory and even the description (!) of the atma.

Some of this ancillary material just represents the world-view on that subject at the time when that particular piece of telling or writing occurred. For instance, when the Upanishads talk about the five primal elements (which are stated as space, air, fire, water and earth) they are not to be taken as the final word on this subject - there is no need to throw out Mendeleev's periodic table of elements which we studied at school. This is because the process of creation of this world and the nature of its constituent elements are *not* the real subject-matters of the Upanishads; information dealing with the five primal elements is included in the Upanishads only to complete a possible model needed to deal with the peripheral curiosity of students.

The guru also needs to deal with apparent contradictions in the core contents of the Upanishads such as when the atma is described as if it has attributes like size and location.[118] This is not to be taken literally but to be regarded partly as poetic license and also an attempt to progress to the attributeless nature of the atma in gradual steps.

If all this is not properly explained by the guru, we could have a situation proverbially described (rather gruesomely) as throwing the baby out with the bath-water; unless suitably guided, a modern student may reject the entire contents of the Upanishads because some peripheral or preliminary contents outrage his common-sense or do not tally with his other valid knowledge.

How does one go about identifying a proper guru? It is difficult (if not impossible) to personally judge a potential guru as well-versed in the vedas and committed only to brahman when one does not know the vedas or brahman oneself. Most of us obviously have to rely on opinions of other persons and the general reputation of a particular guru; a personal meeting further provides inputs based on perceived behaviour, attitudes and some sort of personal chemistry. Ultimately, one has to make a beginning based on practical judgment which may need to be revised later. Even if one begins with a less than perfect guru, there is always a lot to be learnt. A teacher who is just a scholar of the Upanishads will certainly not be as effective as a person who has that knowledge along with direct experience of their insights but, on the other hand, a great deal about the contents of vedantic texts can yet be learnt from a scholarly person. There is no reason not to learn whatever one can from an available teacher and begin dealing

---

118 For instance the Shvetashvatara Upanishad (verse III - 13) says: The purusha (atma), being of the size of the thumb, is concealed by the heart ...

with a better-qualified guru later, whenever that opportunity arises. At the end of it all, finding a proper guru is not entirely a matter of one's own judgment or effort and some of this has to be left to luck; after making suitable efforts to find a guru, it is useful to cultivate the faith that whichever force made one into a spiritual seeker will also lead him to a proper guide. In this context, one of the verses of the *Vivekachudamani*[119] says:

Three rare things become available only due to divine grace:. human hood, the desire for fundamental liberation and the shelter of a great person.

Apart from the good luck in being born a human-being and developing a longing for real freedom, this verse talks about the good fortune in finding a true guru. This fortune is not only in terms of finding a great person who can teach and protect the student with proper knowledge of reality but also in terms of the student himself being able to recognise and surrender his ego to such a guru.

TEACHING METHODOLOGY

How does the guru teach? Where is the long-established teaching tradition of Vedanta codified? Vedanta's teaching methodology is not separately spelt out in any one place but is spread, directly and indirectly, over the Upanishads.

All Upanishads begin with a peace invocation. An example of a well-known invocation is at the beginning of the Katha Upanishad:[120]

---

119 Verse 3: *durlabham trayamevaitdevanugrahahetukam
    manushyatvam mumukshutvam mahapurushsamshrayah.*

120 *om saha navavatu saha naubhunaktu
    saha viryam karvavahai
    tejasvinavadhitamastu ma vidvishavahai
    om shanti shanti shanti.*

May He protect us (both student and teacher).
May He nourish us.
May we acquire the capacity to exert (in the study of
scriptures).
May our study be brilliant (leading to proper
understanding).
May we (student and teacher) not have discord.
May we have peace in all aspects of life.

Such verses are traditionally recited at the commencement of every study period to bring about a settlement of distracting thoughts and emotions and to acknowledge the role of forces beyond our control in the process of studying. This particular verse also warns against the possible tendency of students to unnecessarily disagree with the teacher because of trifling objections and hasty or quibbling arguments.

The primary learning process of Vedanta is set out in this line from the Brihadaranyaka Upanishad:

Atma has to be seen (known) by listening, reflecting and
contemplating.[121]

It starts with an exhortation to the student to know atma and it then lists the three steps of *listening, reflecting and contemplating* which are the backbones in the process of learning Vedanta. The student is first exposed to the teachings by *listening* to the teacher and undergoing a process of self-inquiry.

Next follows *reflection* which refers to the resolution of doubts caused in the student's mind by the teachings. Personal conviction can only be brought about by thinking, bringing up doubts and then getting them satisfactorily resolved. Without this process, the initial teachings would remain only superficial and shaky.

The last step, of *contemplation*, is to repeatedly practice and experience the effect of some of these teachings. (An example here could be a daily period of meditation wherein a person just quietly watches his own body and mind — he becomes an uninvolved and unresisting witness to all sensations and thoughts

121 *atma vare drishtavyah shrotavyo mantavyo nidhidhyasitavyah......*

to bring home the teaching that he is more than just the body or the mind.) This kind of effort is needed not only to assimilate what one has learnt but its repeated practice is essential to counter-act the wrong notions which have been deeply established by initial ignorance and years of conditioning.

This entire process, often referred to as *shravana-manana-nidhidhyasana*,[122] is essential and needs a certain amount of time for it to work. Also, this process is not sequential — we cannot finish all listening first and then start thinking about what we have heard. As we meditate and reflect upon whatever we have learnt, we continue to listen and to learn more and more. Further, listening or learning with regard to any aspect of the teachings is not a one-shot affair. Given the nature of the subject of the teaching and the quality of surrounding ignorance, it is necessary for a student to expose himself to the teachings again and again. Repetition, different frames of mind of the student and different words used by the teacher at different times as well as passage of time all lead to the opening of small and occasional chinks in the layers of conditioning surrounding the student with the possibility of some teachings penetrating and finding their mark.

For the purpose of making the student understand its teachings in different perspectives, Vedanta uses several different frames and examples from our daily experiences. These perspectives, such as *avastha-traya* and *drik-drishya,* are called *prakriyas* or methods. The *avastha-traya* (three states) perspective, for instance, deals with our three common states of being awake, dreaming and in deep-sleep; it argues that because each of these states is known to come and go, there has to be a permanent state to which each of the three inter-changing states are known and which we should discover. The *drik-drishya* (seer–seen) *prakriya*

---

122 It is pertinent to note that for many people who take some interest in Vedanta, their pursuit never really progresses beyond the listening and reading stage. Because of pressures on time and difficulty in having regular association with a good teacher, people often tend to go to sporadic lectures and do random reading. Even regularly attending several public discourses by the same teacher has limitations because wherever a teacher is dealing with a heterogeneous group, his teaching tends to be limited to explaining just the basics. While all such inputs are good, progress does require exposure to more advanced and subtle aspects as well as regular meditation and reflection.

draws upon our common experience of our seeing things and says that the objects seen by us are many but our power of sight is one; it goes further to say that our powers of cognition are many (sight being only one of them) but the mind where cognition occurs is one; ultimately, the mind itself has many states but the knower of all the states of the mind is one and this is the witnessing consciousness, our inner-most truth. There are many other practical perspectives which Vedanta employs to get us to understand our own truth in different ways.

But much more significant than the specific situations and examples used by Vedanta is the appreciation of the fundamental approach of Vedanta. In the words of Shankara:

> *For there is this saying of those who know the true tradition, "That which cannot be expressed (in its true form directly) is expressed (indirectly) through false attribution and subsequent retraction".*[123]

This method of false attribution followed by retraction underlies all forms of Vedanta teachings and is used in different forms throughout the Upanishads, Brahma Sutras and the Bhagavad Gita. It is necessary to do this because there is no way in which the absolute reality, which is the subject-matter of Vedanta, can be directly expressed in its true form.

Vedanta's core teachings deal with a unity which is so complete that *all* duality is ruled out. Words and thoughts can only deal with nouns, adjectives, relationships or activities but how can they cover an all-encompassing unity? Any single word or even a thought represents an apparent departure from brahman because who can speak of or think about anything without a subject-object duality? Vedanta texts contain a story about a qualified student requesting his teacher to teach him about the self. In the story, this teacher maintains his silence in spite of repeated requests for knowledge by the student. Finally he tells the student *"I am telling you, but you do not understand. This self is utter silence."* However, as teaching by silence is not likely to be effective for most people, Vedanta uses the method of false attribution followed by retraction.

123 His bhashya on Verse 13, Chapter XIII of the Bhagavad Gita.

Imaginary characteristics are first attributed to the only reality, to negate whatever is incompatible with those characteristics; subsequently, even the falsely attributed characteristics are negated. For instance in the *karana-karya* (cause-effect) *prakriya*, brahman is stated to be the cause of this entire creation. The purpose of suggesting such a thing is to make sure that brahman is not understood as an effect of any other cause. Later, the real position is clarified in the Upanishads themselves by stating that brahman is *neither an effect nor a cause*. Similarly, when Vedanta texts falsely suggest that the atma (or brahman) is something to be attained or known, it is to emphasise that only the absolute reality is worth knowing. When the atma is spoken of as *the knower*, this too is false and the purpose is only to clarify that the atma is not an object of our knowing. Later, the implication that the atma is a knower (in the sense of an individual performing the activity of knowing) is displaced by calling the atma only a witness. Ultimately even witness-hood has to be denied because that too involves some individuation and duality. This is done by saying at several places in the Upanishads that '*This self is neither this nor that*'. The only reality cannot be anything which is conceived by the mind; whatever is taught about it in a positive sense can only be false attributions and the only thing which can actually be said about it is that '*it is neither this nor that*'. Incidentally, it is this impossibility of saying anything directly about the main subject which makes Vedanta teachers and books seem full of words without, apparently, quite getting to the point.

This fundamental method of false attribution followed by retraction is not only inevitable because of the nature of knowledge sought to be conveyed by Vedanta but also has an accompanying benefit of gradual progression. This process does not completely destroy an individual's existing foundation of notions and beliefs at the very outset; instead, it goes in gradual steps whereby as each false notion is removed, it is replaced with something of greater and more lasting value. This is not only useful for the purpose of easier learning but also benefits those who stop their pursuit of Vedanta mid-way.

While on the subject of teaching methodology, one often hears of well-known saints who have arrived at true understanding without going through any scriptures or any formal teaching process. One also hears of wonderful changes occurring to people after sitting in silence in a sage's presence or on hearing a single phrase (like a *mantra*) or after going into a trance. Several others believe that total devotion to God is the only way to obtain the real truth. These are difficult issues to deal with and just because some of these happenings and beliefs may defy common understanding, this does not necessarily make them untrue or impossible. However, when we study Vedanta, we cannot realistically expect to obtain a mysterious short-cut which will permit us to emulate the examples of a few rare persons. In fact, relying too much on the history of unusual people who seem to be born with an orientation which makes the benefits of Vedanta available to them almost effortlessly could be frustrating and even misleading.

What about total devotion to God as a means of self-knowledge? The ability to completely surrender to God is both beautiful and helpful. *Bhakti* or devotion brings out a whole host of gentler and nobler aspects of any human being; it also brings about a subsidence of the ego as the individual's strong sense of separation gets merged into whichever form of God he relates to. A few very well-prepared and receptive individuals in the highest state of devotion may need only a single (and, perhaps, inadvertently obtained) spark of knowledge to light the fire required to dispel ignorance. For some others, given their emotional and intellectual make-up, devotion may be the only way in which they can express their search for meaning, whether or not this leads to full understanding of reality. However, when we look at Vedanta, we are looking at a means of knowledge which *must* function in all cases and, that too, in a comprehensible and non-miraculous way. In this context, mysterious happenings can only be interesting detours and while devotion is an essential way of preparation and of living, it cannot be consistently used as a substitute for a knowledge-based methodology.

One last thing which needs to be mentioned in the context of Vedanta's teaching methodology is that Vedanta is unique because it is not yet another 'becoming' or 'getting there' but a discovery of what we already are. Nothing is actually needed to make us or to take us to what we have always been. Therefore, though Vedanta's teachings may seem to contain a process, it is a process which gradually cancels itself out. In some ways, and however mysterious or meaningless this may sound, Vedanta is a journey which ends where it begins. As we discover this startling truth we should not let the mechanics, the length and the pace of the 'process' of learning Vedanta detract from the joy of this apparent but marvellous journey.

THE TEXTS

The teachings of Vedanta are contained in a treasure of Sanskrit literature. The apex of this collection of literature is formed by three texts which are of prime importance. These are the Upanishads, the Brahma Sutras and the Bhagavad Gita. The Upanishads are, of course, the first and foremost out of this prime set of texts.

The Upanishads are part of the vedas which are called *shruti,* meaning *heard* texts. As the Upanishads are not ascribed to any known authors they are looked upon as *revealed* texts and, in keeping with the special status accorded to them, they are regarded as holding the highest authority. In fact, as far as Vedanta is concerned, the Upanishads are the full-fledged and unique means of knowledge for knowing the true nature of one's own self.

When something is categorised as a primary means of knowledge, it has a number of significant implications. The first implication is that it can have no substitute. A further implication is that without this specific means of knowledge, it would not be possible to know whatever is to be known by using it. Thus, vision is a specific means of knowledge of colours and it cannot be substituted with another means of knowledge such as hearing; colour cannot be known by somebody who has never had vision.

The subject of Vedanta - our real self - is something which cannot be known by using the usual means of knowledge such as perception and inference, because the senses and the mind cannot operate on something which is the basis of the senses and the mind. Here, the words of the Upanishads are the only means of knowledge.

An ancient sage known as Badarayana reduced the essence of the Upanishads to concise and logically arranged aphorisms in a collection known as the Brahma Sutras. In terms of hierarchy, these Brahma Sutras (also known as Vedanta Sutras) rank in importance next only to the Upanishads. Even though the Brahma Sutras are well-organised, they are still very difficult to understand and assimilate because of their brevity and references to the contents of the Upanishads which are not apparent to the lay reader.

This brings us to the last of the three primary texts and this is the Bhagavad Gita. The Bhagavad Gita is a small part of a gigantic work (of 100,000 verses) called the Mahabharata authored by the famous sage Vyasa. The Gita is much easier to read and to understand compared to the Upanishads and the Brahma Sutras; its setting and tone are much more practical and readily applicable to daily life and its problems. A very significant portion of its contents deals with preparatory matters like devotion and proper understanding of actions and their results. Because of its qualities, its beautiful and powerful poetry and emphasis on the concept of a personified god, for a majority of Hindus the Gita is the only vedantic text that they ever get exposed to.

The Upanishads, the Brahma Sutras and the Bhagavad Gita are collectively called the *prasthana traya* or the three starting points for Vedanta.

A number of well-known teachers have written detailed commentaries on all or some of these three basic texts. Such a commentary is known as a *bhashya*; its contents include breaking-up of compounded words, logically relating different parts of sentences from the original text and unfolding in-depth meanings of words and sentences. Shankara was a prolific *bhashyakara* (commentator) and we have available to us his bhashyas on ten Upanishads, on the Brahma Sutras and on the Bhagavad Gita. His bhashyas are invaluable material for understanding the original texts and so they are very important texts themselves.

Apart from bhashyas, teachers and commentators produced other types of works such as *karikas* (independent expositions in verse on an original text), *vartikas* (verses expounding upon a bhashya to bring out what is not said or what is inadequately said in the bhashya) and *tikas* (explanatory notes along with some additional views on a bhashya or a karika or a vartika).

Bhashyas, karikas, vartikas and tikas are related directly or indirectly to an original and primary text. There is a whole other category of writings which revolve around a specific subject or topic as against one original text. These works are called *prakarana* and they are in the nature of a dissertation on a chosen topic (which could be just one facet of Vedanta or its entire scope). They can be very long and detailed (like the *Vivekachudamani* – attributed with controversy to Shankara – which has 581 verses); others can be concise and yet encapsulate the basic teachings of Vedanta (like the 53 verses of the *Vakyavritti* also ascribed to Shankara). Prakarana books exist in large number and grow continuously by works of new authors in every age.

Apart from the traditional listing of categories of vedantic texts mentioned above, we also have some modern works which do not fall within these categories. These books are compilations of conversations with men of great wisdom who had full understanding of the deepest teachings of Vedanta, but who did not focus on producing elaborate and formal texts. These collections are put together by students and translators associated with men like Ramana Maharshi and Nisargadatta Maharaj. Some works of this category contain piercing insights which ring so clearly of timeless truths that they are a joy to read and provide valuable material for a student of Vedanta.

How does one approach or start with this mass of vedantic literature? There are no simple answers here. The Upanishads were never meant to be available for study by any curious passer-by. They are couched in such language and have such a mystical flavour that for any beginner to just read their bare texts is not only quite meaningless but could also lead to premature and false conclusions or bring about disdain for their contents. Their purpose is not only to instruct but to inspire; their contents are not that of a structured argument but more like a collection of ecstatic snapshots of great truths. Contrary to popular belief, every sentence in the Upanishads is not a statement of the final and absolute truth; there are tentative approaches, interesting debates as well as stories and anecdotes many of which are more to do with questioning and seeking rather than answering and finding. Their unusual and subtle truths are meant for those who combine a burning thirst for their knowledge along with a high level of intellectual and emotional preparation; others are likely to fail in understanding their true message and also face the risk of drawing wrong understanding which could be used to support perverse logic and ethical licentiousness.

The best thing of course is to have selected Upanishads gradually and consistently unfolded to us by an illumined teacher from the basis of his personal experience; this is how they were designed to be taught. However, given the difficulty in spending too much time with a teacher and the ready availability of scores of books on the Upanishads, it would be unrealistic to suggest that one should read nothing on one's own. If possible, only what is recommended by the teacher should be read. If one must read in an unguided fashion then one should begin with prakarana works like *Atma Bodha*, *Vakya Vritti* and *Viveka Chudamani*; in due course, one can then try and read some of the shorter main Upanishads along with Shankara's commentary.

Even though the Brahma Sutras are very concise and logically arranged, attempts to read them on one's own can be even more frustrating than in the case of the Upanishads — their very brevity and a different style of writing and arguing make the Brahma Sutras much more abstruse and are best studied only under the personal guidance of a proper teacher.

The Bhagavad Gita lends itself to much easier reading as it is supposed to; with a commentary it can be an exceptionally valuable text combining, as it does, many of the preparatory and core teachings of Vedanta in a work of magnificence and efficacy.

More modern books containing conversations with and answers from truly evolved persons of this century can be very rewarding reading. Apart from books, we also now have available audio and video formats of teachings of some current teachers of Vedanta. The calibre of such material obviously varies with the teacher concerned and, even with the best of teachers, this is no substitute for live inter-action; however, these media provide a practical and valuable supplement to traditional learning.

In whatever reading we do, we should bear in mind there will be many areas of confusion and apparent contradictions even in authoritative texts; some of this can be avoided by recourse to the teacher and some of it is unavoidable — it almost seems that the struggle and frustration in trying to arrive at some clear and meaningful vision is part of the admission price!

A Different Classification

We have so far been looking at literature and its classification as it pertains to the study of Vedanta. However, if one were to look at the vedic religion (or Hinduism) as a whole, then the way of categorizing the available literature there is different from what we have seen so far. A more general classification of Hindu texts also starts with the four Vedas (*shruti*) as the very top; however, the emphasis here is not only on the portion containing the Upanishads but also on the much larger earlier portions covering worship and rituals.

The Vedas are supplemented by four *upa vedas* (subsidiary *vedas*)[124] and the six *vedangas* (explanatory limbs of the *Vedas*).[125]

The next category of Hindu scriptures is called *smriti* or *that which is remembered*. The *smritis* are ascribed to known authors and cover a very wide range of subjects. An important part of the *smritis* contains rules and regulations governing the conduct of individuals, communities and the state. There are about eighteen such codes given by different law-makers of the past with the best

---

124 *Ayurveda* (the science of promoting and extending a healthy life), *Dhanurveda* (the science of archery and use of many other types of weapons), *Gandharva veda* (relating to music and dance) and *Arthashastra* (dealing with statecraft, politics and administration including economic management).

125 They deal with phonetics, grammar, etymology, prosody, rites & rituals and astronomy & astrology respectively.

known being the *Manu Smriti*; as these texts include conventions which change, portions get outdated from time to time.

The *shrutis* and *smritis* were heard, memorised, interpreted and implemented by rulers, priests and scholars. However, the needs of the man on the street (who may not have the ability or the inclination to get into complex texts) were served by two other categories of texts known as the *itihasas* and the *puranas*. (Both of these are also categorised as *smriti* in a broad sense because they too are of known human composition.)

The itihasas consist of two great epics known as the *Ramayana* and the *Mahabharata*; these are long and complex tales involving a whole gamut of human behaviour and emotions including love, duty, family relations, righteousness, treachery and war. Values encouraged by dharma are highlighted in a poetic and dramatic way here. These two epics are so famous that there is almost nobody, in even the remotest of villages in India, who does not know their stories or who is not aware of the several values preached by them. These epics, apart from popularizing religious stories and values, also contain some gems of great philosophy as well as codes of conduct in well-known portions such as the *Bhagavad Gita* or the *Shantiparva* (both of which happen to be in the *Mahabharata*).

The puranas also contain stories which convey several values and ethics; the stories here are very short and pitched at a level which even children and illiterate adults can understand and enjoy. There are eighteen puranas which contain stories well-known throughout India such as those about Bhakta Dhruva, Satyavan and Savitri, Prahlada, Raja Harishchandra and the like; the better known puranas are the *Bhagavat*, *Vishnu* and *Markandeya* puranas. Each purana tends to emphasise a particular deity.[126]

The last set of traditional texts deals with the *darshanas* (meaning *visions*) which are really schools of philosophy,

---

126 An associated set of scriptures, called the *agamas*, lays down doctrines and disciplines for the worship of particular deities. *Shaiva*, *Vaishnava* and *Shakta*, the three main sects amongst the followers of Hinduism, sprout from the *agamas*.

meant for intellectually-inclined persons and for scholars. Tradition lists six such *astika* schools (those which recognise the final authority of the *vedas*) including Vedanta. Teachers and proponents of each school have produced various texts of different levels of complexity to meet the needs of diverse people included amongst their followers.

This entire treasure of literature is so vast that one can only hope to read and study a small fraction of it; however, it is re-assuring to note that for a prepared student even one small Upanishad studied and understood well is enough to dispel all his self-ignorance and help him find release from unnecessary suffering.

LEARNING FROM VEDANTA

The goal of self-knowledge is very often not accomplished despite Vedanta's excellent teaching traditions and the fortune of finding a proper guru. The primary reason for this is the lack of preparedness of the student, which we have already seen. What we will now consider are less obvious issues which are relevant today.

Let us start with the nature of association between a student of Vedanta and his teacher. In times when traditions were strongly adhered to, Vedanta was not open to everyone; the teacher seriously evaluated the student's readiness in all aspects before exposing him to Vedanta's teachings. There was, thus, a powerful filter at the very outset. Once a student was accepted, the teaching happened over a long time (12 years was the norm) during which the student actually lived with the teacher and learnt constantly, not only in class but throughout all activities of day-to-day living. This not only permitted the student to be immersed in a life of Vedanta and reach a critical mass of learning but also permitted the teacher to fully understand the student's conditioning and capabilities.

Because Vedanta is not only concerned with imparting information but more with re-designing the lens of the student's mind (through which he views himself and the world), an understanding of the student's mind by the teacher is important. It is because of full appreciation of a particular student's needs at a given point in time that a teacher may give different answers to similar questions when such questions come from different students. However, when there is no continuous and lasting relationship between the student and his teacher, the student may wrongly understand a statement meant for someone else and the teacher is not able to calibrate his response to be in tune with the needs of a particular student. This puts much greater responsibility on the student to sift through, evaluate and pick out that material and level of teaching which is appropriate for him at a particular point in time.

Another problem for a student who is not able to make time for a full-time and long-term exposure to the teachings of Vedanta, is the lack of real progression in teaching. In a modern setting, a teacher is confronted with a student body with different levels of eligibility (and, at times, students with no eligibility at all also turn up for a variety of superficial reasons); his teaching then necessarily remains pitched at the lowest common denominator. Such teaching has to dilute the full vision of Vedanta and the progressively rigorous changes it requires[127] do not happen. We, then, virtually spin in the same place, with little progress despite expended time and effort.

Yet another problem in our modern setting is undue emphasis on trying to grasp the concept of wholeness (non-duality or *advaita*). The teaching of Vedanta comprises of two distinct legs:

- Discrimination between the real and the unreal *(viveka prakriya)* which results in *vairagya* or disenchantment

- Appreciation of the common and non-dual reality underlying everything *(sarvatma prakriya)*

Advaita is a fascinating and grand concept which is intellectually challenging; we tend to get into with a lot of enthusiasm right at the beginning of our Vedantic journey and give it undue focus. The *viveka prakriya*, on the other hand, involves dis-identification with things which are dear and close to us, such as our bodies,

---

127 in the ways in which we identify with the world and with our own bodies and minds, in place of desires and the importance of their fulfilment in our lives and in the nature of our associations and relationships.

minds, habits, desires and relationships; this is a laborious and painful task which does not provide quick results or intellectual gratification. However, this is a very critical step and no amount of our cleverness will bring home the benefits of Vedanta if we try to circumvent or compromise *viveka*.

A teacher of Vedanta gives a very helpful analogy here of travellers who have to walk up to the peak of a mountain in darkening twilight. There is a bright flame burning on the mountain top which is our goal, but our path to reach there is full of twists, turns and pitfalls. If we walk with our attention only on the flame on the top, we will stumble and fall at obstacles on the path. However, if we pay careful attention to the path directly in front of us, with perhaps an occasional pause to look at the beckoning flame to keep our orientation and enthusiasm intact, the chances of success are much greater. The flame on the mountain-top is *advaita* or the *sarvatma bhava* while our carefully trudging up the difficult path is the *viveka prakriya*; we have to pay much more attention to the latter, at least initially.

Ironically, absorption of a certain amount of the initial teachings of Vedanta makes our focus on *viveka* and *vairagya* waver. We turn to Vedanta because of pain in significant aspects of our lives or frustration in not experiencing a lasting sense of fulfilment despite many of our desires having been met. With some Vedanta in us, we cultivate a degree of objectivity as well as extra elbow room in our minds. Thus equipped, we can manage our pleasures and pains much better: pleasures became more pleasurable because we can taste them fully, with lesser regrets about the past and lesser fears about the future; disappointments and pain become less intense because of our nascent ability to be witnesses to the states of our own minds as well as the understanding that pleasure and pain move in alternating cycles. However, armed with our new abilities and the comfort they provide, we may become even more committed to transient experiences and pleasures instead of moving forward in the journey to our own truth.

Another aspect of modern teaching, where a teacher has a disparate group of students for short spells of time, is lack of focus on one of Vedanta's three critical processes: *nidhidhyasana* or contemplation. The first two processes - listening and resolving doubts - then get over-emphasised, at the cost of nidhidhyasana which tends to get ignored along with its adjunct which is meditation. Meditation is critical to develop the required focus of the mind (*ekagrata*) while repeated contemplation of the teachings and their implications in our lives is vital if the teachings are to effectively get home. Both meditation and contemplation need to be done rigorously and regularly but many of us today treat these areas lightly and as being optional.

Knowledge and deliverance are not always concurrent; even if we understand the message of Vedanta without any serious doubts or reservation, this does not necessarily mean that we will live in accordance with Vedanta's vision and benefit from it. And this is part of our common experience: we all, for instance, know people who have no doubt that being obese and physically inactive is truly bad for their health but yet will not or cannot do anything to incorporate a sensible diet and exercise regime in their lives. Similarly, our emotions, our ego, our habits and the ingrained strengths of our likes and dislikes may make it very difficult for us to benefit from even a proper understanding of Vedanta, without adequate attention to nidhidhyasana.

Finally, the lessons of Vedanta are subtle and the life-style they require to bear fruit is demanding. These challenges were a bit more manageable in days when the common way of living was not so different compared to that needed for Vedanta and where there was both encouragement and appreciation for its pursuit. In today's set-up, a serious pursuit of Vedanta can be an oddity in many milieus and the people associated with the seeker may be fearful (of that person becoming indifferent to issues and relationships in the world) or derisory. Also, the current way of life in which desires are constantly fanned and egos are encouraged to become larger and larger (by emphasis on consumption, choices and individual rights), makes it that much more difficult to remain balanced and moderated.

All this means that for a student to progress in his study of

Vedanta, there is need to be aware of these factors and deal with them as best as one can.

THE RESULTS

We should now take a look at the results when a duly qualified student is taught by a proper teacher using established methodology. Vedanta is a means of knowledge and it brings about an understanding which was previously absent. Where Vedanta has worked fully, this change in understanding is total (i.e. not subject to any doubts) and permanent (i.e. not capable of being covered or undone).

A person who has completed the entire journey of Vedanta and is established in the understanding which Vedanta provides, is referred to by various terms including *jnani*, *mukta*, *stithaprajna*, *enlightened*, *realised* and *free*. The profound realization of the atma as one's true nature produces a sense of inner freedom, fearlessness and joy; these arise from the knowledge that the atma is forever free (not being subservient even to God), beyond causation or destruction, and the basis for the appearance of the entire world.

With the wisdom of Vedanta, one does not take the world or one's individuality as a serious matter. However, a jnani cannot (and need not) completely give up a functional sense of individuality when he is interacting with the world. A jnani will eat, sleep, plan his activities and respond when called by his individual name, just as any other human being. A jnani's body will feel painful and pleasurable sensations; his mind will experience emotions and will have preferences.

Where he will differ will be in the core of his own awareness or consciousness which now never gets identified with the body and mind. With the freedom and space which become available on dis-identification, the body and mind become privileges and life itself becomes just a game. Most of us can go to a movie and permit a certain amount of identification with the characters and events on the screen so that the show can be enjoyed and yet retain a distance and an unaffected sense of reality. Similarly, a jnani can enjoy life without losing touch with his own truth. He can now inter-act with the world and other people in spontaneous freedom arising from the knowledge that all seemingly individual actions are really a play of a common and impersonal consciousness. He can afford to have preferences because preferences now never become compulsions and the activities of the body and mind do not remain a basis for judging the true self.

The understanding that the doings of the body and mind are not *my* doings cannot stop just there but must lead on to the corollary that the doings of any other body and mind are also not *his* doings. Even with this understanding, the day-to-day behaviour of the jnani may continue as if he and other people are separate individuals but this is only a concession to practicality. In fact, with his own sense of individuality continuing only as a functioning necessity and with other peoples' driving sense of individuality being seen for the error that it is, a jnani can go through life without the pride, guilt and enmity from which the rest of us suffer because we take our egos as the real "I".

The equanimity of a jnani, his composure in the face of changing currents of life and his indifference to concerns and issues which whip up emotions in others may be mistaken for inertness, insensitivity and laziness. There are many people who are physically slothful, emotionally less sensitive and intellectually dull; superficially, some of their actions and reactions (or lack thereof) may seem to resemble a jnani's behaviour. However, the core teachings of Vedanta have little validity or relevance for someone of diminished sensitivity. After all, there is a vast gulf between a person who is incapable of mourning and someone else who transcends mourning as a result of proper understanding while retaining the emotional potential to feel deep grief. A jnani's equanimity is different because it is not a result of heaviness and deadening which makes disequilibrium difficult; his equanimity arises from knowledge and objectivity which, in fact, quicken his perceptions and sharpen his sensitivity.

To get away from some more stereo-typed images, a jnani need not be a sanayasi, i.e. he can have a family, wear normal clothes and need not sport matted hair or have a beard. Also, he need not be a teacher of Vedanta. In fact, he can appear so ordinary that most people may not even know that he is a rare one who has pursued and completed the entire journey of Vedanta. The only visible signs of his knowledge may be a certain poise, naturalness and spontaneity; a non-defensive cheerfulness; a light touch in dealings with others; a gentle kindliness which is perceptive but not intrusive or sentimental — an increased generosity of spirit which is unsanctimonious and non-evangelical.

Let us now turn our attention away from the jnani and consider the results of Vedanta for even those of us who have not completed the full course. Some results of the partial and superficial understanding of Vedanta's teachings can be a bit unsettling to begin with. Some people, as they start imbibing the initial concepts and terminology of Vedanta, tend to develop a certain amount of arrogance based on self-righteousness or pseudo-intellectualism or both. A patronizing attitude may also develop from the notion that Vedanta is the elite primacy which includes all other religions and philosophies and then transcends them. Some others, who may already have other significant intellectual attainments, can make Vedanta into just another scholarly pursuit; they end up reading more and more scriptures, remembering reams of Sanskrit *mantras* and *shlokas* and entering into interminable arguments on obscure points without ever letting the true feel of Vedanta enter their own lives.

Unfortunately, while some familiarity with the scriptures is useful, being a vedantic scholar is quite different from learning the message of Vedanta; here, any learning which does not work in every-day life and in every moment of living is no learning.

There is a completely different type of problem which may arise especially with the family, friends and close associates of the student of Vedanta. Even at the preparatory stage of learning, a certain sense of discrimination and dispassion tends to develop in the student. He may then begin to raise uncomfortable questions or express unpalatable opinions; these could relate to behaviour, attitudes and goals which others in his social milieu consider normal and which he himself had espoused. He may also appear indifferent to company and pastimes which he had once enjoyed and may seem strangely reticent and unmoved in the face of several events affecting himself and others around him.

All this can be very trying for others who may be justifiably confused and even pained. All that can be said here is that as the student's learning progresses, people around may begin to understand the nature of the change which that individual is undergoing and, ultimately, see the value of that change not only for the individual but even for those around him. In this context, it also needs to be said that the worthiest of goals — knowledge of the self leading to freedom and tranquility — does demand objective assessment and even sacrifice in the area of our close relationships. In the process of becoming proficient in the art of living with wisdom, there may be need to reconsider whom one associates with. Our friends and associates need to be worthy people whose influence elevates us instead of reinforcing ignorant and slovenly habits which impede our growth.

As we get further and further into the teachings of Vedanta, the first inkling that there is more to life and to our own selves than what we had ever imagined, brings about a great sense of hope and purpose. As it dawns upon us (even temporarily such as during periods of meditation) that our reality goes beyond our bodies and minds, there is a sense of freedom and an increased sense of understanding and acceptance of people and events around us. As we begin to understand the inherent tendency of our bodies and minds to try and overcome their own limitations and the ultimate futility of efforts in this direction, we gain a new perspective from which to view not only our usual efforts but also the efforts of those around us. Very often, this kind of understanding makes us into non-judgemental and empathetic listeners to whom people instinctively turn to for help and advice.

The preparatory stage Vedanta also helps in cultivating an attitude of gratitude and devotion based on a meaningful understanding of God which provides relief and composure at the level of emotions. On the day-to-day plane, a combination of admitting God into our lives and a realistic understanding of our authorship of only actions but not their results, brings about a sea-change in our attitude to successes and failures. More objective understanding of those we deal with resolves a number of invalid problems in inter-personal relationships because human behaviour is understood in a different perspective and many previously vexing issues lose their relevance. A person who has imbibed only some of Vedanta's preparatory teachings, can still be significantly more happy and balanced.

NOT YET CONVINCED?

There are several good and compelling reasons for us to understand the world for what it really is and to get proper insights into our own truth. The teachings of Vedanta are indispensable here. People turn to Vedanta for a variety of reasons. A large number seek the wisdom of Vedanta when they are in distress: either because of some major upheaval in their lives or when the weight of unanswered existential questions becomes just too much for comfort. For others, the pursuit of Vedanta is a natural extension of their religious leanings and cultural conditioning. For yet others, the logical approach of Vedanta provides a reassuring way of dealing with their curiosity and also promises intellectual pleasure.

But, yet, the fact is that very few people at any time and in any age have had the inclination to undertake a serious pursuit of Vedanta.[128] That this has been so and will continue to be so is recognised by Vedanta itself. Vedantic tradition has, in fact, been against general dissemination of this knowledge. This is because if a seeker is not duly qualified, the teachings of Vedanta will not only be ineffective but can also be harmful either in terms of encouraging perverse thinking or by causing a break-down of an individual's comforting infrastructure of beliefs and conditioning. Partial or defective knowledge, if not recognised as incomplete, can actually be much more damaging than no knowledge. In the words of Alexander Pope:

> *A little learning is a dangerous thing;*
> *Drink deep, or taste not the Pierian Spring;*
> *There shallow draughts intoxicate the brain;*
> *And drinking largely sobers us again.*

Leaving aside Vedanta's own safeguards, we have to recognise that no amount of persuasion and argument will convince some of us to expose ourselves to this knowledge. Further, even from

---

128 What is meant here by Vedanta is any means of obtaining true knowledge of our self and achieving complete growth and freedom. Whether this effort is labeled Vedanta or not and whether or not Sanskrit terminology is used, does not really matter.

amongst those who actually begin the pursuit of Vedanta, only a few will have the inclination and capacity to run the full course. Where does all this lead us to? What happens if we just cannot get interested enough in Vedanta to make it into a meaningful pursuit? What happens if even after pursuing Vedanta for some time, its teachings do not seem to take hold and work for us in our daily lives?

Looking at these problems from the impersonal (and seemingly harsh) view-point of the totality of creation, both our individual fate and the message of Vedanta are of no particular consequence. An individual's personal potential, problems and agenda are not significant issues from that perspective. The scale and mystery of creation are immensely large and complex. On that scale entire stellar systems come into being and are destroyed without any noticeable consequence, just as tiny grass flowers are born and die unnoticed in our forests. In terms of the history of this small planet alone, the human race has been in existence for a length of time which could be spoken of as the twinkling of an eye. In another twinkling of an eye our entire race could be wiped out and become a historical foot-note as an interesting (and perhaps dangerous) experiment. On their own time-scale, our planet and the universe will be undisturbed in their own path irrespective of our doings.

We need to be aware of our own reality not as pinnacles of creation weighed down by a heavy sense of cosmic responsibility, but as individuals who need to solve their own problems of finding meaning and of living in happiness. This solution can ultimately come from knowing and understanding our own selves. If we cannot or do not make this effort, only we as individuals will be losers and nothing else will be affected. In the ultimate analysis, one can only say that, like everything else, the inability or unwillingness to grow in this direction has also to be part of the scheme of creation which must be unfolding as it should. Beyond a point, one need not read anything very individual or personal into all this. While it is good for us to try and apply ourselves with diligence to the task of gaining self knowledge, we must temper our endeavours and aspirations with humility. Such humility can only come from the understanding that our choices and actual results depend upon a host of factors (and we can call them fate, circumstances, God's grace, luck or whatever else we may like), many of which are beyond our control and even beyond our knowledge.

To turn to Vedanta to find an answer to our sense of limitation and to then let Vedanta become a source of further complexes which increase the sense of inadequacy or limitation, would really be a cruel case of jumping from the proverbial frying pan into the fire. One can only pray, in the words of this well-known prayer:

> *God give me the courage to change the things I can,*
> *The serenity to accept the things I cannot, and*
> *The wisdom to know the difference*

and understand, as we pray, that there is no guarantee that the required wisdom will be necessarily available to us.

There is another important factor here. This is a crucial truth about Vedanta, which we understand only when we are some way down its path: the journey of Vedanta is only an apparent journey. Paradoxical or even nonsensical as it may sound, Vedanta ends where it begins – with us as we actually are, here and now. Vedanta's achievement is not an actual change in our reality or the gain of some hidden gem wrested from our mystical depths. All that Vedanta does is to bring about a change in our understanding and save us from unnecessary suffering which arises out of a wrong conclusion. To use an analogy, we are like the person who has pushed his glasses up to his forehead and then gets into a frenzied search for them; as soon as this person glances into a mirror, he sees the glasses perched on his own forehead and stops his silly hunt. The mirror did not produce the glasses or bring this person closer to them, it only provided knowledge of an already existing situation. Without the mirror, he would have suffered further from the apparent loss of the glasses and expended more energy in a search in the wrong direction; however, in reality, the glasses were never away from him. In the same way, Vedanta is very useful in freeing us from unnecessary and painful efforts but yet, at our fundamental level, we really lose nothing even if we are not able to incorporate all the teachings of Vedanta into our lives. The teachings of Vedanta only bring about a cognitive change; while this change immensely benefits the state of our minds, our reality remains what it always is, whether before or after Vedanta. After all, when we have a cracked pot, it is the pot which is cracked and not the clay; Vedanta only teaches us to understand clay minus its 'potness'.

On a more positive note, the very fact that we have taken any interest at all in a subject like Vedanta goes to show that a certain amount of good fortune is already working for us. Even casual interest in Vedanta very often provides an opportunity to examine the frame-work of our usual understanding and efforts. If this interest can be sustained and if the blessing of finding a real teacher happens to us then we are truly hooked – our weaknesses and past conditioning may hold us back and make us struggle but, in the long run, they cannot keep us away from our destiny of freedom by self-knowledge. As Khalil Gibran said, *"In your longing for your giant self lies your goodness; and that longing is in all of you. But in some of you that longing is a torrent rushing with might to the sea ... and in others it is a flat stream that loses itself in angles and bends and lingers before it reaches the shore."*

So with faith and effort, let us persevere in our attempts to share the vision of the seers recorded in the Upanishads and, in the process, enjoy the journey of life and learning. Let us pray in the words of the Upanishads:

> *asatoma sadgamaya*
> *tamasoma jyotirgamaya*
> *mrityorma amritamgamaya*
> *om shanti shanti shanti*

> *From untruth, lead me to truth*
> *From darkness, lead me to light*
> *From mortality, lead me to immortality.*
> *May there be peace in all aspects of life.*

adah	-	that (pronoun)
adharma	-	opposed to or contrary to dharma
adhikari	-	one qualified or eligible (for self-knowledge)
Adi Shankara	-	see *Shankara*
advaita	-	non-dual
ahamkara	-	sense of individuality, ego
ahimsa	-	non-violence; a way of life in which injury to others is kept to the minimum possible
anadi	-	without a beginning, timeless
ananda	-	bliss or fullness
ananta	-	unending, limitless
anirvachaniya	-	inexplicable
anrtam	-	false
apaureshya	-	not of human origin
artha	-	security, wealth
asana	-	posture for stretching and meditation
atma	-	the true self which is not different from *brahman;* inner-most essence of man unfolded by Vedanta, the nature of which is *sat-chit-ananda*
avarana	-	covering
avastha-traya	-	three states (of wakefulness, dreaming and deep sleep)
Bhagavad Gita	-	well-known Hindu scripture which is part of a large epic called the *Mahabharata;* one of the three starting points of vedantic philosophy
bhagawan	-	God, usually in a personalized form

bhakti	- worship
bhashya	- commentary (on the primary scriptures of Vedanta)
Brahma Sutras	- concise and logically arranged aphorisms written by Badarayana, containing the essence of the *Upanishads*; one of the three starting points of vedantic philosophy
brahman	- non-dual fundamental reality which is the truth of everything and defined as *satyam-jnanam-anantam*
carvaka	- an ancient philosophy of materialism
dharma	- righteousness, propriety, virtue, duty
dvaita	- duality
Gita	- see *Bhagavad Gita*
guru	- teacher of self-knowledge (remover of darkness)
Hindu	- refers to an adherent of *Hinduism*; the word is derived from *Sindhu* which is the Sanskrit name for the Indus river which flows in the north-western part of the Indian sub-continent
Hinduism	- refers to what is considered to be the world's oldest religion which developed in the Indian sub-continent in pre-historic times; this religious tradition was known as *sanatana dharma* (eternal way) and the term 'Hinduism' came into use only in the 1800's
idam	- this (pronoun)

Ishwara	-	God as the combined material and intelligent cause of creation
jagat	-	world, the created universe
jnana	-	knowledge
jnani	-	the one who knows
kala	-	time
kama	-	desire, pleasure
karana	-	cause
karma	-	action; result of action which may fructify in this life or in any subsequent life of the same soul
karma yoga	-	a way of living a normal, worldly life but without focus on personal pleasure and security because liberation (by self-knowledge) is seen as the only worthwhile goal
mahabhutas	-	the five basic elements which are *akasha* (space), *vayu* (air), *agni* (fire), *apa* (water) and *prithvi* (earth)
mahavakya		great statement; refers to four statements (from the *Upanishads* portion of each one of the four Vedas) which individually encapsulate the essence of Vedanta's vision
mala	-	dirt, impurity
manana	-	reflecting over the teachings to check and resolve doubts
maya	-	the indescribable power which brings about the apparent appearance of the world

mithya	-	anything which has no independent existence but depends on something else
moksha	-	liberation (from the sense of limitation in general)
mumukshu	-	seeker of *moksha*; one with a burning desire for liberation
murti	-	statue, figure
neti neti	-	not this, not this; used to describe *atma* whose infinity is beyond positive description because any thought or concept is limited to the finite
nidhidhyasana	-	contemplation or meditation to overcome contrary tendencies of the mind
nimitta karana	-	the efficient or intelligent cause
nitya	-	permanent, eternal, unchanging
parampara	-	tradition, lineage, uninterrupted succession
parmarthika	-	the absolutely real
pramana	-	means of valid knowledge
prarabhda	-	'ripened' actions; accumulated past actions whose fruits are experienced now
prasada	-	gift from God
pratibhasika	-	apparent, illusory
purna	-	full, complete
rajas	-	one of the three basic qualities (*gunas*); activity, energy, passion
rishi	-	seer of truth; Vedic sage
samsara	-	the flow of the world; life of coercive and

	perpetual becoming
sanyasa	- renunciation of all worldly possessions and ties
sanyasi	- one who has renounced all worldly possessions and ties; a monk
sat	- existence, reality, being
sat chit ananda -	description of *atma* as timeless existence, self-evident consciousness and limitlessness
sattva	- one of the three basic qualities (*gunas*); purity, balance, harmony
satyam jnanam anantam	- description of *brahman* as timeless existence, self-evident consciousness and limitlessness
Shankara	- an Indian philosopher of the 8th century CE who consolidated the doctrine of advaita Vedanta; author of seminal commentaries on ten Upanishads, the Brahma Sutras and the Bhagavad Gita as well as several other works
Shankaracharya	- see *Shankara*
shloka	- a Sanskrit verse-form
shravana	- hearing, study
shruti	- that which is heard; revealed scripture; Vedas
smriti	- that which is remembered; a group of traditional scriptures other than the Vedas
stithaprajna	- one who is stable in knowledge and constant awareness of reality

Sufism	- an inner and mystical dimension of Islam with a philosophy which is universal in nature; some Muslims consider it to be outside the sphere of Islam
tamas	- one of the three basic qualities (*gunas*); indolence, ignorance, bestiality
Taoism	- literally, 'the way'; expanded meanings include 'the natural and spontaneous way in which things begin and pursue their course' and ' the source of both existence and non-existence'
tat tvam asi	- famous mahavakya meaning 'you are that'
trigunas	- the three basic qualities of *sattva, rajas* and *tamas*
Upanishads	- philosophical portions found at the end of the four *Vedas* and collectively also called Vedanta
upadana karana	- the material or substantial cause
vairagya	- dispassion, disenchantment
vastu	- object; another name for the only reality which is also called *brahman* or *atma*
Veda(s)	- a compilation of that which is known; a summary name for four sacred scriptures of Hinduism regarded as divine revelation
Vedanta	- a collective name for the philosophical portions found at the end of the four *Vedas*; a school of philosophy which accepts the authority of the *Vedas* with

		special emphasis on the contents of the *Upanishads*
vikshepa	-	division, distraction, projection
viveka	-	discrimination, discernment
vyahavarika	-	the relative, empirical and transactional
yoga	-	to unite or yoke; a means for accomplishing something; one of the six traditional schools of philosophy

BOOKS OF RELATED INTEREST

THE ESSENTIAL VEDANTA: A New Source Book of Advaita Vedanta
—*Eliot Deutsch & Rohit Dalvi (eds.)*
This book is a comprehensive introduction to the tradition of Advaita Vedanta based upon primary sources and makes possible a study of it in its classical form. Translations from all major Sanskrit writings are included here along with the selections from all of the most important representatives of this central philosophy of India.

ISBN: 978-81-7822-265-3

THE HINDU MIND:Fundamentals of Hindu Religion and Philosophy for All Ages
—*Bansi Pandit*
The Hindu Mind provides an excellent introduction to the historical, philosophical, ritualistic, social, and ethical dimensions of Hinduism. The major contribution of the book is that it shows the interconnections among these diverse dimensions. The author brings to the people the key concepts such as Brahman, karma, dharma, maya and samskara, which constitute the foundational beliefs of Hinduism.

ISBN: 978-81-7822-007-9

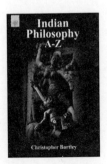

INDIAN PHILOSOPHY A-Z
—*Christopher Bartley*
This alphabetical handbook defines and explains key concepts in classical Indian philosophy, identifies controversial issues, describes major traditions of thought, and locates influential thinkers in their intellectual and religious contexts. They introduce the central concepts of the various branches of philosophy written by established philosophers, covering both traditional and contemporary terminology.

ISBN: 978-81-7822-313-1